1 & 2
Corinthians

ABOUT THE AUTHORS

General Editor

Clinton E. Arnold (Ph.D., University of Aberdeen), professor and chairman, department of New Testament, Talbot School of Theology, Biola University, Los Angeles, California

1 Corinthians:

David W. J. Gill (DPhil, University of Oxford), Sub-dean of the faculty of arts and social studies and senior lecturer, department of classics and ancient history, University of Wales Swansea, United Kingdom

2 Corinthians

Moyer V. Hubbard (DPhil, University of Oxford), assistant professor of New Testament, Talbot School of Theology, Biola University, Los Angeles, California

Zondervan Illustrated Bible Backgrounds Commentary

1 & 2 Corinthians

David W. J. Gill
Moyer V. Hubbard

Clinton E. Arnold   *general editor*

ZONDERVAN

1 Corinthians—Copyright © 2002 by David Gill
2 Corinthians—Copyright © 2002 by Moyer Hubbard

Requests for information should be addressed to:
Zondervan, 3900 *Sparks Dr. SE, Grand Rapids, Michigan 49546*

This edition: ISBN 978-0310-52304-8

Library of Congress Cataloging-in-Publication Data
    Zondervan illustrated Bible backgrounds commentary / Clinton E. Arnold, general editor.
        p.   cm.
    Includes bibliographical references.
    ISBN 978-0310-27822-1
    1. Bible. N.T. — Commentaries.   I. Arnold, Clinton E.
    BS2341.52.Z66 2001
    225.7 — dc21   2001046801

Interior design by Sherri L. Hoffman

Printed in the United States of America

CONTENTS

INTRODUCTION

All readers of the Bible have a tendency to view what it says through their own culture and life circumstances. This can happen almost subconsiously as we read the pages of the text.

When most people in the church read about the thief on the cross, for instance, they immediately think of a burglar that held up a store or broke into a home. They may be rather shocked to find out that the guy was actually a Jewish revolutionary figure who was part of a growing movement in Palestine eager to throw off Roman rule.

It also comes as something of a surprise to contemporary Christians that "cursing" in the New Testament era had little or nothing to do with cussing somebody out. It had far more to do with the invocation of spirits to cause someone harm.

No doubt there is a need in the church for learning more about the world of the New Testament to avoid erroneous interpretations of the text of Scripture. But relevant historical and cultural insights also provide an added dimension of perspective to the words of the Bible. This kind of information often functions in the same way as watching a movie in color rather than in black and white. Finding out, for instance, how Paul compared Christ's victory on the cross to a joyous celebration parade in honor of a Roman general after winning an extraordinary battle brings does indeed magnify the profundity and implications of Jesus' work on the cross. Discovering that the factions at Corinth ("I follow Paul . . . I follow Apollos . . .") had plenty of precedent in the local cults ("I follow Aphrodite; I follow Apollo . . .") helps us understand the "why" of a particular problem. Learning about the water supply from the springs of Hierapolis that flowed into Laodicea as "lukewarm" water enables us to appreciate the relevance of the metaphor Jesus used when he addressed the spiritual laxity of this church.

My sense is that most Christians are eager to learn more about the real life setting of the New Testament. In the preaching and teaching of the Bible in the church, congregants are always grateful when they learn something of the background and historical context of the text. It not only helps them understand the text more accurately, but often enables them to identify with the people and circumstances of the Bible. I have been asked on countless occasions by Christians, "Where can I get access to good historical background information about this passage?" Earnest Christians are hungry for information that makes their Bibles come alive.

The stimulus for this commentary came from the church and the aim is to serve the church. The contributors to this series have sought to provide illuminating and interesting historical/cultural background information. The intent was to draw upon relevant papyri, inscriptions, archaeological discoveries, and the numerous studies of Judaism, Roman culture, Hellenism, and other features of the world of the New Testament and to make the results accessible to people in the church. We recognize that some readers of the commentary will want to go further, and so the sources of the information have been carefully documented in endnotes.

The written information has been supplemented with hundreds of photographs, maps, charts, artwork, and other graphics that help the reader better understand the world of the New Testament. Each of the writers was given an opportunity to dream up a "wish list" of illustrations that he thought would help to illustrate the passages in the New Testament book for which he was writing commentary. Although we were not able to obtain everything they were looking for, we came close.

The team of commentators are writing for the benefit of the broad array of Christians who simply want to better understand their Bibles from the vantage point of the historical context. This is an installment in a new genre of "Bible background" commentaries that was kicked off by Craig Keener's fine volume. Consequently, this is not an "exegetical" commentary that provides linguistic insight and background into Greek constructions and verb tenses. Neither is this work an "expository" commentary that provides a verse-by-verse exposition of the text; for in-depth philological or theological insight, readers will need to have other more specialized or comprehensive commentaries available. Nor is this an "historical-critical" commentary, although the contributors are all scholars and have already made substantial academic contributions on the New Testament books they are writing on for this set. The team intentionally does not engage all of the issues that are discussed in the scholarly guild.

Rather, our goal is to offer a reading and interpretation of the text informed by what we regard as the most relevant historical information. For many in the church, this commentary will serve as an important entry point into the interpretation and appreciation of the text. For other more serious students of the Word, these volumes will provide an important supplement to many of the fine exegetical, expository, and critical available.

The contributors represent a group of scholars who embrace the Bible as the Word of God and believe that the message of its pages has life-changing relevance for faith and practice today. Accordingly, we offer "Reflections" on the relevance of the Scripture to life for every chapter of the New Testament.

I pray that this commentary brings you both delight and insight in digging deeper into the Word of God.

Clinton E. Arnold
General Editor

LIST OF SIDEBARS

INDEX OF PHOTOS
AND MAPS

ABBREVIATIONS

1. Books of the Bible and Apocrypha

1 Chron.	1 Chronicles
2 Chron.	2 Chronicles
1 Cor.	1 Corinthians
2 Cor.	2 Corinthians
1 Esd.	1 Esdras
2 Esd.	2 Esdras
1 John	1 John
2 John	2 John
3 John	3 John
1 Kings	1 Kings
2 Kings	2 Kings
1 Macc.	1 Maccabees
2 Macc.	2 Maccabees
1 Peter	1 Peter
2 Peter	2 Peter
1 Sam.	1 Samuel
2 Sam.	2 Samuel
1 Thess.	1 Thessalonians
2 Thess.	2 Thessalonians
1 Tim.	1 Timothy
2 Tim.	2 Timothy
Acts	Acts
Amos	Amos
Bar.	Baruch
Bel	Bel and the Dragon
Col.	Colossians
Dan.	Daniel
Deut.	Deuteronomy
Eccl.	Ecclesiastes
Ep. Jer.	Epistle of Jeremiah
Eph.	Ephesians
Est.	Esther
Ezek.	Ezekiel
Ex.	Exodus
Ezra	Ezra
Gal.	Galatians
Gen.	Genesis
Hab.	Habakkuk
Hag.	Haggai
Heb.	Hebrews
Hos.	Hosea
Isa.	Isaiah
James	James
Jer.	Jeremiah
Job	Job
Joel	Joel
John	John
Jonah	Jonah
Josh.	Joshua
Jude	Jude
Judg.	Judges
Judith	Judith
Lam.	Lamentations
Lev.	Leviticus
Luke	Luke
Mal.	Malachi
Mark	Mark
Matt.	Matthew
Mic.	Micah
Nah.	Nahum
Neh.	Nehemiah
Num.	Numbers
Obad.	Obadiah
Phil.	Philippians
Philem.	Philemon
Pr. Man.	Prayer of Manassah
Prov.	Proverbs
Ps.	Psalm
Rest. of Est.	The Rest of Esther
Rev.	Revelation
Rom.	Romans
Ruth	Ruth
S. of III Ch.	The Song of the Three Holy Children
Sir.	Sirach/Ecclesiasticus
Song	Song of Songs
Sus.	Susanna
Titus	Titus
Tobit	Tobit
Wisd. Sol.	The Wisdom of Solomon
Zech.	Zechariah
Zeph.	Zephaniah

2. Old and New Testament Pseudepigrapha and Rabbinic Literature

Individual tractates of rabbinic literature follow the abbreviations of the *SBL Handbook of Style*, pp. 79–80. Qumran documents follow standard Dead Sea Scroll conventions.

2 Bar.	*2 Baruch*
3 Bar.	*3 Baruch*
4 Bar.	*4 Baruch*
1 En.	*1 Enoch*
2 En.	*2 Enoch*
3 En.	*3 Enoch*
4 Ezra	*4 Ezra*

3 Macc.	3 Maccabees
4 Macc.	4 Maccabees
5 Macc.	5 Maccabees
Acts Phil.	Acts of Philip
Acts Pet.	Acts of Peter and the 12 Apostles
Apoc. Elijah	Apocalypse of Elijah
As. Mos.	Assumption of Moses
b.	Babylonian Talmud (+ tractate)
Gos. Thom.	Gospel of Thomas
Jos. Asen.	Joseph and Aseneth
Jub.	Jubilees
Let. Aris.	Letter of Aristeas
m.	Mishnah (+ tractate)
Mek.	Mekilta
Midr.	Midrash I (+ biblical book)
Odes Sol.	Odes of Solomon
Pesiq. Rab.	Pesiqta Rabbati
Pirqe. R. El.	Pirqe Rabbi Eliezer
Pss. Sol.	Psalms of Solomon
Rab.	Rabbah (+biblical book); (e.g., Gen. Rab.=Genesis Rabbah)
S. ʿOlam Rab.	Seder ʿOlam Rabbah
Sem.	Semahot
Sib. Or.	Sibylline Oracles
T. Ab.	Testament of Abraham
T. Adam	Testament of Adam
T. Ash.	Testament of Asher
T. Benj.	Testament of Benjamin
T. Dan	Testament of Dan
T. Gad	Testament of Gad
T. Hez.	Testament of Hezekiah
T. Isaac	Testament of Isaac
T. Iss.	Testament of Issachar
T. Jac.	Testament of Jacob
T. Job	Testament of Job
T. Jos.	Testament of Joseph
T. Jud.	Testament of Judah
T. Levi	Testament of Levi
T. Mos.	Testament of Moses
T. Naph.	Testament of Naphtali
T. Reu.	Testament of Reuben
T. Sim.	Testament of Simeon
T. Sol.	Testament of Solomon
T. Zeb.	Testament of Zebulum
Tanh.	Tanhuma
Tg. Isa.	Targum of Isaiah
Tg. Lam.	Targum of Lamentations
Tg. Neof.	Targum Neofiti
Tg. Onq.	Targum Onqelos
Tg. Ps.-J	Targum Pseudo-Jonathan
y.	Jerusalem Talmud (+ tractate)

3. Classical Historians

For an extended list of classical historians and church fathers, see *SBL Handbook of Style*, pp. 84–87. For many works of classical antiquity, the abbreviations have been subjected to the author's discretion; the names of these works should be obvious upon consulting entries of the classical writers in classical dictionaries or encyclopedias.

Eusebius

Eccl. Hist.	Ecclesiastical History

Josephus

Ag. Ap.	Against Apion
Ant.	Jewish Antiquities
J.W.	Jewish War
Life	The Life

Philo

Abraham	On the Life of Abraham
Agriculture	On Agriculture
Alleg. Interp	Allegorical Interpretation
Animals	Whether Animals Have Reason
Cherubim	On the Cherubim
Confusion	On the Confusion of Thomas
Contempl. Life	On the Contemplative Life
Creation	On the Creation of the World
Curses	On Curses
Decalogue	On the Decalogue
Dreams	On Dreams
Drunkenness	On Drunkenness
Embassy	On the Embassy to Gaius
Eternity	On the Eternity of the World
Flaccus	Against Flaccus
Flight	On Flight and Finding
Giants	On Giants
God	On God
Heir	Who Is the Heir?
Hypothetica	Hypothetica
Joseph	On the Life of Joseph
Migration	On the Migration of Abraham
Moses	On the Life of Moses
Names	On the Change of Names
Person	That Every Good Person Is Free
Planting	On Planting
Posterity	On the Posterity of Cain
Prelim. Studies	On the Preliminary Studies
Providence	On Providence
QE	Questions and Answers on Exodus
QG	Questions and Answers on Genesis
Rewards	On Rewards and Punishments
Sacrifices	On the Sacrifices of Cain and Abel
Sobriety	On Sobriety
Spec. Laws	On the Special Laws
Unchangeable	That God Is Unchangeable
Virtues	On the Virtues

Worse	*That the Worse Attacks the Better*

Apostolic Fathers

1 Clem.	*First Letter of Clement*
Barn.	*Epistle of Barnabas*
Clem. Hom.	*Ancient Homily of Clement (also called 2 Clement)*
Did.	*Didache*
Herm. Vis.;	*Shepherd of Hermas,*
Sim.	*Visions; Similitudes*
Ignatius	*Epistles of Ignatius (followed by the letter's name)*
Mart. Pol.	*Martyrdom of Polycarp*

4. Modern Abbreviations

AASOR	Annual of the American Schools of Oriental Research
AB	Anchor Bible
ABD	*Anchor Bible Dictionary*
ABRL	Anchor Bible Reference Library
AGJU	Arbeiten zur Geschichte des antiken Judentums und des Urchristentums
AH	*Agricultural History*
ALGHJ	Arbeiten zur Literatur und Geschichte des Hellenistischen Judentums
AnBib	Analecta biblica
ANRW	*Aufstieg und Niedergang der römischen Welt*
ANTC	Abingdon New Testament Commentaries
BAGD	Bauer, W., W. F. Arndt, F. W. Gingrich, and F. W. Danker. *Greek-English Lexicon of the New Testament and Other Early Christina Literature* (2d. ed.)
BA	*Biblical Archaeologist*
BAFCS	Book of Acts in Its First Century Setting
BAR	*Biblical Archaeology Review*
BASOR	*Bulletin of the American Schools of Oriental Research*
BBC	Bible Background Commentary
BBR	*Bulletin for Biblical Research*
BDB	Brown, F., S. R. Driver, and C. A. Briggs. *A Hebrew and English Lexicon of the Old Testament*
BDF	Blass, F., A. Debrunner, and R. W. Funk. *A Greek Grammar of the New Testament and Other Early Christian Literature*
BECNT	Baker Exegetical Commentary on the New Testament
BI	*Biblical Illustrator*
Bib	*Biblica*
BibSac	*Bibliotheca Sacra*

BLT	Brethren Life and Thought
BNTC	Black's New Testament Commentary
BRev	*Bible Review*
BSHJ	Baltimore Studies in the History of Judaism
BST	The Bible Speaks Today
BSV	Biblical Social Values
BT	*The Bible Translator*
BTB	Biblical Theology Bulletin
BZ	*Biblische Zeitschrift*
CBQ	*Catholic Biblical Quarterly*
CBTJ	*Calvary Baptist Theological Journal*
CGTC	Cambridge Greek Testament Commentary
CH	*Church History*
CIL	*Corpus inscriptionum latinarum*
CPJ	*Corpus papyrorum judaicorum*
CRINT	*Compendia rerum iudaicarum ad Novum Testamentum*
CTJ	*Calvin Theological Journal*
CTM	*Concordia Theological Monthly*
CTT	Contours of Christian Theology
DBI	*Dictionary of Biblical Imagery*
DCM	*Dictionary of Classical Mythology.*
DDD	*Dictionary of Deities and Demons in the Bible*
DJBP	*Dictionary of Judaism in the Biblical Period*
DJG	*Dictionary of Jesus and the Gospels*
DLNT	*Dictionary of the Later New Testament and Its Developments*
DNTB	*Dictionary of New Testament Background*
DPL	*Dictionary of Paul and His Letters*
EBC	*Expositor's Bible Commentary*
EDBT	*Evangelical Dictionary of Biblical Theology*
EDNT	*Exegetical Dictionary of the New Testament*
EJR	*Encyclopedia of the Jewish Religion*
EPRO	Études préliminaires aux religions orientales dans l'empire romain
EvQ	*Evangelical Quarterly*
ExpTim	*Expository Times*
FRLANT	Forsuchungen zur Religion und Literatur des Alten und Neuen Testament
GNC	Good News Commentary
GNS	Good News Studies
HCNT	*Hellenistic Commentary to the New Testament*
HDB	*Hastings Dictionary of the Bible*

HJP	History of the Jewish People in the Age of Jesus Christ, by E. Schürer
HTR	Harvard Theological Review
HTS	Harvard Theological Studies
HUCA	Hebrew Union College Annual
IBD	Illustrated Bible Dictionary
IBS	Irish Biblical Studies
ICC	International Critical Commentary
IDB	The Interpreter's Dictionary of the Bible
IEJ	Israel Exploration Journal
IG	Inscriptiones graecae
IGRR	Inscriptiones graecae ad res romanas pertinentes
ILS	Inscriptiones Latinae Selectae
Imm	Immanuel
ISBE	International Standard Bible Encyclopedia
Int	Interpretation
IvE	Inschriften von Ephesos
IVPNTC	InterVarsity Press New Testament Commentary
JAC	Jahrbuch fur Antike und Christentum
JBL	Journal of Biblical Literature
JETS	Journal of the Evangelical Theological Society
JHS	Journal of Hellenic Studies
JJS	Journal of Jewish Studies
JOAIW	Jahreshefte des Osterreeichischen Archaologischen Instites in Wien
JSJ	Journal for the Study of Judaism in the Persian, Hellenistic, and Roman Periods
JRS	Journal of Roman Studies
JSNT	Journal for the Study of the New Testament
JSNTSup	Journal for the Study of the New Testament: Supplement Series
JSOT	Journal for the Study of the Old Testament
JSOTSup	Journal for the Study of the Old Testament: Supplement Series
JTS	Journal of Theological Studies
KTR	Kings Theological Review
LCL	Loeb Classical Library
LEC	Library of Early Christianity
LSJ	Liddell, H. G., R. Scott, H. S. Jones. A Greek-English Lexicon
MM	Moulton, J. H., and G. Milligan. The Vocabulary of the Greek Testament
MNTC	Moffatt New Testament Commentary
NBD	New Bible Dictionary
NC	Narrative Commentaries
NCBC	New Century Bible Commentary Eerdmans

NEAE	New Encyclopedia of Archaeological Excavations in the Holy Land
NEASB	Near East Archaeological Society Bulletin
New Docs	New Documents Illustrating Early Christianity
NIBC	New International Biblical Commentary
NICNT	New International Commentary on the New Testament
NIDNTT	New International Dictionary of New Testament Theology
NIGTC	New International Greek Testament Commentary
NIVAC	NIV Application Commentary
NorTT	Norsk Teologisk Tidsskrift
NoT	Notes on Translation
NovT	Novum Testamentum
NovTSup	Novum Testamentum Supplements
NTAbh	Neutestamentliche Abhandlungen
NTS	New Testament Studies
NTT	New Testament Theology
NTTS	New Testament Tools and Studies
OAG	Oxford Archaeological Guides
OCCC	Oxford Companion to Classical Civilization
OCD	Oxford Classical Dictionary
ODCC	The Oxford Dictionary of the Christian Church
OGIS	Orientis graeci inscriptiones selectae
OHCW	The Oxford History of the Classical World
OHRW	Oxford History of the Roman World
OTP	Old Testament Pseudepigrapha, ed. by J. H. Charlesworth
PEQ	Palestine Exploration Quarterly
PG	Patrologia graeca
PGM	Papyri graecae magicae: Die griechischen Zauberpapyri
PL	Patrologia latina
PNTC	Pelican New Testament Commentaries
Rb	Revista biblica
RB	Revue biblique
RivB	Rivista biblica italiana
RTR	Reformed Theological Review
SB	Sources bibliques
SBL	Society of Biblical Literature
SBLDS	Society of Biblical Literature Dissertation Series
SBLMS	Society of Biblical Literature Monograph Series

SBLSP	*Society of Biblical Literature Seminar Papers*
SBS	Stuttgarter Bibelstudien
SBT	Studies in Biblical Theology
SCJ	*Stone-Campbell Journal*
Scr	*Scripture*
SE	*Studia Evangelica*
SEG	*Supplementum epigraphicum graecum*
SJLA	Studies in Judaism in Late Antiquity
SJT	*Scottish Journal of Theology*
SNTSMS	Society for New Testament Studies Monograph Series
SSC	Social Science Commentary
SSCSSG	Social-Science Commentary on the Synoptic Gospels
Str-B	Strack, H. L., and P. Billerbeck. *Kommentar zum Neuen Testament aus Talmud und Midrasch*
TC	Thornapple Commentaries
TDNT	*Theological Dictionary of the New Testament*
TDOT	*Theological Dictionary of the Old Testament*
TLNT	*Theological Lexicon of the New Testament*
TLZ	*Theologische Literaturzeitung*
TNTC	Tyndale New Testament Commentary
TrinJ	*Trinity Journal*
TS	*Theological Studies*
TSAJ	Texte und Studien zum antiken Judentum
TWNT	*Theologische Wörterbuch zum Neuen Testament*
TynBul	*Tyndale Bulletin*
WBC	Word Biblical Commentary Waco: Word, 1982
WMANT	Wissenschaftliche Monographien zum Alten und Neuen Testament
WUNT	Wissenschaftliche Untersuchungen zum Neuen Testament
YJS	Yale Judaica Series
ZNW	*Zeitschrift fur die neutestamentliche Wissenschaft und die Junde der alteren Kirche*
ZPE	*Zeischrift der Papyrolgie und Epigraphkik*
ZPEB	*Zondervan Pictorial Encyclopedia of the Bible*

5. General Abbreviations

ad. loc.	in the place cited
b.	born
c., ca.	circa
cf.	compare
d.	died
ed(s).	editors(s), edited by
e.g.	for example
ET	English translation
frg.	fragment
i.e.	that is
ibid.	in the same place
idem	the same (author)
lit.	literally
l(l)	line(s)
MSS	manuscripts
n.d.	no date
NS	New Series
par.	parallel
passim	here and there
repr.	reprint
ser.	series
s.v.	*sub verbo*, under the word
trans.	translator, translated by; transitive

Zondervan Illustrated Bible Backgrounds Commentary

1 CORINTHIANS

by David W. J. Gill

Corinth was a major city in the eastern Peloponnese of Greece.[1] It lay near the narrow isthmus that joined the Peloponnese to the mainland. The city lay at the foot of a mountain, Akrocorinth (elevation 1883 feet), which also served as a location for some of the cults of the city.

The City of Corinth

The history of the city of Corinth can be traced back to the earliest periods of Greek history. In the archaic period (6th cent. B.C.) it was ruled by the Kypselid family. During the Peloponnesian War (late 5th cent. B.C.) Corinth fought against Athens. During the second century B.C. Corinth joined other Greek states to fight against the domination of Rome, and in 146 B.C. the city was captured and razed to the ground by the Roman general Mummius. As a result, the city was left derelict for over a hundred years until Julius Caesar decided to found a colony, with the full Latin title of *Colonia Laus Iulia Corinthienses,*

CORINTH

◀

▶ **1 Corinthians**
IMPORTANT FACTS:

- **AUTHOR:** The apostle Paul and Sosthenes.
- **DATE:** c. A.D. 55 (Paul writing from Ephesus).
- **OCCASION:**
  - To respond to information that there had been quarrels in the church.
  - To prepare for a visit from Timothy and Paul himself.
- **KEY THEMES:**
  1. The impact of the Christian gospel on the life of the Christian.
  2. The ordering of the local church.

in 44 B.C. As Caesar was assassinated in March of that year, it seems likely that Mark Antony, Caesar's co-consul, may have been responsible for implementing the legislation. Some of the Roman sources suggest that the colony was established with Italian freedmen, that is, former slaves, though they probably only formed a small part of the overall population. The geographer Strabo records some of the details of the colony at this time:

> Now after Corinth had remained deserted for a long time, it was restored again, because of its favourable position, by the deified Caesar, who colonised it with people that belonged for the most part to the freedman class. And when these were removing the ruins and at the same time digging open the graves, they found numbers of terracotta reliefs, and also many bronze vessels. And since they admired the worksmanship they left no grave unransacked.[2]

It is important to stress the lack of continuity between the Greek and Roman city. A number of buildings were demolished and the archaic temple in the heart of the town may have had its roof timbers removed. One of the famous descriptions of the ruined city occurs in a letter from Ser. Sulpicius to the Roman orator Cicero in 45 B.C.[3] There are other references to individuals living among the ruins[4], but the key point is that Corinth no longer existed as a political entity.

Corinth was one of a number of city-states (Gk. *polis*) in the Greek world. Her territory, the Corinthia, bordered on that of a number of other city-states. To the east along the isthmus that joined the Peloponnese to the Greek mainland was Megara. Northwards, along the coast of the Corinthian Gulf, was Sikyon. Along the southern side of the Corinthia was the Argolid, with cities such as Argos and Epidauros (where there was a major sanctuary for the healing-god Asklepios). Within the Corinthia were two main harbors, Lechaeum and Cenchreae, giving access respectively to the Corinthian Gulf (and Italy) and the Saronic Gulf and the eastern Mediterranean. These were some of the major harbors of the Mediterranean, rivaling those of Ostia (the port of Rome), Alexandria in Egypt, and Caesarea (the major port that gave access to Judea).

▶
CORINTH AND ITS ENVIRONS

▶ **The City of Corinth IMPORTANT FACTS:**

- Population: Approximately 100,000 (80,000 colony, 20,000 *territorium*).
- Religion: Patron deity Aphrodite; major sanctuary of Poseidon at nearby Isthmia; numerous other deities worshiped.
- Port city.
- Seat of the Roman governor for the province of Achaia.

▶ Strabo in Corinth

One of the earliest accounts of the Roman colony at Corinth was by the geographer Strabo (c. 64 B.C. – A.D. 21), who came from Amaseia in Pontus (northwest Asia Minor). The account is based on a personal autopsy "from what I myself saw after the recent restoration of the city by the Romans."[A-1] Strabo may have been visiting the colony when Octavian — the future emperor Augustus — was on his way back to Italy after the battle of Actium (Sept. 2, 31 B.C.) and the capture of Alexandria (Aug. 1, 30 B.C.) for his triple triumph (held Aug. 13 – 15, 29 B.C.). Octavian is known to have stopped at Corinth at this time. One of Strabo's vantage points was the Acrocorinth: "I myself have looked down at the settlement from Acrocorinth."[A-2] From the mountain he could look across the Corinthian Gulf to the mountains of Parnassos and Helikon on the Greek mainland. Strabo apparently made use of earlier accounts of the colony, including Apollodoros's commentary on the Homeric *Catalogue of the Ships* (written in the second century B.C. on the eve of the Roman destruction of the colony), Hieronymos of Cardia (300 B.C.), and the fourth-century B.C. geographer Eudoxos of Knidos.

CORINTH

▼

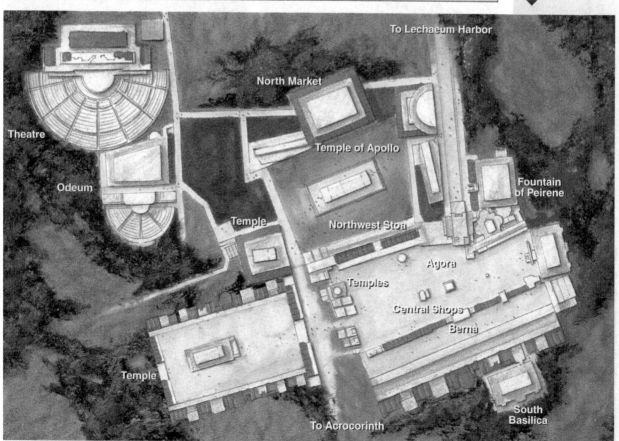

1 Corinthians

(clockwise from top)

CORINTH

Aerial view of the remains of the ancient city.

A Corinthian inscription with a list of victors in the Isthmian games.

The *diolkos* — a rock road that the Romans built enabling them to drag boats across the narrowest point of the isthmus.

The Acrocorinth with some of the ruins of ancient Corinth in the foreground.

View from the Lechaeum, Corinth's western port, toward Corinth and the Acrocorinth.

Corinth became the residence for the Roman governor of the senatorial province of Achaia, which was reestablished by Claudius in A.D. 44. Prior to that, the province had been combined with Macedonia as one of the military "imperial" provinces (see comments on 16:15). This administrative function allowed Corinth to become the leading city in the province. It seems to have attracted members of elite families to reside there, such as the Euryclids from Sparta. It also meant that individual cities would need to consult the governor at Corinth; thus, members of the Corinthian elite allowed themselves to be used as intermediaries or *proxenoi*. One of these *proxenoi*, L. Licinnius Anteros, was honored by the city of Methana near Troezen in A.D. 1/2.[5]

The Spiritual Climate of the Area

The second-century A.D. Roman orator Favorinus of Arles (in the south of France) praised Corinth as a city "favoured by Aphrodite."[6] Certainly in the Hellenistic period before the sack of the city, the sanctuary of Aphrodite on the Acrocorinth had been a complex affair. Strabo, probably drawing on classical or Hellenistic historians of the city, noted that at this earlier time, "the temple of Aphrodite was so rich that it owned more than a thousand temple-slaves, courtesans, whom both men and women had dedicated to the goddess."[7] However, Strabo's own visit to the Acrocorinth showed that the Roman temple was far more modest: "The summit has a small temple of Aphrodite."[8] Aphrodite or Venus (her Roman name) was seen as the ancestor of Julius Caesar, the founder of the Roman colony. Indeed

in the Julian Forum at Rome, completed by Caesar's adopted son Augustus, there was a temple to Venus Genetrix. A further temple of Aphrodite at Corinth appears to have been located on a terrace at the west end of the forum, as part of an inscription has been found that links the structure to Venus.[9] The second-century A.D. travel writer Pausanias also noted that this part of the forum contained a statue of Aphrodite made by the sculptor Hermogenes of Kythera (an island off the south coast of the Peloponnese).[10]

The forum of Corinth today is dominated by the columns of a Greek temple of the Doric order of architecture, probably erected in the sixth century B.C. It survived the sack of the city and was adapted in the Roman period for a new type of cult. Some of the earlier cults of the Greek city may have been reestablished, though it is not clear how much continuity there was with cult practice of the second century B.C. The sanctuary of Demeter and Kore (Persephone) on the slopes of the Acrocorinth may not have been revived until the second century A.D.

The colony also housed the cult to the Roman emperors. This may have been focused on the temple that coins of the colony show was dedicated to the Gens Iulia (the Julian family); Julius Caesar was deified after his assassination in March 44 B.C. and his adopted son Augustus was able to enjoy the associated benefits of divinity.[11]

One of the most important cults of the Corinthia was that of Poseidon (Lat. Neptune), a god associated with the sea and earthquakes. His cult was located at Isthmia at the neck of the Corinthian isthmus. This sanctuary, with a temple to the god, was associated with one of the sets of Panhellenic games that attracted people

**TEMPLE OF
APHRODITE**

The scant remains
of this famous
temple on top of
the Acrocorinth.
▼

to attend from all over the Greek world. Such games, like those at Olympia, Delphi, and Nemea, continued in the Roman period and became the model for the establishment of festivals in the cities of the Greek east. While the emperor Nero was taking part in the Isthmian games in November 67, he declared Greece to be free from taxes — a right later removed by the emperor Vespasian.[12] The responsibility of the games had been transferred to nearby Sikyon after Corinth was sacked, but was restored to the colony some time after its foundation.

Eastern deities are known from Corinth, though it is not always easy to decide when in the Roman period they were introduced. Often the main source for information is Pausanias, writing some 120 years after the establishment of the church at Corinth. One of the most colorful accounts of the Egyptian deity Isis in the Corinthia is contained in the work of Lucius Apuleius, in his visions of the goddess at Cenchreae described in his work, *The Golden Ass*.[13] Certainly the worship of Isis and Serapis can be traced back to the Hellenistic period, and Corinth, as a major port, would have been in contact with Egypt. A similar phenomenon for these Egyptian deities can be found on the island of Crete.[14]

The Introduction of Christianity to Corinth

The church had been established at Corinth after Paul's visit to Macedonia and Athens (Acts 18). Paul possibly arrived at Corinth by sea, in which case he would have sailed from the Piraeus, the port of Athens, and arrived at Cenchrea, the eastern port of Corinth. The land route along the isthmus of Corinth was not an easy one. The date can be fixed by the mention of the presence of the Roman governor of the province of Achaia, L. Junius Gallio. An inscription

▶ Pausanias in Corinth

Pausanias probably came from Lydia in modern Turkey, in the region of Mount Sipylus, as it is a feature regularly mentioned in the text.[A-3] A likely city for his upbringing is Magnesia on the Sipylus.[A-4] Pausanias's discussion of the refoundation of Corinth, 217 years before his day, provides a date of A.D. 174 for the writing of this part of the work.[A-5] Scholars think he completed his writing by around 180. The colony of Corinth is discussed in Book 2 of his travel guide to the Greek world. As in many places, he notes "things worthy of mention" — the "starred" sites still common in modern travel accounts, including "the extant remains of antiquity," that is, the pre-Roman city. Pausanias qualifies his recommendation by noting that "the greater number of them belong to the period of its second ascendancy."[A-6] Like Strabo he likely ascended Acrocorinth and commented on the sanctuary of Aphrodite found there. He left Corinth by traveling up the coast of the Corinthian Gulf toward neighboring Sikyon.

from the sanctuary of Apollo at Delphi shows that he was governor in Greece when Claudius had obtained "tribunician power" twelve times and had been acclaimed emperor twenty-six times. From other inscriptions, these events place the Delphi inscription between the end of 51 and August 52 (when he was acclaimed emperor for the twenty-seventh time). An undated statue base, originally no doubt bearing a portrait of the governor, was erected in honor of Gallio at Plataia in Boiotia (central Greece). Paul stayed in the city for some eighteen months. Early members of the church included Priscilla and Aquila, who had been expelled from Rome by Emperor Claudius.

Issues in the Church at Corinth

It was perhaps at Corinth that Christianity came into contact with a city that was mainly Italian in culture and with a population that, officially at least, was Latin-speaking. It was to Corinth that those who had aspirations in the province of Achaia moved, and it had become fashionable to adopt Roman culture. Perhaps this accounts for the personal rivalry that becomes such an issue in 1 Corinthians. The ambitions and emphasis on status so clear in the colony were being transferred to the church community. Thus we also find issues of dress being used to make statements about positions in society. Even Paul's role as preacher and apostle

▶ Archaeological Prospects at Corinth

Since 1895 Corinth has been explored by the American School of Classical Studies at Athens, in conjunction with the Archaeological Institute of America, though excavations have focused on the area of the forum.[A-7] Changes in sea levels have taken place since antiquity, which has hindered the exploration of the two harbors of Corinth. Cenchrea, the eastern port of Corinth, is now partly submerged, but it has been the focus of excavations by an American team, including staff of Chicago and Indiana Universities.[A-8] Lechaeum, on the Gulf of Corinth, has been the subject of limited excavation by a team from the Greek archaeological service.[A-9] The Panhellenic sanctuary of Poseidon at Isthmia has been excavated by an American team from the University of Chicago.[A-10]

ARCHAEOLOGICAL SITES

(left) The remains of the harbor at Cenchrae. The partially submerged foundations are the remnants of a temple of Isis.

(right) The forum at Corinth.

▼

were questioned in the light of the expectation from the educated elite of what a good public orator should be like.[15]

The letter is a response to specific issues raised by the church as well as to more informal information that has reached Paul in the province of Asia. In chapter 7 Paul mentions "the matters you wrote about" (7:1), which perhaps include marriage (7:1), single people (7:25), food sacrificed to pagan gods (8:1), spiritual gifts (12:1), and a collection for God's people (16:1). Paul writes to a dynamic church that is trying to find its feet in an alien culture.

Introduction to the Letter (1:1 – 3)

Paul . . . and our brother Sosthenes (1:1). The opening sentence of the letter shows that it was jointly written by Paul and Sosthenes. Paul emphasizes his authoritative position by drawing attention to his role as an apostle of Jesus Christ; the central role of Jesus Christ is underscored throughout this opening chapter. Sosthenes is designated not as an apostle but as "our brother." A possible candidate for this individual is the Corinthian synagogue ruler, Sosthenes, who was beaten during Paul's time in Corinth (Acts 18:17). Other individuals of this name are known from Corinth, including a magistrate possibly during the reign of Emperor Trajan.[16] Paul, however, is the main correspondent, for later he instructs them "to imitate me" (4:16).

To the church of God in Corinth (1:2). This letter is addressed to the church at Corinth in contrast to the second letter, which was also to "the saints" throughout the Roman province of Achaia. Paul uses a Greek political word for the church, *ekklēsia*; it implies the whole body of

Christ's people in the city. Paul provides a list of reasons why individuals could call themselves members of the church in the same way that citizens of Corinth would be able to point to certain criteria by which they could call themselves Corinthians.

Grace and peace to you from God our Father and the Lord Jesus Christ (1:3). The combination of grace and peace is a common formula in New Testament letters. The more usual Greek greeting, *chaire*, has been transformed to the Christian word for grace, *charis*, and linked to the Greek word for the Hebrew *shalom*.

Thanksgiving (1:4 – 9)

I always thank God . . . because of his grace given you (1:4). Paul follows a standard pattern in his thanksgiving for the church at Corinth. He gives particular thanks for the grace they have received undeservedly from God. In a church characterized by boasting, the members need to be reminded of what they have already received.

You have been enriched in every way (1:5). In a church that contained every shade of society (1:26), all have been enriched, not in a worldly way, but with two specific characteristics, speaking (*logos*) and knowledge (*gnōsis*). *Logos* and *gnōsis* were both characteristics valued by the elite in the Roman colony; within the church such gifts are open to all, regardless of status. The Roman orator Favorinus visited Corinth in the first part of the second century A.D. and recorded a love of public-speaking in the city.[17] Paul may be placing an emphasis on speaking with meetings of the church.

Our testimony . . . was confirmed in you (1:6). The Greek word for "confirmed" suggests that Paul is using a legal metaphor to illustrate that God has completed a contract with the church at Corinth, marked by the evidence of the gifts of "speaking" and "knowledge."

As you eagerly wait for our Lord Jesus Christ to be revealed (1:7). The view that the present world will come to an end with the appearing of Jesus Christ is in marked contrast to the Roman worldview, which expected an unchecked continuation of its empire's domination and authority.

That you will be blameless on the day of our Lord Jesus Christ (1:8). Paul continues the legal metaphor by using the word "blameless." The "day of the Lord" is an expression drawn from the Old Testament prophets (Amos 5:18 – 20; Joel 2:31), which suggests that part of the readership of Paul's letter is Jewish.

God, who has called you into fellowship with his Son Jesus Christ our Lord, is faithful (1:9). This verse draws on the imagery of the Mosaic law: "Know therefore that the LORD your God is God; he is the faithful God" (Deut. 7:9). Paul

is reminding individual members of the Corinthian church that whatever their social status, a faithful God will equip them for service.

Loyalties and Divisions (1:10 – 17)

Paul now starts a section in the letter where he responds to issues in the church brought to his attention both by a report from "Chloe's household" (1:12) and from the personal report of Stephanas, Fortunatus, and Achaicus (16:15 – 17).

I appeal . . . that . . . you agree with one another so that there may be no divisions among you and that you may be perfectly united in mind and thought (1:10). This issue of divisions in the church was clearly known by the early Christian writer Clement (c. A.D. 95). Paul uses the verb "appeal," which usually had the meaning of writing with authority; this is no empty rhetoric, but an appeal coming from an apostle of Jesus Christ. The Corinthian church needs to take note. Paul uses two metaphors in his appeal. The word "divisions" recalls the furrows created by ploughing, whereas the vision of being "perfectly united" recalls the mending of nets (Mark 1:19).

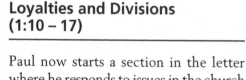

CORINTH

(left) Corinthian columns on a temple dedicated to Octavia, the sister of Caesar Augustus.

(right) The well-preserved structure of the Fountain of Peirene.

Some from Chloe's household have informed me that there are quarrels among you (1:11). The members of Chloe's household are likely domestic servants — either slaves or former slaves (so-called freedmen). Insofar as Paul writes the letter from Asia (16:19) — which probably means the city of Ephesus — the movement of slaves or freedmen between Corinth and western Turkey has been plausibly interpreted as indicating that Chloe was in fact from Asia but had settled in Corinth. A first-century example of such an individual is presented by the case of Junia Theodora, originally from Lycia (in southwestern Turkey), but who had settled in the colony and proudly called herself "resident of Corinth."[18] The word *eris* ("quarrels") is often linked to divisions and strife, frequently within the political sphere. Such quarrels were characteristics of pupils in the intellectual world of the first century, where great emphasis was placed on loyalty to the master or teacher. Paul urges the Corinthians to look away from their spiritual teachers and rather to Jesus Christ.

I follow Paul . . . Apollos . . . Cephas . . . Christ (1:12).

Paul lists the different named leaders within the Corinthian church. Apollos was a Jew from Alexandria (in Egypt), who is described as "learned" or "eloquent" (Acts 18:24). He had come under the influence of Priscilla and Aquila at Ephesus and from there had moved to Corinth. Cephas is the Aramaic name for Peter. The Greek phrase translated as "I follow" (or equally well as "I belong to") is sometimes found inscribed on objects dedicated to the pagan gods of the Greek world. For example, an archaic column-krater (a two-handled bowl) found on the site of the later Asklepieion carries the inscription "I belong to Apollo."[19] Thus, there may be different groups within the church at Corinth who are more keen to support their own theological position than to be united in Jesus Christ. These divisions or parties are of the same sort as found in contemporary political bodies.

Is Christ divided? (1:13). Paul uses a series of rhetorical questions to confront the church with the foolishness of their position. Thus Paul uses a means of communication that was familiar to the well educated.

Crispus and Gaius (1:14). Crispus is almost certainly to be identified with the synagogue ruler at Corinth, who with "his entire household believed in

APHRODITE

Statue of the goddess, also known as Venus to the Romans.

▶ **"I Belong to Aphrodite"**

The series of slogans found at the beginning of 1 Corinthians showing allegiance to individuals ("I follow Paul"; "I follow Apollos"; etc.) use the same Greek phrase found on objects dedicated in sanctuaries in Corinth. A bronze dedication found in the excavations carries the statement "I belong to Aphrodite," thereby signifying that an individual had offered it to the goddess in her sanctuary at Corinth. Although this came from the archaic city, it is possible that individuals at Corinth have adopted slogans ultimately derived from the religious language of the colony.

REFLECTIONS

IT IS EASY TO FALL INTO THE TRAP of preferring the leadership style of one person over the other. Perhaps one individual's preaching speaks more directly to us, or his or her pastoral concern is more relevant. Such split allegiances can divide a church community. We need to ensure that our main commitment is to Jesus Christ.

the Lord" during Paul's first visit to the city (Acts 18:8). A synagogue ruler at Corinth is likely to have been a wealthy individual, for he was responsible for the upkeep of the building. Gaius was not only a common Roman name (note the Macedonian Gaius who accompanied Paul; Acts 19:29; 20:4), but inscriptions from Corinth show that it was a relatively common name in first-century Corinth. This Gaius is likely the same person "whose hospitality I [Paul] and the whole church here enjoy" (Rom. 16:23, a letter written from Corinth). Gaius almost certainly holds Roman citizenship; it is undoubtedly the praenomen of those freedmen who received their citizenship from Gaius Julius Caesar.

The household of Stephanas (1:16). In addition to Crispus and Gaius Paul has also baptized "the household of Stephanas" while at Corinth. The term "household" (*oikos*) is likely to have included not only Stephanas's immediate family, but also those attached to the household, perhaps including slaves. This same household is mentioned later in the letter, when Paul records the delegation sent to him (16:15, 17). Stephanas, along with Crispus and Gaius, are likely to have been among the

"wise," "influential," and those of "noble birth" (1:26) of the colony.

Not with words of human wisdom (1:17). Paul makes a distinction between using sophisticated rhetorical techniques and the preaching of the Christian gospel. He challenges the Corinthian church not to use the techniques of contemporary oratory unless they retain the cross as a central feature of their message. Paul's worry is that if he uses special rhetorical techniques, members of the church might admire him rather than heed his message.

Wisdom and Rhetoric (1:18 – 31)

Paul now develops the contrast between the wisdom of the age and the message of the cross. The background to this section is perhaps the way that itinerant speakers of his day, so-called sophists, used rhetorical techniques to influence their audiences. Such oratory was widely valued, and Paul has to remind the Corinthian church that the content matters more than the presentation.

The message of the cross (1:18). The word "message" translates the Greek word *logos*. As such, it allows a distinc-

ROMAN CROSS

A model of a typical Roman cross with a nameplate on the top and two wooden beams for the arms and legs.

tion to be drawn between the "words of human wisdom" (1:17) and the "word" or "message" of the cross. Indeed, it is the "oratory" of the cross itself that becomes central in communication.

Those who are perishing, but to us who are being saved (1:18). Paul presents the church with a new vision of world order. A Roman colony like Corinth has certain social distinctions: Roman citizen and noncitizen, slave and free, male and female. For Paul the Jew (and at the same time Roman citizen) there is the distinction between Jews and Gentiles. The Greeks made a distinction between themselves and those who do not speak Greek, whom they called by the word *barbaros* (see comments on 14:11). However, the new way of perceiving the world must ignore these worldly distinctions. Society consisted of two groups: those like Paul and the members of the Corinthian church ("but to us") who can be described as "being saved," and those outside the church "who are perishing." Note too that those in the colony who have power but are outside the church view the cross as "foolishness"; in contrast, those considered to be foolish have experienced the power of God.

I will destroy the wisdom of the wise; the intelligence of the intelligent I will frustrate (1:19). Paul appeals to Isaiah 29:14 to support his argument. He quotes the Greek Septuagint version of the prophecy, although he changes the last word; the LXX reads "I will hide" rather than "I will frustrate." The "wise" was a recognized Greek term for members of the social elite; thus, Paul is applying Old Testament Scripture to the Corinthian situation. Such an appeal would suggest that

members of the Corinthian church were conversant with the Jewish Scriptures.

The wise man . . . the scholar . . . the philosopher of this age (1:20). Paul uses four rhetorical questions, which may be a deliberate allusion to another passage of Isaiah (33:18): "Where is that chief officer? Where is the one who took the revenue? Where is the officer in charge of the towers?" However, there are key differences. Paul chooses three figures representative of education in the Greek provinces of the eastern Mediterranean. The "wise man" (*sophos*) can be understood as a Greek philosopher. The "scholar" (*grammateus*) can have two meanings. In a Jewish setting, the *grammateus* was an expert in the Mosaic law; in the Gospels the word is translated as "the teachers of the law" (e.g., Matt. 5:20). A *grammateus* in the Greek

world was the normal term for a "city clerk"; such a figure features in the riot in Ephesus (Acts 19:35). As Paul goes on to make a distinction between Jews and Greeks (1:22), it is likely that he has in mind Jewish "teachers of the law." "The philosopher [*syzētētēs*] of this age" means "the disputer of this age"; it seems likely that Paul is alluding to the emergence of itinerant orators or sophists.[20]

The world through its wisdom (1:21). The "wisdom of the world," alluded to in the previous verse, may refer to the intellectual climate of the Roman empire. The "world" (*kosmos*) was a way of defining the limit of Roman rule. For example, in a decree passed by the provincial council of Asia c. A.D. 15 and found at Halikarnassos (in western Turkey), the emperor Augustus was described as "father of his country and of the whole world."[21]

Jews demand miraculous signs and Greeks look for wisdom (1:22). Paul identifies two main cultural groups, "Jews" and "Greeks," while ignoring the Romans; both Jews and Greeks could hold Roman citizenship. Paul characterizes the Jews as looking for "miraculous signs" that authenticate the coming of their Messiah. Such an interest is reflected in the Gospel of Mark, where the Pharisees, in order to test Jesus,

"asked him for a sign from heaven"; Jesus replied, "Why does this generation ask for a miraculous sign? I tell you the truth, no sign will be given to it" (Mark 8:11 – 12). The Greeks had a reputation, which can be traced back to the Greek historian Herodotus, of a love for wisdom (*sophia*). Herodotus tells the story that the king of Scythia (an area adjoining the Black Sea) once sent to find out what the Greeks were like; it was reported, "all Greeks were keen for every kind of learning, except the Lacedaemonians."[22] Particular groups of Greek philosophers, such as the Stoics and Epicureans, gave discourses on "the nature of the gods" as part of their search for wisdom.

We preach Christ crucified: a stumbling block to Jews and foolishness to Gentiles (1:23). "Stumbling block" (*skandalon*) in fact implies that for the Jews the cross was a literal scandal or an offensive action. Since the Jews believed that "anyone who is hung on a tree is under God's curse" (Deut. 21:23), the thought of the promised Messiah being crucified on a wooden cross was scandalous. For the Gentiles (i.e., non-Jews), the preaching of the crucified Christ seemed ridiculous. Jesus had been convicted by the Roman governor of a province of the empire and had been crucified according to Roman law. The idea that a criminal could be

▶ Coins at Corinth

Corinth, in common with other Roman colonies, issued coinage with the names of the two chief magistrates, the *duovirs*. Such coinage helps to provide a list of the names of wealthy individuals who dominated the political life of the colony, and as such help to date some of the buildings they helped build. The coins sometimes carried images of new buildings in the colony, such as the temple of the Divine Julius Caesar. Such local coinage emphasizes the identity and status of the colony within the province of Achaia and the wider Roman empire.

the Christ was regarded as foolish. Such views about Christianity can be detected in the correspondence between Pliny the Younger, governor of the province of Bithynia (in northwest Turkey), and the Roman emperor Trajan.[23]

Not many of you were wise by human standards; not many were influential; not many were of noble birth (1:26). Paul makes an important statement here about the status of members of the Corinthian church. In a Roman colony organized in terms of citizenship, birth, and wealth, membership of the church was purely on the basis of calling (a theme first developed at 1:24). Paul identifies three groups here: the "wise" (*sophoi*), the "influential" or those who held power (*dynatoi*) in the colony, and those of "noble birth" (lit., "well born"). These three terms describe the social elite of the Roman colony and may have been used as marks of pride. The fact that "not many" were called does imply that a few members of the Corinthian church were drawn from the elite of Corinthian society. In other words, the message of Jesus Christ was reaching the full range of social strata at Corinth (and presumably elsewhere).

The foolish things of the world . . . the weak things of the world . . . the lowly things of this world and the despised things — and the things that are not (1:27 – 28). The elite of Corinthian society may well have despised the lower members who perhaps did not hold Roman citizenship. Certainly the orators or sophists of the day would have ridiculed the foolish, the weak, the lowly, the despised, and the nobodies. Yet it was this latter group who had been chosen by God. Paul is using a recognized rhetorical technique of constructing arguments from opposites. The Greek uses the neuter — conveyed by the translation "things" — to outline the attributes of the individuals called by God.[24]

No one may boast before him (1:29). "To boast" regularly features in the Corinthian letters. The sophists regularly boasted of their status. If educated members of the social elite were taking positions of leadership in the Corinthian church, they may have being using oratorical skills to "boast" of their own social position, emphasizing that they were "wise," "influential," or of "noble birth." Paul makes it clear that such boasting has no place in the church.

Let him who boasts boast in the Lord (1:31). Paul supports his argument with Jeremiah 9:24, but replaces "about this" with "in the Lord." Those familiar with the Old Testament would be able to complete

---

▶ Jews at Corinth

According to Acts 18:4, Corinth had a Jewish synagogue. Among the early converts was the *archisynagōgos* (the "ruler of the synagogue"), Crispus, who has a suggestively Roman name. Philo also mentions Corinth as one of the cities of the province of Achaia that had a synagogue.[A-11] A synagogue inscription, almost certainly dating to several hundred years after Paul's time, has been found at Corinth. The location of Corinth, with its contacts with both the eastern Mediterranean and Italy, make it a likely place for a Jewish community. Paul's frequent reference and allusion to the Old Testament suggest that the Christian community there included members who were Jewish by background.

the quotation that resonates with the issues of the preceding verses: "Let not the wise man boast of his wisdom or the strong man boast of his strength but let him who boasts boast about this: that he understands and knows me, that I am the LORD, who exercises kindness, justice and righteousness on earth, for in these I delight" (Jer. 9:23 – 24).

Paul's Arrival at Corinth (2:1 – 5)

Paul turns from considering the way in which the Corinthians have considered wisdom and rhetoric and instead focuses on the content of his own ministry. He presents a preaching style that may have become less familiar to the Corinthian Christians.

I did not come with eloquence or superior wisdom (2:1). Paul refers here to his original arrival in the colony, probably in the fall of A.D. 50 (Acts 18). He had "reasoned in the synagogue, trying to persuade Jews and Greeks" (18:4), trying to draw attention to Jesus Christ. He is drawing a contrast with the way that public speakers in the ancient world — sophists and orators — would arrive in a city and follow a set (and expected) protocol of heaping praise on the city and its achievements; in using such "eloquence" and "superior wisdom", these sophists tried both to win an audience and to draw attention to themselves.[25] So, for example, Favorinus, who visited Corinth probably in the early second century A.D., observed, "When I first visited your city [polis] the first time . . . and gave your people [dēmos] and magistrates a sample of my eloquence [lit., words], I seemed to be on friendly, yes intimate, terms with you."[26] Dio Chrysostom, addressing the assembly of his own city Prusa in Bithynia (northwest-

ern Turkey), observed that in his travels he could visit "the greatest cities" — including Rome — and his arrival was "escorted with much enthusiasm and éclat [philotimia], the recipients of my visits being grateful for my presence and begging me to address them and advise them and flocking about my doors from early dawn, all without my having incurred any expense or having made any contribution, with the result that all would admire me."[27]

Paul followed a different strategy, for his oratory proclaimed "the testimony about God." The Greek words translated as "superior" are better translated as "according to excellence" and apply both to the "oratory" ("eloquence") and to the "wisdom."[28] The stress on excellence was familiar to an elite group at Corinth.

For I resolved to know nothing while I was with you except Jesus Christ and him crucified (2:2). Paul had made his mind up that his arrival at Corinth would be marked by a presentation of Jesus Christ. He did not want his preaching to be confused with the oratory of a sophist, which would be done merely for its own sake. An orator might, for example, have included praise of the colony at Corinth, but Paul's emphasis was on the cross.

I came to you in weakness and fear, and with much trembling (2:3). In contrast to the sophists and orators, who arrived in Corinth with what might be termed "presence," Paul describes himself in some negative terms. "Weakness" is probably better translated "hardships," reflecting the difficulties he faced through his traveling ministry. "With much trembling" is not found in the Greek, which rather links "fear" and "trembling" — words that in the Old Testament reflect the presence of God. Such words contrast with the first-century speaker Scopelian, who used an "extremely melodious voice" and certainly could not be seen as a "timid speaker."[29] Thus, Paul was a man in whose message his hearers could detect the word of God.

My message and my preaching were not with wise and persuasive words, but with a demonstration of the Spirit's power (2:4). Paul's message (or "oratory") led to his preaching; by contrast, the Corinthians were familiar with the sophists of their day, who used "wise and persuasive words" to bring their hearers to wisdom.[30] "Demonstration" (*apodeixis*) is a word Paul has borrowed from oratory itself. Cicero defines this term as "a process of reasoning that leads from things

> **WISDOM AND RHETORIC**
>
> *(left)* A statue of Sophia in the Celsus library façade in Ephesus.
>
> *(right)* Aristotle (384 – 322 B.C.), the father of rhetoric.

▶ Oratory in Corinth

Public speaking or oratory is one of the issues lying behind the letter. A speech by the orator Favorinus (c. A.D. 80 – 150), who came from Arles in the south of France, is preserved in the corpus of speeches by his teacher Dio Chrysostom.[A-12] Although the speech was delivered some time after Paul's day and in a period when the colony was becoming more Greek, it provides detail about the way in which orators addressed their audiences. After talking about the colorful and eminent visitors who had visited the city — including Arion, who was saved by a dolphin, Solon, the great lawgiver of the city of Athens, and the historian Herodotus — Favorinus recalled this about his second visit to the city:

You were so glad to see me that you did your best to get me to stay with you, but seeing that to be impossible, you did have a likeness made of me, and you took this and set it up in your Library, a front row seat as it were, where you felt it would most effectively stimulate the youth to persevere in the same pursuits as myself.[A-13]

Favorinus was himself a great rival of another orator, Polemo of Laodicea,[A-14] and through this speech it is possible to detect the way that Favorinus used his speech to promote himself — and in this case to have the Corinthians reinstate his statue.

perceived to something not previously perceived."[31] In Quintilian's study of oratory the "demonstration" or "proof" is seen as "a method of proving what is not certain by means of what is certain."[32] Paul's technique is essentially a "proof" of the Spirit's power.

So that your faith might not rest on men's wisdom, but on God's power (2:5). Paul warns the Corinthians about allowing their faith to be based on the hearing of fine oratory; faith comes as a result of hearing the message and by God's intervention. The word "power" (*dynamis*) was used by ancient rhetoricians, such as Dio Chrysostom, for eloquence in oratory.[33] Christian preachers are not in the business of using persuasive techniques; rather, they persuade people by relying on God's, not their own, power.

God's Wisdom and Human Wisdom (2:6–16)

Paul has refuted the wisdom being presented to the Corinthians by contemporary orators. He has demonstrated that he is different from such speakers. Paul now picks on a word much loved by the Corinthians, "wisdom," but uses it to point them to God.

We do . . . speak a message of wisdom among the mature, but not the wisdom of this age or of the rulers of this age (2:6). "Mature" (*teleios*) was a word the public orators of Paul's day used about themselves; as they gathered followers — or disciples — around them, they progressed into maturity. Such "mature" people, no doubt from elite families, would go on to hold magistracies in the colony. For Paul, however, the "mature" are those who hear and respond to his message about "Jesus Christ and him crucified" (2:2). "Rulers of this age" also occurs a few lines later (2:8), which suggests he has in mind the Jewish and Roman authorities responsible for Jesus' death. Corinth, as the seat of the provincial governor of Achaia, was one of the centers for "rulers" of the Roman empire.

A wisdom . . . hidden (2:7). There is a sense of irony here, for as the Corinthian elite seek wisdom by listening to the sophists and orators and thus grow into maturity, they have failed to understand the nature of true "wisdom."

None of the rulers of this age understood it, for if they had, they would not have crucified the Lord of glory (2:8). The Roman governor Pontius Pilate and the educated Jewish elite had put Jesus to death; in spite of their "wisdom" they did not recognize the "Lord of glory." Paul demonstrates that members of the Corinthian church who wish to follow the type of wisdom recommended by their secular society are no different from those who crucified the Christ. Wise Corinthian Christians will not be uncritical followers of the "rulers of the age." Interestingly, Paul used a similar argument about rulers failing to recognize Christ in his sermon preached at Pisidian Antioch (Acts 13:27).

No eye has seen, no ear has heard, no mind has conceived what God has prepared for those who love him (2:9). Paul alludes to Isaiah 64:4, which, although not a precise quotation, makes the point that God's grace will be given to those who love him.

God has revealed it to us by his Spirit (2:10). God's grace has been revealed to the Corinthian Christians. In other words, Paul's poor oratorical style has nevertheless conveyed the message about "Jesus Christ and him crucified" that was endorsed by "the Spirit's power." There is no point for seeking more mature "wisdom."

Not in words taught us by human wisdom (2:13). The "words" to which Paul alludes are those presented by the secular orators; it is interchangeable with "speech." They must be cautious about adopting the techniques devised by orators, which were intended to generate admiration among the listeners. The contrast is made with the words taught by the Holy Spirit.

For who has known the mind of the Lord that he may instruct him? (2:16). Paul quotes here from Isaiah 40:13, though in an adapted form, "Who has understood the mind of the LORD, or instructed him as his counselor?" Such a change allows Paul to turn the quotation into a rhetorical device that requires the Corinthians to answer that nobody is in that position.

Spiritual or Worldly Members of the Church (3:1 – 4)

I could not address you as spiritual but as worldly (3:1). Paul is describing the time when he was originally with the Corinthian Christians. He describes them at that time as "worldly" — more accurately "fleshly" or even "those composed of flesh." The Corinthian Christians may have described themselves as "the spiritual ones" (*pneumatikoi*). Paul's implication is that the Corinthian Christians are un-spiritual, by which he means that their lives are unworthy of the Spirit who has made them believers in Christ. The "infants" contrast with the "mature" (2:6). Paul uses imagery found in both Hellenistic[34] and Jewish philosophy[35] to show the growth of maturity. His argument is that whereas the Corinthians would describe themselves as "spiritual" and "mature," Paul would describe them as "fleshly" and "immature."

Not solid food (3:2). Would the Corinthians have accused Paul of not offering them wisdom, which they considered to be "solid food"? Yet if this section develops Paul's preceding arguments (2:6 – 16), then the milk is the good news that allowed the Corinthians to become Christians, and the solid food is a developed understanding of the Cross. Paul's concern is that the Corinthians consume the "solid food" of the gospel (even if in the form of milk!), not the "solid food" of wisdom that inhibits Christian or spiritual growth.

You are still worldly (3:3). "Worldly" contrasts with the Greek word used at 3:1 and here effectively means, "You are still characteristic of flesh." The Corinthian Christians have not taken on the characteristics of the Spirit but rather of the world.

There is jealousy and quarreling among you (3:3). Paul introduces a new word, "jealousy," alongside that of "quarreling" (see 1:11). This combination is found elsewhere in Paul (2 Cor. 12:20; Gal. 5:20). Such jealousy is akin to "rivalry," a characteristic of those who follow the sophists; such behavior can be described as "worldly" (or "fleshly") or of "men" (i.e., a common human trait). Christian maturity leads men and women to reject the partisanship found in secular society. Faith rests on the power of the Spirit; human values rest on wisdom (1 Cor. 2:4 – 5). Paul's imagery sees life as a walk (NIV "acting"), a process informed by sophists or by the Spirit.

"I follow Paul," and another, "I follow Apollos" (3:4). Paul returns to his earlier argument (1:12) and shows that those who seek to follow specific Christian leaders or teachers (as opposed to Christ or the Spirit) are adopting secular values. Paul's concern is for all Christian people to be recognized and characterized by a spiritual (i.e., Spirit-led) life.

Images of Christian Ministry and the Church (3:5 – 17)

Paul is concerned that the Corinthian church realizes the meaning of Christian ministry and the church.

What, after all, is Apollos? And what is Paul? (3:5). At the beginning of the letter Paul introduced himself as "an apostle of Christ Jesus" (1:1). Now he brackets himself with Apollos — who is not described in the New Testament as an apostle and here is deliberately given primacy before Paul — as one of the "servants" (*diakonos*, the equivalent of "deacon"). All Christian ministers are primarily subject to God's authority: God allocates the tasks in his fields (3:9). As a "servant" of the Lord, both Paul and Apollos, indeed all Chris-

tian ministers, have a duty to present the Christian gospel so that individuals come to believe in Jesus Christ. Paul emphasizes that Christian belief is not in the minister who brings the good news, but rather through the minister.

I planted the seed, Apollos watered it, but God made it grow (3:6). Christian ministers have different functions or ministries; Paul shows the differences between himself and Apollos by using an agricultural metaphor. The territory of ancient Corinth was rich in agriculture. Yet it still needed individuals to plant and irrigate the crop. Without watering, the crop would fail; without planting, there would be nothing to water. Thus both Paul and Apollos have valid and mutually dependent ministries, and both are subject to God, who in fact brings the growth. Christian ministers need to be obedient to the task that the Lord has allocated to them (3:5) in the same way as those working in the fields need to obey the owner if there is to be a crop.

So neither he who plants nor he who waters is anything, but only God, who makes things grow (3:7). Individuals at Corinth may say they follow a specific individual, but Paul insists that true Christian ministers are in fact "nobodies" because it is Christ who brings the growth. When we eat a loaf of bread, the name of the man or woman who planted the seed is unimportant. So in the church, the personality who brings the good news is unimportant compared to the God whose Son died on the cross for us.

Each will be rewarded according to his own labor (3:8). Those working in the fields around Corinth have a united purpose: to ensure there is a crop to provide themselves with food and a livelihood; that is their reward (or "pay"). Those ministering in the church likewise have a single purpose; thus, it is foolish to be partisan because all ministers are working — or should be working — toward a common goal.

You are God's field, God's building (3:9). Once again Paul emphasizes that all who work in God's field must have a sense of working together with others who seek to present the same gospel of Jesus Christ. Note too that those who work in the field have no claim to it; that right belongs to God alone — Christian ministers can hold no claim on the church in which they serve. Paul places an emphasis on "we," not just the minister, but all who are involved in the life of the church. Paul then switches the imagery from the fields of Corinth to a city with God's building.

I laid a foundation as an expert builder (3:10). Paul uses an image taken from the urban landscape of the Roman colony. Since the creation of the colony in 44 B.C. wealthy benefactors had been giving new buildings, which had decorated the space around the forum at the heart of the colony (see "Buildings at Corinth"). Paul

is alluding to such building projects. Like the agricultural metaphor, two people are involved in the construction of the building: the first lays a foundation, the second builds up the walls. As in the previous metaphor, Paul is addressing the issue of how to build up the church at Corinth. The grace of God has been given to Paul specifically to found the church. He describes himself as an "expert" builder, using the Greek word *sophos*, which resonates and contrasts with the way that the elite members of the church have described themselves (1:20). The word "builder" literally means "chief builder" (i.e., architect), which suggests that Paul has been given specific responsibility for the building project. "Someone else" probably refers to various teachers in Corinth who are moving away from what Paul originally taught.

No one can lay any foundation other than the one already laid (3:11). Foundations are prepared for specific buildings anticipated by the chief builder; any other construction would be inappropriate. For example, if the architects of Corinth had prepared foundations for a substantial Roman temple and somebody built a house instead, there would have been a scandal. Likewise, Paul has prepared foundations based on Jesus Christ, and those seeking to develop the church must continue to encourage the church to focus on the crucified Jesus (1:23).

Using gold, silver, costly stones, wood, hay or straw (3:12). All buildings need a foundation, but once that has been established the superstructure can be built from a range of materials. At the bottom end is the simple house of mud-brick, which used hay or straw as a binding agent; the house would be equipped with

THE FORUM

A portion of the forum with the Apollo temple in the background.

▼

wooden doors and lintels (which were often removed when the house was abandoned). At the other end of the scale are the major public buildings, which could have gilded features or other metallic attachments. These buildings were made of stone. A particularly wealthy benefactor might bring in marble over some distance to enhance a building; this may be hinted at by the "costly stones." For example, the temple of Apollo at Delphi had stone brought from near Corinth when it was rebuilt in the fourth century B.C.[36] In the Roman period the colored marble *laconia* was particularly valued and quarried extensively. "Costly stones" may also refer to gemstones used to decorate parts of the building. The range of such materials — gold, silver, and precious stones — may also be a deliberate allusion to the materials used for the temple at Jerusalem (e.g., 1 Chron. 29:2).

The Day will bring it to light (3:13). The "Day" refers to the "day of our Lord Jesus Christ" (1:8), that is, the Day of Judgment. The fire, which is a Jewish image for what will happen on that day, will reveal whether the superstructure of the building — that is, the body of the

believing Christians at Corinth — has been built with gospel or worldly wisdom material.

If what he has built survives, he will receive his reward (3:14). The architect or chief builder on a project would receive his payment ("reward") on its completion. Some of the most detailed building accounts from the ancient world relate to the classical period, in particular to projects at Athens like the building of the Parthenon, but also to work at the sanctuary of Asclepius at Epidauros.[37] Paul's comment resonates with the situation at Rome under Tiberius, who "restored all

THE *BĒMA*

The judgment seat in the forum at Corinth.

▼

▶ Buildings at Corinth

One of the ways that individuals could express their position in Roman society was to become benefactors of the city in which they lived and where they might also serve as magistrates. The American excavations at Corinth have concentrated on the main public area of the colony, the forum, where a large number of inscriptions have been found. Many of these come from buildings around the forum and record the details of the benefaction. According to one inscription from the mid-first century A.D., a benefactor whose name is lost paid for the revetment of the *bēma*, the

public platform in the forum, and "paid personally the expense of making all its marble."[A-15] One of the chief magistrates of the colony, an *aedile* by name of Gnaeus Babbius Philinus, seems to have made a major building dedication in the forum in the early first century A.D.[A-16] These include basilicas for legal hearings as well as temples. What is clear from the archaeological record as well as the building inscriptions is that by the middle of the first century the colony had been endowed with a number of significant buildings, largely paid for by private individuals.[A-17]

the buildings which had suffered damage (he himself built no completely new building, except the temple of Augustus), he claimed none of them as his own, but rather he bestowed the names of the original builders on all of them."[38] Although the names of architects are rare in the Roman world, it is likely that those involved in major building projects at Corinth would be celebrated by the local community for enhancing their city.

If it is burned up, he will suffer loss; he himself will be saved, but only as one escaping through the flames (3:15). In contrast to the architect who completes his project and is paid, if the builder who follows on from Paul uses inappropriate materials, such as wisdom, the day of reckoning will find him out. Certainly the builder has not been saved by his works, but by the grace of God.

Don't you know that you yourselves are God's temple and that God's Spirit lives in you? (3:16). This third image tries to explain to the Corinthian churches what is meant by the "temple of God." Jewish members of the church will identify "temple" (*naos*) with the temple at Jerusalem, whereas Gentile members would

associate that word with the religious structures that dotted their city, such as the archaic temple dominating the forum. In both cases, it is the place where God or a god dwelt. This new temple is something very different, however, as it is a temple made of living stones, that is, the Christian community at Corinth. The definition of members of the church is that God's Spirit dwells in them; in other words, they are "spiritual." "Fleshly" or "worldly" individuals (3:1, 3) need to think whether their lives are suitable for this holy building. There is also the implication that as there can only be one temple of God at Jerusalem or one temple for a particular god in Corinth, so there can only be one church at Corinth.[39]

If anyone destroys God's temple, God will destroy him (3:17). The jealousy and quarrelling in the Corinthian church (3:3) is damaging God's holy temple, the body of believers. If there is only one church, partisanship can only be damaging and unworthy of something that is holy. There is a great emphasis on individual members seeking to maintain the unity of the church.

"You Are of Christ" (3:18 – 23)

This paragraph concludes the argument about those who allow jealousy and quarrelling to divide the church. The section divides into two, introduced by parallel constructions in the Greek that can be translated, "Let no one deceive himself" (3:18 RSV) and "Let no one boast of men (3:21 RSV).

If any one of you thinks he is wise by the standards of this age, he should become a "fool" so that he may become wise (3:18). The deception of the church comes not

APOLLO TEMPLE

▼

from outside, but from within the Christian community. Paul returns to the theme he started in 2:8, where wisdom was a sign of Christian maturity, not a mark of the spirit of the age. The foolishness refers back to 1:25, where "the foolishness of God is wiser than man's wisdom."

The wisdom of this world is foolishness in God's sight. As it is written: "He catches the wise in their craftiness" (3:19). Paul reverses the argument of 1:25. The Corinthian Christians are now forced to see their position and quarrelling from God's perspective. Paul quotes, perhaps using his own Greek translation from the Hebrew, from the words of Eliphaz in Job 5:13; the verse continues "and the schemes of the wily are swept away," reminding the Corinthians of the foolishness of the position of those who wish to follow human wisdom.

"The Lord knows that the thoughts of the wise are futile." (3:20). Paul quotes from the LXX of Psalm 94:1, except that he replaces "the thoughts of men" with "the thoughts of the wise," thereby applying this verse to his specific situation. From God's perspective a love of the wisdom of the age is foolish or futile.

So then, no more boasting about men! (3:21). Paul returns the Corinthians' attention to Jeremiah 9:24 (cf. 1 Cor. 1:31), showing that boasting should only be in the Lord. The partisanship of 1:12 with different groups following Paul, Apollos, or Cephas is now obsolete, for Christians are "of Christ." It is Jesus Christ, the Son of God, who gives the Corinthian believers their identity.

All are yours (3:22). Paul stresses that allegiance to Christ is universal (lit., the *kosmos*); it is for all time, even in death, and is as relevant now as it will be in the future without the need for development along the lines of human wisdom.

Fools for Christ (4:1 – 13)

Men ought to regard us as servants of Christ and as those entrusted with the secret things of God (4:1). In 3:5 Paul used the Greek word *diakonos* ("servant") to describe his ministry. Now he emphasizes that he is one of several people working for Christ among the Corinthian Christians. The word translated "servants" here is *hyperetēs*. The word literally means an "under rower," but came to mean a servant. In a many-oared ship it was important to have everyone pulling in time; no doubt Paul is here thinking of a team of Christian ministers working in cooperation and collaboration. The word "entrusted" (*oikonomos*) was commonly used in the Hellenistic period of the person in charge of an estate belonging to an absentee landlord. For example, on the Saronic Gulf, not far from Corinth, the Methana peninsula was under the

---

REFLECTIONS

THE IMAGERY OF PAUL REMINDS us that the common starting point for all Christians is our shared faith in Jesus Christ. We are fellow workers for him. It may be tempting to slip into our denominations and separate forms of worship. Instead, we should never forget that as Christians we are united, that Jesus Christ is our foundation.

care of an *oikonomos* who looked after the city for the Ptolemies of Egypt. The term *mystēria* ("secret things") picks up on 2:7. In the ancient world so-called mystery cults from the eastern Mediterranean became popular at Rome. Though much of the evidence is after this time, the Anatolian deity Cybele seems to have been particularly popular. She was worshiped not in human form but as a rock or *baetyl*, which was moved to Rome in 204 B.C.[40]

Those who have been given a trust must prove faithful (4:2). The *oikonomos* looking after estates was in a position of great trust, especially if the absentee landlord was far removed. Paul is highlighting the characteristic of those entrusted with Christian responsibility to be "faithful." This characteristic is very different from the eloquence and wisdom expected by some in the church at Corinth.

I care very little if I am judged by you or by any human court; indeed, I do not even judge myself (4:3). The Greek idiom translated "by any human court" refers to having one's day in court. Such a "day" resonates with the Day of Judgment (3:13; 4:5). In a city dominated by the law of Rome, Paul reminds the Corinthians that there is a judge above human magistrates and that his actions are ones he wants to be judged in this higher court.

My conscience is clear, but that does not make me innocent. It is the Lord who judges me (4:4). "The Lord" here clearly means Christ, but in the secular world, the *oikonomos* would be looking after the estate for his absent "lord" or *kyrios*. In legal terms only the "lord" has the right to judge his servants. Christians must remember that their actions will be judged by God, not by their peers within the church.

So that you may learn from us the meaning of the saying, "Do not go beyond what is written." Then you will not take pride in one man over against another (4:6). The Corinthians have been emphasizing "pride." Part of this was extended to comparing Paul and Apollos, debating who was the most effective servant of Christ. Indeed, later in the letter it appears as if the Corinthian church may have requested a return visit from Apollos (16:12). "Do not go beyond what is written" is an allusion to the Old Testament writings. Scripture is meant to form the boundary for the conduct of the Christian life.

You have become rich! You have become kings (4:8). Professional orators were able to command large sums where they presented their speeches. Philo commented that such wealth "exist[s] not only for our security, but also for our happiness."[41] In other words, oratory could give an individual high status. The Corinthians placed so much emphasis on this skill that Paul comments they had become as rich as kings. Perhaps he has in mind the legendary riches of the now dead Hellenistic rulers or the riches of the Roman emperor. Though the concept of kingship was abhorrent to Romans after the expulsion of the Tarquins as kings of Rome at the end of the sixth century B.C., more recently *basileus* ("king") was being applied to the emperor.

Like men condemned to die in the arena (4:9). Paul takes as his imagery the spectacle of the Roman arena, where criminals or captives of war were paraded in triumph by the conquering commander — at this date only the emperor had that privilege — before fighting each other to death to entertain the people. Such gladiatorial shows were uncommon in the Greek east, but would, perhaps, have appealed to the people of a Roman colony. It is ironic that the Roman emperor, sometimes designated as "master of the universe,"[42] had his show viewed by a different "universe" or *kosmos*. The spectacle resonates with the word *theatron* ("arena"), the place where the spectacle takes place (more accurately the amphitheater, of which Corinth was in fact equipped). This lay to the northeast of the city, outside the line of the later city wall.[43] Roman testimony makes reference to "the Corinthians watch[ing] these combats outside the city in a ravine, a place that is able to hold a large crowd, but otherwise is sordid and such that no one would even bury there a freeborn citizen."[44] The earliest structure may have been temporary, but as Corinth became the focus for games associated with the imperial cult, a more permanent structure would have been needed.[45]

We are fools for Christ, but you are so wise in Christ! We are weak, but you are strong! You are honored, we are dishonored! (4:10). Paul uses a series of contrasts that indicates that the Corinthian Christians are using words of high status about themselves — "wise," "strong," "honored" — whereas Paul uses low status terms for himself and those who maintain an apostolic ministry — "fools," "weak," "dishonored" (cf. also 1:26).

We go hungry and thirsty, we are in rags, we are brutally treated, we are homeless (4:11). This image is one that picks up on the theme that these are men con-demned to die. The contrast would be to the emperor leading the procession.

We work hard with our own hands (4:12). The social elite were scornful of those who worked for a living. Roman social hierarchy in fact precluded some groups — notably those at the top of the social scale — from handling money or conducting business, which was the preserve of members of the equestrian order. The believers in Corinthians are unlikely to have been wealthy enough to be patricians, but they would have adopted wider Roman values towards wealth.

When we are cursed, we bless (4:12b). The first of these three pairs of contrasting actions reflects the teaching of Jesus in Luke: "Bless those who curse you" (Luke 4:28). Paul is presenting a model for the church at Corinth.

The scum of the earth, the refuse of the world (4:13). Paul alludes to Lamentations 3:45: "You have made us scum and refuse among the nations," though his words differ from the LXX.

Paul as Founder and Father (4:14 – 17)

I am not writing this to shame you (4:14). Shame was to be avoided in Roman society, so Paul makes it clear that he was only writing as a warning.

Ten thousand guardians in Christ . . . in Christ Jesus I became your father through the gospel (4:15). "Guardians" translates a word for the person who accompanied the children of wealthy families to school. Paul describes himself as the *patēr* ("father") of the Christian community. In the same way, members of the colony looked to Julius Caesar as the founding father of the colony at Corinth, or to the emperor himself, who carried the honorific title "father of the country."

Therefore I urge you to imitate me (4:16). There was considerable pressure in Roman society to aspire to a set career and to follow set patterns of behavior; Paul is urging the Corinthians to set themselves free by following his pattern of example. Unfortunately, already some of the Christians had become imitators of the orators.

I am sending to you Timothy (4:17). This is one of two mentions of Timothy in this letter. Paul, writing from Ephesus, dispatched Timothy and Erastus to Macedonia while he himself stayed in the province of Asia (Acts 19:22). Although Erastus is not mentioned here, he set out from Ephesus with Timothy; a man of the same name is also mentioned in Romans 16:23 (see "Paul Quotes an Athenian Playwright" at 15:33).

A Kingdom of Power (4:18 – 21)

As if I were not coming to you (4:18). The Corinthian Christians presumably expected Paul, now in Ephesus, to have returned, just as one of the orators on the circuit of the great cities of the Greek east might return to Corinth.

I will come to you very soon (4:19). Paul provides the details of his plans and those of Timothy later (16:5 – 9).

I will find out not only how these arrogant people are talking, but what power they have (4:19). A contrast is made between the "talk" (*logos*) of the arrogant and their "power." Paul's preaching (*logos*) at Corinth may not have had the eloquence of traveling orators, but the result of the preaching was that a Corinthian Christian's faith rested on God's power (1:17 – 18).

For the kingdom of God is not a matter of talk but of power (4:20). The "kingdom of God" is a major theme of Jesus' teaching in the Gospels. The linking of the kingdom with power recalls Jesus' words: "I tell you the truth, some who are standing here will not taste death before they see the kingdom of God come with power" (Mark 9:1).

Shall I come to you with a whip (4:21). The Greek word translated "whip" (*rhabdos*) is the same used as the "rod" used for

▶ Timothy in Corinth

Timothy came from Lystra in the province of Galatia. He was the son of a Greek father and a Jewish mother, Eunice (Acts 16:1; 2 Tim. 1:5). He had accompanied Paul in his travels through Macedonia (Acts 17:14). Timothy arrived at Corinth along with Silas when Paul first came to the colony (18:5) and so was known to the congregation. Timothy is also mentioned in other Corinthian contexts. He is one of the people who sends greetings in the concluding section of the letter to the Romans (Rom. 16:21), written from Corinth, and he is the cowriter of the second letter to the Corinthians (2 Cor. 1:1).

correction; for example, "I will punish their sin with the rod, their iniquity with flogging" (Ps. 89:32). In ancient Greece, the *rhabdos* was the stick that was struck rhythmically during the recitation of poetic works by a rhapsode.

Immorality and the Church's Response (5:1 – 8)

It is actually reported that there is sexual immorality among you, and of a kind that does not occur even among pagans (5:1). A situation of sexual immorality (*porneia*) seems to be common knowledge within the Corinthian church. The Jewish world considered *porneia* as a regular feature of the surrounding pagan cultures. Thus the council of Jerusalem asked the Gentile Christians "to abstain from food sacrificed to idols, from blood, from the meat of strangled animals and from sexual immorality [*porneia*]" (Acts 15:29; cf. 15:20; 21:25). Although this word is associated with "prostitution," it could also be extended to homosexual acts (Jude 7). It is ironic that within the Corinthian church, such a hallmark of pagan society is in fact of a type not found among the pagans.

A man has his father's wife (5:1). Paul now spells out the nature of this *porneia*: A man

has an ongoing sexual relationship — implied by the Greek word translated as "has" — with his father's wife — that is, undoubtedly this man's stepmother. This would be shocking to Jewish society as such a relationship was forbidden: "Do not have sexual relations with your father's wife; that would dishonor your father" (Lev. 18:8). But such a liaison was also banned under Roman law — in particular, the *lex Iulia de adulteriis* introduced by Augustus between 18 and 16 B.C. The punishment for such activity was exile to an island. The incentive for such a relationship may have been in the hope of retaining the woman's marriage dowry to her family when perhaps her husband died. It may have been hoped that the son and stepmother might have had children, thereby increasing the claim for retaining the dowry within the present family.[46]

You are proud! (5:2). Paul describes the Corinthian Christians as "proud" or "puffed up with pride"; the term used here is translated "arrogant" earlier in 4:18 – 19. Paul would prefer a response of grief. Such pride may be explained if the man in the incestuous relationship has high status within the colony, perhaps a Roman citizen of high standing. Indeed, he may well have been the patron of the church. Such patron-client relationships were important mechanisms of control within Roman society, and members of the church may have felt it inappropriate to question the sexual morals of such a high-standing individual. But rather than being proud that such a high-profile individual was a member of their Christian community, Paul insists they should be ashamed at tolerating such activity. If this is the scenario, Paul's criticism is aimed as much at the attitude of the Corinthian Christians toward status as it is toward sexual immorality. The word translated as "filled with grief" conveys the meaning of "mourning." It was as if this individual in the colony has died and the church — and indeed the wider colony — should be grieving.

Even though I am not physically present, I am with you in spirit. And I have already passed judgment on the one who did this, just as if I were present (5:3). Paul reacts to the Corinthian response by his own personal comment (emphasized in the Greek by introducing this sentence with *egō men*, "And I for my part"). Paul, the apostle who established the Corinthian church, may not be present in person, but he has the right and authority to intervene in the situation. Paul then uses legal language. A case has been reported to him and the hearing has started. In Roman society one could only bring lawsuits against one's peers. Thus, if the man involved in the incestuous relationship was of high status, the Corinthian Christians, especially if they were in a client-patron relationship with him, would not wish to initiate proceedings. But the case has been reported (5:1) to the apostle.

When you are assembled in the name of our Lord Jesus and I am with you in spirit, and the power of our Lord Jesus is present (5:4). Paul in effect is calling the Christian community together to make a corporate act. What characterizes the members of the gathering is that each one bears the name of the Lord Jesus; status in the wider community does not matter. Paul the apostle of Jesus Christ (1:1) is with them "in spirit," a phrase that on the one hand may mean he identifies with them in the decision they have to make, and on the other endorses the

fact that each one has been empowered by the Spirit of God. The "power of our Lord Jesus" contrasts with the wider perception of power in the Roman colony that normally went with high status.

Hand this man over to Satan (5:5). A similar expression of handing individuals over to Satan occurs in 1 Timothy 1:20, where Hymenaeus and Alexander are cited. "That the sinful nature may be destroyed" is a translation of the Greek equivalent of "the destruction of the flesh." A physical death may be expected, and a parallel can be drawn with the deaths of Ananias and Sapphira in Acts 5:1 – 11 or the incorrect use of the Lord's Supper in 1 Corinthians 11:30 – 32. Clearly the intention is that this man must be excluded from the fellowship with the goal of putting to death that part of his sinful nature so that on the Day of Judgment he will be saved. The loss of status as a Christian is not implied.

Your boasting is not good. Don't you know that a little yeast works through the whole batch of dough? (5:6). Paul draws attention to one of the unacceptable characteristics of the Christian community at Corinth: their boasting especially about human beings (see also 3:21). Such a feature is similar to their arrogance or the way in which they are puffed up with pride (5:2). "Don't you know that" is a rhetorical device Paul uses twice more in the letter (3:16; 9:13). The expression "a little yeast works through the whole batch of dough" may have been a well-known saying, perhaps Jewish in origin. The word *zymē* is best translated as "leaven" rather than yeast. In other words, a piece of fermented dough is kept back from the baking so that it can be used to "leaven" the next batch of dough. Paul here is using the image of baking to show that even a small amount of evil will permeate the whole church.

Get rid of the old yeast that you may be a new batch without yeast — as you really are. For Christ, our Passover lamb, has been sacrificed (5:7). The reference to being rid of old "yeast" or (better) "leaven" is an allusion to the Feast of Unleavened Bread, when God's people left Egypt: "For seven days you are to eat bread made without yeast. On the first day remove the yeast from your houses, for whoever eats anything with yeast in it from the first day through the seventh must be cut off from Israel" (Ex. 12:15). "Leaven" was not to be added to grain offerings (cited throughout Leviticus), no doubt because it detracted from the purity, and therefore holiness, of the offering. Paul's powerful image, which in fact makes the Corinthian Christians the new batch of dough (without the impurity of the incestuous man), develops into the full Passover image with Christ as the lamb. It was the slaying of the Passover lamb (cf. Ex. 12:21) that gave the purity to the people of God as they left Egypt; in effect, they were unleavened.

Therefore let us keep the Festival, not with the old yeast, the yeast of malice and wickedness, but with bread without yeast, the bread of sincerity and truth (5:8). Paul contrasts the leavened bread with the unleavened. The former contains all types of bad things ("malice") and iniquities ("wickedness"), whereas the latter contains pure things ("sincerity and truth"). By using the present tense, Paul urges the Corinthian Christians to celebrate "the Festival," that is, to lead a life that day by day is unpermeated by "malice and wickedness" and is characterized by "sincerity and truth."

Limiting Associations (5:9 – 13)

I have written you in my letter not to associate with sexually immoral people (5:9). Paul continues on the theme of the incestuous man who has already been described as "sexually immoral." Clearly this issue has been raised by Paul beforehand in an earlier letter that has not survived. The key issue is that the Corinthian churches should not get mixed up with sexually immoral people; just as leaven should not be added to pure dough.

The people of this world who are immoral, or the greedy and swindlers, or idolaters (5:10). The Corinthian Christians should not take on the secular values

of the world around them; at the same time, they must be an integrated part of society as a witness to it. Apparently the Corinthians have misunderstood Paul's earlier letter. Their response to his desire for them not to associate with sexually immoral people was to ask, "But how can we do that, when we rub shoulders with such people in the forum and other public spaces?" Paul's intention was not for them to cut themselves off from the world. Notice his characterization of pagan Roman society as people who are "[sexually] immoral . . . greedy . . . swindlers, or idolaters." Such issues were as prevalent in mid-first-century Corinth as they are in our own societies. The issue of idolatry will be picked up later in the letter (chs. 8 – 10). The Jewish world was familiar with groups such as the Essenes, who took themselves into the desert to remove themselves from the pressures and iniquities of society.

You must not associate with anyone who calls himself a brother but is sexually immoral or greedy, an idolater or a slanderer, a drunkard or a swindler (5:11). The list of "vices" in pagan society is repeated and expanded to include drunkards and slanderers; this list will be augmented even further in 6:9 – 10. Such lists are common in Jewish characterizations of the society around them, such as Philo,[47] as well as in other Pauline letters. Such individuals are to be excluded from common meals, which presumably include the Lord's Supper. Drinking was an integral part of the ancient banquet, and drunkenness could allow such functions to degenerate into orgies. In a thriving commercial center like Corinth, with its active shipping interest, swindling is perhaps linked to business interests of members of the church.

"Expel the wicked man from among you" (5:13). The Mosaic law insisted that God's people "must purge the evil from among you" (or "from Israel"); this included worshiping other gods (Deut. 17:7), giving false testimony or witness in a court of law (19:19), premarital sexual relations (22:21), adultery (22:22, 24), and abduction (24:7). Paul quotes from the Mosaic law here to suggest that the wicked man should be expelled from the Christian community. As such it picks up and concludes earlier remarks throughout this chapter (5:2, 5, 7). Notice the way that the Christian community is first to deal with sin within itself.

Civil Litigation in Corinth (6:1 – 11)

If any of you has a dispute with another, dare he take it before the ungodly for judgment instead of before the saints? (6:1). The Roman legal system prevented those of inferior status from prosecuting their "superiors," such as patrons and magistrates.[48] Thus these disputes are likely to have been between those of the

---

REFLECTIONS

IT IS EASY TO BE SHOCKED ABOUT the latest revelation of sexual impropriety in the church community when we see it on TV. Yet there is nothing new; it was there in Corinth. What is important is our attitude towards immorality that we encounter among fellow Christians. We need to ask ourselves how we can become God's holy people in our communities, unpermeated by the wickedness that surrounds us.

same social status within the Roman colony; no doubt they are drawn from those who would consider themselves as "powerful" (*dynatoi*, 1:26). Alternatively they could be cases brought by an individual with high social status against someone with a lower social status — for example, a magistrate against a freedman. The case would be initiated by taking the matter before one of the two main magistrates in the colony, one of the *duovirs*. The case would be heard before a judge or a jury of one's peers.[49] Jurors were selected from wealthier social groups; in Cyrenaica (North Africa) jurors had to have a property value of 7,500 *denarii*.[50] The Cyrene edict of Augustus dating to 7/6 B.C. suggests that juries could sometimes act in an unjust way, constituting some form of cliques.[51] Later sources show that Corinth itself suffered from such legal corruption.[52] The word "ungodly" can also be translated "unrighteous" (or perhaps "corrupt"). Since Paul himself used the Roman legal system from time to time, it is unlikely that he is recommending a distancing from it; he is more likely drawing attention to the potentially corrupt nature of the system.

Do you not know that the saints will judge the world? (6:2). Paul asks a rhetorical question that seems to draw on the LXX of Daniel 7:22, which provides the context of the Day of Judgment. This implies that some of the readers of this letter are familiar with Jewish writings and theology surrounding the end of the world.

If you are to judge the world, are you not competent to judge trivial cases? (6:2). "Trivial cases" indicates that the disputes between the Corinthian Christians come under the aegis of civil law rather than criminal law (which would cover things such as acts of treason and murder[53]). Civil law included areas such as "legal possession, breach of contract, damages, fraud and injury."[54] Young men drawn from the social elite might bring "trivial cases" to demonstrate their forensic skills. Perhaps some of the social elite from the church at Corinth are bringing "trivial" civil cases against fellow Christians in order to establish their own position (and harm their opponents), and this has caused tensions within the church.

Appoint as judges even men of little account in the church! (6:4). The "men of little account" or of "small esteem" contrast with the social elite who are in fact bringing such cases and who are indeed able to judge them. The Greek word translated here as church, *ekklēsia*, is the same word used for the secular gathering of the citizen body. Thus, there is irony that those unable to participate in the public *ekklēsia* are nevertheless suitable judges in the Christian *ekklēsia*.

I say this to shame you (6:5). Shame was something that members of the Corinthian elite would want to avoid. It contrasts with Paul's earlier comment that he is not writing to shame them (4:14). Shame continues to be an important aspect of Paul's instruction to the Corinthian church (15:34).

Is it possible that there is nobody among you wise enough to judge a dispute between believers? (6:5). Since the Corinthian church contains members of the social elite — the powerful and well-born (1:26) — they have been educated to judge such legal cases. Among this group should be some "capable"[55] enough to have become arbitrators in the

▶ Roman Civil Law in Corinth

Roman legal arrangements in the Augustan period — for the province of Crete and Cyrene — can be detected in a decree of 7/6 B.C. preserved at Cyrene, where Augustus stated:

Regarding disputes which occur . . . excluding indictments for capital crimes, where the governor must himself conduct the inquiry and render a decision or else set up a panel of jurors — for all other cases it is my pleasure that Greek jurors shall be assigned unless some defendant or accused desires to have Roman citizens as jurors.[A-18]

Although Corinth was a Roman colony, it seems likely that such civil cases would be heard before judges and juries rather than before the governor. In the Greek east it seems to have been common for personal enmity to have been continued through bringing civil actions, thus damaging an opponent's reputation; such actions were described by the Latin terms *reprehension vitae* or *vituperatio.*

disagreements among Christians, thereby diffusing the situation before divisions occur. Those who are educated, however, would consider themselves to be wise (*sophos*) or sophisticated, a danger Paul earlier pointed out in the life of the church (1:27; 3:18).

One brother goes to law against another — and this in front of unbelievers! (6:6). The unbelievers refer to the civic magistrates of the Roman colony who are not part of the Christian community. This means that cases brought by Christians against fellow Christians are being heard in a public court.

The very fact that you have lawsuits among you means you have been completely defeated already (6:7). These words are aimed at the plaintiff, who has not seen that by taking action against the defendant, members of the Christian community are being presented as law-breakers in the colony. Such a publicly held view is detrimental to the church.

You yourselves cheat and do wrong, and you do this to your brothers (6:8). "Do wrong" carries the meaning of "defraud." These words are clearly aimed at the defendant and imply that there may have been some wrong-doing. Christians have an ethical imperative laid on them to abide by the law.

Do you not know that the wicked will not inherit the kingdom of God? Do not be deceived: Neither the sexually immoral nor idolaters nor adulterers nor male prostitutes nor homosexual offenders (6:9). Paul introduces a range of people whose lifestyles may have been accepted in wider Roman and Greek society, but which was defined as "wicked" by God's standards. The "sexually immoral" (*pornoi*) include Christians who are sexually active before marriage; this contrasts with "adulterers" (*moichoi*), who have sexual partners outside marriage. In Roman elite society it was acceptable for the husband to have sexual relations outside marriage, but such standards were not to be tolerated within the Christian community.

Paul uses specialized terminology here.[56] Roman law, in particular the *lex Scantinia* of the mid-second century

B.C., legislated about homosexual behavior.[57] Such laws protected Roman citizens against homosexual acts. Corinth as a Roman colony would thus consider homosexual acts with fellow citizens as illegal, but not with noncitizens (i.e., non-Romans) and slaves.

Male prostitutes (6:9). This expression translates *malakoi*. The Greek word *malakos* transferred to the Latin *malacus*. It means in effect "a soft person" and took on the meaning of somebody effeminate. The fact that Latin has no indigenous word for such a person may suggest that a passive participant in a homosexual relationship was not condemned by Roman law so long as he was not a Roman citizen.

Homosexual offenders (6:9). This expression translates the Greek word *arsenokoitai*. This may be a word derived from the LXX of Leviticus 18:22: "Do not lie with a man as one lies with a woman; that is detestable." The *malakos* (see previous comment) is probably the passive participant, whereas the *arsenokoitēs* is the active participant. Thus, both stand criticized by Paul within the Christian community. Note, however, that these are but two areas of life that Paul highlights, and the church has not always had the right balance.

Nor thieves nor the greedy nor drunkards nor slanderers nor swindlers will inherit the kingdom of God (6:10). The "greedy" are literally those "who wish to have more"; in other words they are covetous. In spite of what God has given to them, they want more. "Drunkards" probably implies those people who regularly attend the drinking parties of the colony, whether in private homes or at public festivals. "Swindlers" are those who snatch things from others and perhaps reflects on the fact that those involved in the trading life of this busy city with its two ports were less than honest.

That is what some of you were (6:11). At the beginning of the letter Paul characterized the church as having few who "were wise by human standards; not many were influential; not many were of noble birth" (1:26). Now it becomes clear that although a few members of the church came from elite backgrounds, a cross-section of the members of the church had morally questionable backgrounds.

But you were washed (6:11). This is clearly a reference to baptism after repentance (cf. Paul's use of this same verb in one of his accounts of his conversion on the road to Damascus, Acts 22:16). This is a reminder that whatever our backgrounds, we are new creations in Christ.

Immorality (6:12 – 20)

"Everything is permissible for me" (6:12). Paul seems to be quoting a phrase used by the Corinthian church, which he repeats later in the letter (10:23).

"Food for the stomach and the stomach for food" — but God will destroy them both. The body is not meant for sexual immorality, but for the Lord, and the Lord for the body (6:13). The Roman love of food is reflected in the cookbooks that have survived from antiquity, such as that attributed to Apicius. His recipes include, "Numidian chicken," "rabbit with fruit sauce," "liver sausage," "anchovy delight without the anchovies," and "sweet and sour pork."[58] By reminding the Corinthian Christians that their bodies belonged to

God, Paul counters the claim that if sexual liberty was acceptable in the colony, it could also be acceptable in the Christian community. Believers are not free to do as they please. Paul may be quoting one of the sayings of the Corinthian church.

By his power God raised the Lord from the dead, and he will raise us also (6:14). Corinthian Christians, drawing on Platonic philosophy, may have tried to separate the soul from the body so that they could partake in sexual immorality without feeling that it mattered to their soul. Paul stresses the importance of the human body by referring them to the idea of the bodily resurrection of Jesus Christ from the grave and our own bodily resurrection at the last day.

Never! (6:15). Paul uses the Greek words translated as "Never!" (*mē genoito*) in other letters (e.g., Romans, Galatians). It may be a rhetorical device, as it is a phrase used in diatribe.

Do you not know that he who unites himself with a prostitute is one with her in body? For it is said, "The two will become one flesh." (6:16). It has been suggested that prostitutes would have been made available at the banquet when young men came of age.[59] Paul uses the LXX of Genesis 2:24 to make the theological point that sexual intercourse institutes a bond between the two people. Sexual activity outside marriage cannot be justified.

Your body is a temple of the Holy Spirit (6:19). In the pagan urban landscape of the Roman colony, the temples on their high podia were the places where the gods — in the form of their cult-statues — were thought to dwell. In

contrast, the bodies of Christians are the temple of the Holy Spirit.

You were bought at a price. Therefore honor God with your body (6:20). Christ's death on the cross has "bought" the lives of Christians as it removed them from the ownership of "sin." The Greek verb "honor" can also be translated "glorify"; earlier Paul talked about Jesus as the "Lord of glory" (2:8).

Sexual Abstinence, Singleness, and Marriage (7:1 – 16)

Now for the matters you wrote about (7:1). Paul turns to issues raised in a letter ("you wrote about") by the Corinthian church. In the remaining chapters there are five distinct issues he addresses:

1. "It is good for a man not to marry" (7:1).
2. "Now about virgins" (7:25).
3. "Now about food sacrificed to idols" (8:1).
4. "Now about spiritual gifts" (12:1).
5. "Now about the collection for God's people" (16:1).

A sixth issue may concern Apollos (16:12). It is important to understand the issues raised with Paul against the background of "the present crisis" (7:26).

It is good for a man not to marry (7:1). The Greek in this sentence ("to marry," lit. trans., is "to touch a woman") is at first sight ambiguous in that there is no distinction in the Greek word *gynē* between "a wife" or "a woman"; the NIV takes the noun with the verb as "to marry." However the Greek can be taken to mean, "It is a fine thing/good for a man not to touch a woman/(his) wife." The Greek verb (*haptomai*) in this clause means to touch or grasp and was used in Greek athletics when two wrestlers came together in the ring. The sense here implies a sexual relationship.

Since there is so much immorality, each man should have his own wife, and each woman her own husband (7:2). The Greek verb translated as "have" implies a sexual relationship. Because of the sexual immorality (*porneia*) in Corinthian society, husbands and wives should be faithful to their partner in sexual matters. This sentence picks up the language of Paul's earlier argument about the sexual immorality concerning the man having an incestuous relationship with his stepmother (5:1). Roman epitaphs often speak of the relationship between husband and wife. For example, in a first century B.C. example from Rome, the husband talks of his wife Aurelia Philematium, who died aged forty, as "chaste in body, with a loving spirit, she lived faithful to her faithful husband, always optimistic, even in bitter times, she never shirked her duties."[60]

The husband should fulfill his marital duty to his wife, and likewise the wife to her husband (7:3). Paul is moving away from the usual Roman norm, in which the husband dominated the wife; in Christian marriage there is to be a mutuality of relations.

The wife's body does not belong to her alone but also to her husband. In the same way, the husband's body does not belong to him alone but also to his wife (7:4). This teaching is radical for a Roman audience. Men felt free to have sexual intercourse with slaves or other women. Sexual fulfillment was seen as an end in itself. According to ancient marriage contracts, of which a number have survived on papyri from Egypt, male promiscuity was acceptable.[61] Paul is reminding husbands and wives of the exclusivity of their relationship. Extramarital activity is not acceptable for Christians.

Do not deprive each other except by mutual consent and for a time, so that you may devote yourselves to prayer. Then come together again (7:5). Paul may be addressing the issue of married couples abstaining from sexual intercourse in the light of the "present crisis" (7:26). In the ancient world the only effective form of contraception was not to engage in sexual activity. Soranus, writing in the second century A.D., noted that "it is safer to prevent conception from occurring than to destroy the fetus through abortion."[62] Yet Paul reminds such couples that sexual relations ("come together") are part of marriage.

I say this as a concession, not as a command (7:6). The "concession" refers to Paul's own singleness (7:7). The "command" refers to the issues in the preceding verses, especially indicated by the word "should" (7:2, 3).

I wish that all men were as I am. But each man has his own gift from God (7:7). Paul recognizes that singleness can be a gift from God. Roman citizens were encouraged to marry (and by implication have children) through Roman legislation. Emperor Augustus had initiated such laws partly to increase the citizen body in the face of depletions during the civil wars of the first century B.C., notably the great struggle against Antony and Cleopatra that culminated in the battle of Actium in 31 B.C. and the fall of Alexandria in 30 B.C. The church needs to recognize the gift of singleness even if the social norm is for individuals to marry.

Now to the unmarried and the widows I say: It is good for them to stay unmarried, as I am (7:8). Paul turns from issues for those who are already married to those who have yet to marry or who have been widowed. Paul's advice is the same as that given to the virgins, namely, to stay in the state of singlehood in which Paul himself is. It has been suggested that the Greek word for "the unmarried" (*agamoi*) may refer to (male) widowers, for "virgins" (i.e., those never married) are dealt with in 7:25 – 26.[63]

Given "the present crisis" Paul is advocating that this group not marry because if they have children, they will have to live through troubled times. Paul's language reflects that of the disciples when they responded to Jesus' teaching on divorce: "If this is the situation between a husband and a wife, it is better not to marry" (Matt. 19:10). Marriage should not be undertaken lightly, as it has personal and social consequences.

But if they cannot control themselves, they should marry, for it is better to marry than to burn with passion (7:9). Women tended to marry in their teens, though their husbands were often older.

To the married I give this command (not I, but the Lord): A wife must not separate from her husband (7:10). Paul turns to the sensitive issue of separation in marriage and divorce. His teaching is clear, and the authority he takes is not ultimately his own but that of Jesus Christ ("the Lord"; see also 9:14; 11:23). Subsequent verses make it clear that both husband and wife referred to in this verse are Christians. The "command" does not appear elsewhere in the New Testament as a quotation of Jesus, but it is a summary of teaching found in the Gospels. In Mark 10:1 – 12 (see also Matt. 19:1 – 12) Jesus is confronted by the Pharisees, who asked him, "Is it lawful for a man to divorce his wife?" (Mark 10:2). Jesus then clarified his teaching with the disciples: "Anyone who divorces his wife and marries another woman commits adultery against her. And if she divorces her husband and marries another man, she commits adultery" (10:11 – 12; see also Luke 16:18). This command, given originally in the context of Jewish marriage, is applicable to Christians. Roman

law might allow divorce, but not Jesus' teaching. Still, some Roman marriages were long-lasting. Pliny the Younger, governor of the province of Bithynia under the emperor Trajan, wrote about his friend Macrinus, whose wife had died after thirty-nine years of marriage "without a single quarrel or bitter word."[64]

If she does, she must remain unmarried or else be reconciled to her husband. And a husband must not divorce his wife (7:11). Paul lays out the two options available to Christians if they separate from their spouses: either remain unmarried or seek reconciliation. Remarriage of a Christian divorcee comes under Jesus' specific teaching (e.g., Luke 16:18). This is in contrast with the Roman legal situation. A divorce settlement from Egypt dated 13 B.C. (after it became a Roman province) declared, "From this day it will be lawful for Zois to marry another man and for Antipater to marry another woman, with neither party being liable to prosecution."[65]

If any brother has a wife who is not a believer and she is willing to live with him, he must not divorce her. And if a woman has a husband who is not a believer and he is willing to live with her, she must not divorce him (7:12 – 13). Within the Christian community at Corinth, and almost certainly elsewhere, Paul faces the issue of men and women converted to Jesus Christ but the spouse remains an unbeliever. Clearly this may cause tensions within the marriage. If the unbelieving partner is willing to remain married, there should be no move to seek a divorce. The Christians at Corinth may have pointed to Old Testament examples where Jews married non-Jews and brought God's displeasure (e.g., 2 Chron.

21:6) and therefore thought it appropriate for a Christian to seek a divorce.

If the unbeliever leaves, let him do so. . . . God has called us to live in peace (7:15). In a divorce the husband was expected to hand back the dowry he had received over from the bride's family at the time of marriage. For example in a divorce settlement of 13 B.C., the husband had to hand back "the items he received as her dowry, namely, clothing valued at 120 silver drachmas and a pair of gold earrings."[66] A (Christian) husband might try to be difficult and retain such a dowry, but Paul reminds the Christian to live in peace and to let the (unbelieving) wife go.

How do you know, wife, whether you will save your husband? Or, how do you know, husband, whether you will save your wife? (7:16). Paul can give no guarantees about the future destiny of an unbelieving marriage partner, but the hope of conversion is there.

Status and Calling in the Secular World (7:17 – 24)

Each one should retain the place in life that the Lord assigned to him and to which God has called him. This is the rule I lay down in all the churches (7:17). Paul the apostle presented standard guidelines or rules in each of the churches, not just the ones he founded.[67] In the Roman east there were aspirations for upward social mobility, with the main goal to gain Roman citizenship that was relatively rare in the eastern Mediterranean outside Roman colonies. It may be that some of the Corinthian Christians had been drawn to live in the colony from other cities of the province of Achaia, but that did not make them

Roman citizens. The calling (*klēsis*) can also take the meaning of social class.[68]

Was a man already circumcised when he was called? He should not become uncircumcised. Was a man uncircumcised when he was called? He should not be circumcised (7:18). Within the Corinthian church there were Christian Jews who bore the marks of circumcision. They may have been tempted to undergo surgery — epispasm — to disguise their circumcision. This operation is discussed in a medical treatise, *De Medicina*, by Celsus, written during the Julio-Claudian period.[69]

Each one should remain in the situation which he was in when God called him (7:20). The Christian should be satisfied with the position or status he or she held prior to conversion. There is no advantage of trying to appear a former Jew.

Were you a slave when you were called? Don't let it trouble you — although if you can gain your freedom, do so (7:21). The second group within the church who have aspirations are slaves. They might hope to be manumitted by their owners and gain the status of being a freedman. The cost of receiving their freedom would allow their owner to buy a replacement slave. Slaves were able to earn money and amass money, which could be used to pay for their freedom. Paul is merely describing a common practice in the ancient world.

For he who was a slave when he was called by the Lord is the Lord's freedman; similarly, he who was a free man when he was called is Christ's slave (7:22). Paul uses the Greek technical word for a "freedman," the status to which a slave might aspire. Paul makes the point that those who have been called by Christ are already freedmen (and women). On receiving their freedom, former slaves became clients of their former masters, who were then considered their patron and who could expect support from them. Paul stresses that the Christian's patron is the Lord; thus, there is a duty to put oneself in his service. A number of individuals at Corinth with the status of "freedman" can be identified in surviving inscriptions, for they have the three Roman names. Former slaves tended to take on the *praenomen* and *nomen* of their former master.

▶ Jewish Circumcision and the Gymnasium

Circumcision was viewed with suspicion by Roman citizens, in part because it identified Jews (and Egyptians) as having separate ethnic origins. Ancient authors such as Martial[A-19] and the Jewish Philo[A-20] record Jews taking part in the gymnasium of their communities. This establishment was more than an exercise area and often included lecture rooms and other educational and cultural facilities. If Jews wished to take part in civic institutions such as the gymnasium or adopt the Roman cultural habit of taking hot baths, they would be easily identified when stripped naked.[A-21] Young men were usually enrolled as *ephēboi* in the gymnasium if they were entitled, whether or not they were Jews, and thus it may be that the reversal of the circumcision would be undertaken before the age of puberty; certainly Celsus indicates that this was the preferable age for such an operation. Such enrollment would give the young men opportunities, and some Jews did gain important positions of authority, such as Tiberius Claudius Alexander, who became governor of Judea.

You were bought at a price; do not become slaves of men (7:23). Some free-born Christians seemed to be willing to sell themselves into slavery. Such individuals, usually from poorer backgrounds, could then join the household of high-status individuals and, on paying for their freedom, could gain a higher status as a freedman; certainly their sons would be full, free-born Roman citizens if their patron was one. Some freedmen had considerable status and money. One of the best caricatures of a free-born man selling himself into slavery and then gaining his freedom appears in Petronius' *Satyricon*, written about the same time as 1 Corinthians.[70] The man would also be expected to worship his new master as a god, something that may have given concern to Paul.[71] The phrase "bought at a price" repeats that of 6:20.

Each man, as responsible to God, should remain in the situation God called him to (7:24). Paul has been discussing those who might wish to hide the fact that they were Jews so that they could progress in Gentile society (7:18), or slaves who aspired to have the status of "freedman" or "freedwoman" in Roman law (7:22). His concern is that ambition for promotion and elevation in the wider society should not interfere with one's Christian service.

Between Betrothal and Consummation (7:25 – 40)

Now about virgins: I have no command from the Lord, but I give a judgment (7:25). A group has raised the issue of "virgins" and marriage with Paul and he is responding. It seems that the group asking the question does not consist of the girls' fathers, but rather of young men within the church seeking to marry (7:28, 36 – 37). Girls were usually given in marriage at a young age.[72]

Because of the present crisis, I think that it is good for you to remain as you are (7:26). The "present crisis" or "dislocation" may refer to a period of food shortages in the Mediterranean.[73] At this time a certain Tiberius Claudius Dinippus was honored by elements within Corinth for acting as *curator* of the grain supply on three different occasions.[74] The Roman historian Tacitus has also recorded food shortages at this time.[75] Food shortages could induce social unrest and even riots. Such food shortages as well as earthquakes were seen by Christians as indicators that Christ would return (Matt. 24:7; Mark 13:8; Luke 21:11).

Are you married? Do not seek a divorce. Are you unmarried? Do not look for a wife (7:27). In Roman elite society men were encouraged to marry. Tacitus records that "towards the end of his life, Augustus passed the Papia-Poppaean Law, which supplemented the earlier Julian Laws, to encourage the enforcement of penalties for celibacy and to enrich the Treasury."[76]

But if you do marry, you have not sinned; and if a virgin marries, she has not sinned. But those who marry will face many troubles in this life (7:28). Paul's advice stems from his understanding of "the present crisis" (7:26), which he thinks will bring food shortages and other traumas. Marriage is not sinful, but Paul recognizes that if Corinthian Christians marry in the face of the present crisis, their children may suffer.

The time is short (7:29). The rise of Augustus created a new starting point

▶ The Dinippus Inscriptions

During excavations in the central part of Corinth at least ten inscriptions have been found that serve as the bases for honorific statues to Tiberius Claudius Dinippus.[A-22] This individual, who originally served as a military tribune in the Legion VI Hispanensis ("Spanish") as well as *agōnothetēs* ("official in charge of the games") in the city, appears to have been honored by each of the tribes of which the citizen body of the colony of Corinth was composed. The inscriptions record that he had held the post of *curator annonae* three times. This post involved the supervision of the grain supply and implies that there had been a period of grain shortage. Since Dinippus apparently held the post of quinquennial *duovir* in A.D. 52/53, it is reasonable to suppose that he held the curatorship in the 50s, a period known to have been one of famines or food shortages.[A-23] His generosity led the different tribes of the colony to show their appreciation of his role.

for time; note the inscriptions from the province of Achaia, such as the honorific inscription of the Corinthian citizen L. Licinnius Anteros from Methana on the Saronic Gulf, dated (using the new calendar initiated after the battle of Actium) to A.D. 1/2.[77] Paul emphasizes here that the time "has been shortened" (not as in NIV, "the time is short"). He encourages Christians to move away from the worries of the "present crisis" (7:26) to a Christian perspective on time.

Those who have wives should live as if they had none; those who mourn, as if they did not; those who are happy, as if they were not (7:29 – 30). Paul refers to the "seasons" in life, derived from Ecclesiastes 3:1 – 8:[78]

> There is a time for everything,
> and a season for every activity under
>   heaven:
> a time to be born and a time to die,
> a time to plant and a time to uproot,
> a time to kill and a time to heal,
> a time to tear down and a time to
>   build,
> a time to weep and a time to laugh,
> a time to mourn and a time to dance,
> a time to scatter stones and a time to
>   gather them,
> a time to embrace and a time to
>   refrain,
> a time to search and a time to give up,
> a time to keep and a time to throw
>   away,
> a time to tear and a time to mend,
> a time to be silent and a time to
>   speak,
> a time to love and a time to hate,
> a time for war and a time for peace.

This world in its present form is passing away (7:31). The social consequences of the "present crisis" (7:26) mean changes in the world order. In one sense Roman rule has brought order, at least to the Mediterranean world, but that too will be thrown into crisis as military commanders seek to wrestle power from the dynastic emperor, as was the case with the fall of Nero in A.D. 69, the year of the four emperors.

An unmarried man is concerned about the Lord's affairs — how he can please the Lord (7:32). Paul reminds unmarried men that without the responsibility of wife and family, they will be free to concentrate on Christian work. In a world where travel was difficult, single men were best equipped to move from city to city, province to province.

A married man is concerned about the affairs of this world — how he can please his wife — and his interests are divided (7:33 – 34a). Paul does not want the Christian husband to neglect his wife and family because of Christian ministry and work. He recognizes there will be a division of interests and time, and it is up to the Christian to find the right balance of commitments. An unmarried man can be more single-minded in his work for the kingdom of God.

Undivided devotion to the Lord (7:35). Christian devotion is expressed through honoring marriage commitments made before conversion.

If anyone thinks he is acting improperly toward the virgin he is engaged to, and if she is getting along in years and he feels he ought to marry, he should do as he wants (7:36). The term "improperly" can also be translated "in an unseemly way."[79] First-century use suggests it includes acts of immodesty as well as fornication, but may also include acts considered unacceptable in wider society.[80] In the Roman world it was acceptable for some sort of sexual contact between a betrothed couple, although there was protection for women from those who might be trying to seduce them.[81] However, it seems that in this context there has been no contact of a sexual nature,

for Paul has already condemned fornication (6:9).

The term "virgin" (*parthenos*) refers to the unmarried status of a woman. "Getting along in years" (*hyperakmos*) can also be translated as "past the bloom of youth."[82] The term was used by the Ephesian medical writer Soranus in his work on gynecology dating to the late first century A.D.[83] He uses the term to refer to women after the onset of menstruation, around age fourteen. A later source suggests that the term could also have the meaning of passion.[84]

But the man . . . who has made up his mind not to marry the virgin . . . also does the right thing (7:37). Given the present crisis, the man who had been planning to marry is under no obligation as long as all parties, especially the fiancée's family, understand his reason for the decision.

So then, he who marries the virgin does right, but he who does not marry her does even better (7:38). If after consideration it is thought appropriate to marry, Paul is happy for the marriage to proceed. The central issue is that the decision is taken after weighing the options.

A woman is bound to her husband as long as he lives. But if her husband dies, she is free to marry anyone she wishes, but he must belong to the Lord (7:39). Christians are not free to marry whomever they would choose, but only other Christians. The context here is for those who have been widowed, but it is equally true for those who have never married. The Julian Law of 18 B.C. (*Lex Iulia de maritandis ordinibus*) allowed a widow to be exempt from marriage for one year after her husband's death, and the Papia-Poppaean Law of A.D. 9 two years.[85]

In my judgment, she is happier if she stays as she is — and I think that I too have the Spirit of God (7:40). Paul is contrasting himself with those in the Corinthian church who claimed to be "spiritual" (cf. 1 Cor. 2:15). Paul is "spiritual" in the sense that he is filled with the Spirit of God. This may be compared with his claim to have "the mind of Christ" (1 Cor. 2:16).

Food Sacrificed to Idols (8:1 – 13)

This is another issue raised by the Corinthians in a letter to Paul (see 7:1). Parts of this letter may be quoted (e.g., 8:5 – 6). The issue in this section relates to food eaten in the precinct of the temple (8:10), rather than the issue discussed later (10:25 – 11:1) about eating food offered to an idol in a private home.

Now about food sacrificed to idols (8:1). The food offered to idols may be linked to major civic festivals. Meat was not a common item in the ancient diet and was usually only consumed as part of a religious ceremony. At Corinth some of the wealthy magistrates were known to give such banquets. Lucius Castricius Reg-

ulus, probably dating to the early first century A.D., who was the first president (*agōnothetēs*) of the Panhellenic Games within the territory of Corinth, once gave a banquet for all the "inhabitants of the colony"[86]; those who were not Roman citizens and who were merely considered residents would have been excluded. A similar banquet was given by Sospis, president of the Isthmian Games and friend of Plutarch.[87]

We know that we all possess knowledge (8:1). This may be a quotation from the letter written by the Corinthians to Paul. The "knowledge" (*gnōsis*) of the Christian is ultimately derived from Jesus Christ, as Paul emphasized at the beginning of the letter (1:5). This word was common in philosophical language, ultimately deriving from individuals like Plato. The members of the elite within the church at Corinth are likely to have been instructed in philosophy as part of their general education. The knowledge the Corinthian

right ▶

A POPULAR IDOL

A statue of the goddess Persephone.

Christians display is developed later in the chapter (8:4).

We know that an idol is nothing at all in the world and that there is no God but one (8:4). The Corinthians have boasted about their knowledge, and this is clearly a quotation from their letter. No doubt Paul had to address this issue when he was at Corinth, as many converts would have been involved with pagan deities. The same was true in the Macedonian city of Thessalonica, where the Christians there had "turned to God from idols to serve the living and true God" (1 Thess. 1:9). Some Christians may have believed that it meant nothing if they entered a pagan sanctuary and consumed meat that was explicitly linked to sacrifice. Paul quotes from the law of Moses: "Hear, O Israel: The Lord our God, the Lord is one" (Deut. 6:4).

For even if there are so-called gods, whether in heaven or on earth (as indeed there are many "gods" and many "lords") (8:5). Paul is making the point that *even though* there are so-called gods, their claim is false.[88] The gods "in heaven" would include deities such as Jupiter,

the chief of the pagan gods, and Aphrodite, the patron deity of the colony. The gods "on earth" may be an allusion to the way the Roman imperial family was worshiped and considered to be divine. At Corinth there was a temple of Octavia, dedicated to the sister of the emperor Augustus. The focus for a provincial imperial cult, based at Corinth, was established about A.D. 54.[89] There was a regular festival celebrating the imperial family; thus a Christian attending a banquet in honor of the deified emperor might be compromised.[90]

One God, the Father, from whom all things came and for whom we live; and . . . one Lord, Jesus Christ, through whom all things came and through whom we live (8:6). Paul turns the language widespread in the ancient world to show that there is only one God and one Lord. Before Paul was shipwrecked on the way to Rome, he addressed his fellows with the statement about "God whose I am and whom I serve" (Acts 27:23).

Some people are still so accustomed to idols that when they eat such food they think of it as having been sacrificed to

CANAANITE IDOLS

(left) Images of Astarte, a Canaanite fertility goddess (13th – 10th century B.C.).

(right) Statue of an Ammonite deity (8th – 7th century B.C.).

an idol, and since their conscience is weak, it is defiled (8:7). When people in the ancient world described a cult statue to be displayed in a temple, they would drop the word "statue." Thus at Olympia in the Peloponnese, the seated figure in the temple was Zeus; Strabo, writing during the reign of Augustus, made the comment that if the god were to stand up, "he would take the roof off the temple"![91] Those believers who had been brought up to believe in the presence of a god within pagan sanctuaries would feel defiled if they continued to participate in such ritual meals.

Food does not bring us near to God (8:8). The partaking of food offered to idols makes no material difference to the standing of a Christian before God. It is the attitude with which a Corinthian believer is involved with such meals that is significant.

Be careful, however, that the exercise of your freedom does not become a stumbling block to the weak (8:9). The phrase translated as "the exercise of your freedom" can in fact mean "this right of yours." One's right (*exousia*) can be equated with civic privilege held by leading citizens within the colony.[92] This can be compared with the rights of an apostle in the next chapter (which uses the same Greek word). As citizens and Greeks, the leading members of the city may have had the right to participate in the festivals and associated athletic events, such as at Isthmia.

For if anyone with a weak conscience sees you who have this knowledge eating in an idol's temple, won't he be emboldened to eat what has been sacrificed to idols? (8:10). Some of the Corinthian

Christians were clearly attending feasts within the precincts of the cult centers of Corinth and its territory. A number of dining rooms linked to sanctuaries are known in the Corinthia, though not all date to the first century.[93] Dining rooms formed part of the complex of the Asklepieion at Corinth. Dining rooms were usually small, sometimes for only seven reclining individuals; thus, banquets were intimate occasions. The Greek word translated "eating" means reclining; the picture is of an individual reclining on a couch, arranged around the outer wall of a small room, to eat.

Not all such feasts were eaten in sanctuaries. A mass of animal bones were found near the theater, and it seems possible that the meat was distributed to the people and consumed within the theater itself. But note that the issue being discussed is about eating food within the pagan sanctuary, not eating food that has been sacrificed (this is dealt with separately at 10:14–22). The result of one Christian eating within the sanctuary is that a weaker Christian may see him and

"DO AS I SAY, NOT AS I DO!" HOW often have we heard that piece of advice? If we are serious about helping young Christians to grow, we must consider carefully our own lifestyles and see what things might be sending out unhelpful signals. We may, of course, come to a mature decision; but the young Christian might not see it like that!

be, literally, "built up" to go and do the same.

So this weak brother, for whom Christ died, is destroyed by your knowledge (8:11). The destruction for the "weak brother" is that he reverts to his old pagan ways.

When you sin against your brothers in this way and wound their weak conscience, you sin against Christ (8:12). When Paul was confronted by Jesus on the road to Damascus, Jesus asked him, "Saul, Saul, why do you persecute me?" (Acts 9:4). Actions against our brothers and sisters in Christ are actions against the person of Jesus Christ.

Paul the Apostle (9:1 – 27)

Have I not seen Jesus our Lord? (9:1). Paul considered the events on the Damascus road not as a vision but as a real encounter with the risen Lord Jesus.

For you are the seal of my apostleship in the Lord (9:2). To deny Paul's apostleship, as some at Corinth clearly did, is to deny the validity of the church at Corinth.

This is my defense to those who sit in judgment on me (9:3). This verse introduces a series of questions intended to defend Paul from criticisms being made against him.

Don't we have the right to food and drink? (9:4). As the Corinthian Christians considered themselves to have

ASCLEPIUS

(left) The theater at Epidaurus, the center for the worship of Asclepius.

(right) Statue of Asclepius at the Epidaurus museum.

rights (8:9), so Paul as an apostle considers he has rights.

Don't we have the right to take a believing wife along with us, as do the other apostles and the Lord's brothers and Cephas? (9:5). Notice that the wife of an apostle comes from the community of Christians. Jesus' brothers appear as a distinct group within the early church (Acts 1:14).

Barnabas (9:6). Barnabas, originally from the island of Cyprus, was a Levite (Acts 4:36). He accompanied Paul on his first missionary journey until they had a disagreement over John Mark (Acts 15:37).

Who serves as a soldier (9:7). Achaia was a senatorial province and had no legionary garrison. However, soldiers from neighboring provinces were seconded to the provincial administration at Corinth. A first-century example of this is the tombstone of Caius Valerius Valens, found at Kranion.[94] The text reads:

> C[aius] Valerius Valens, son of C[aius], Quirinan tribe, from the Cam[unni] people, a soldier [*miles*] of the 8th Augustan legion, century of Senucius [or Senucus], he lived 35 years, he was a soldier for 14 years. *Heres ex testamento.*

The abbreviation "Cam" on the tombstone may indicate that he came from the Alpine tribe of the Camunni, who had been incorporated into the empire in 16 B.C.; members of the tribe were enrolled in the Roman Quirinan tribe when they became Roman citizens. Valens's legion is known to have served in Moesia (the lower Danube) from A.D. 45 to 69, and it is possible that Valens

was seconded to the governor's staff of Achaia. Although he is described as a soldier, Valens is shown in the grave relief as an officer, perhaps holding the rank of *optio*.[95]

Who plants a vineyard and does not eat of its grapes? Who tends a flock and does not drink of the milk? (9:7). Archaeological field survey in Greece has done much to throw light on ancient agricultural practice. The situation is likely to be with absentee landlords and tenant farmers. In other words, the social elite at Corinth may have owned land in different parts of the province, such as Laconia, and had tenants to plant their vineyards. Others, such as L. Licinnius Anteros in the Augustan period, resided at Corinth and were given the privilege of grazing their flocks elsewhere (e.g., on the Methana peninsula near Troezen).[96] It would be unreasonable for the landlord to expect his tenants not to eat some of the grapes or to drink some of the milk.

Doesn't the Law say the same thing? (9:8). Paul turns from secular illustrations that could be observed in contemporary Corinth to examples from the Old Testament.

Do not muzzle an ox while it is treading out the grain (9:9). Paul quotes from Deuteronomy 25:4. The ox is representative of those who work to bring in the harvest.

This was written for us, because when the plowman plows and the thresher threshes, they ought to do so in the hope of sharing in the harvest (9:10). Paul goes from the text to the application of the law to the people in Corinth. The Christian community needs to recognize that those who minister to them deserve material and financial support.

We did not use this right. On the contrary, we put up with anything rather than hinder the gospel of Christ (9:12). When Paul bade farewell to the elders at Ephesus, he reminded them of the words of Jesus, "It is more blessed to give than to receive" (Acts 20:35). This was one principle for his apostolic ministry — in sharp contrast with the roving professional speakers, the sophists, who expected honors and financial gain from their public speaking.

Those who work in the temple get their food from the temple, and those who serve at the altar share in what is offered on the altar (9:13). It is not clear if the intended background is Jewish or Gentile. Jews knew that the priests in the temple at Jerusalem were allowed to share in a proportion of what was offered (e.g., Num. 1:8 – 19). Those involved

with the pagan temples of the Roman colony knew that any engaged in the sacrifices received a share of the sacrifice; it was, of course, going to be a specific issue in the church about "food offered to idols" (8:1 – 13).

The Lord has commanded that those who preach the gospel should receive their living from the gospel (9:14). When Jesus sent out his disciples to preach the gospel, he commanded them, "Do not take along any gold or silver or copper in your belts; take no bag for the journey, or extra tunic, or sandals or a staff; for the worker is worth his keep" (Matt. 10:10).

I have not used any of these rights. And I am not writing this in the hope that you will do such things for me. I would rather die than have anyone deprive me of this boast (9:15). In the ancient world a discussion of money led to the feeling that money was being sought. Paul distances

◀

ALTAR OF SACRIFICE

A model of the altar in the Court of Priests in the Jerusalem temple.

himself from such expectation. The Greek sentence is left hanging to emphasize Paul's unwillingness to accept money in response to this teaching: "For it is good for me rather to die than. . . ."[97] In Paul's mind, the integrity of the gospel is at stake here.

I am compelled to preach. Woe to me if I do not preach the gospel! (9:16). Paul refers to this compulsion to preach in 2 Corinthians 5:14: "For Christ's love compels us, because we are convinced that one died for all, and therefore all died."

What then is my reward? Just this: that in preaching the gospel I may offer it free of charge (9:18). Travelling orators or sophists might come to Corinth and make a fine speech in the hope of being honored by the colony or receiving some financial reward. Paul's preaching stands in marked contrast because it is done with no expectation of human reward.

Though I am free and belong to no man, I make myself a slave to everyone, to win as many as possible (9:19). Tutors might be engaged by a wealthy family for the education of children. Although Paul has links with some of the wealthy households of Corinth, such as that of Stephanas (1:16; 16:15), he can state unequivocally that he is independent.

To the Jews I became like a Jew, to win the Jews. To those under the law I became like one under the law . . . so as to win those under the law (9:20). Paul is sensitive to Jewish culture so as to present the gospel of Jesus Christ to the Jews.

To those not having the law I became like one not having the law . . . so as to win those not having the law (9:21). Paul

recognizes that the Christian gospel is relevant to the Gentiles (i.e., non-Jews), and so he seeks to find points of contact with their culture.

To the weak I became weak, to win the weak. I have become all things to all men so that by all possible means I might save some (9:22). Although "the weak" may refer to the "weak brother" of 8:9 – 13, this group are among those who have yet to respond to the gospel. A possible third group might be those who hold to various ancient superstitions.

I do all this for the sake of the gospel, that I may share in its blessings (9:23). Paul's life has been committed to sharing the good news of Jesus Christ with the different groups he has encountered in

right ▶

ATHLETE HOLDING A CROWN

his journeys through the provinces of the eastern Roman empire.

All the runners run, but only one gets the prize? Run in such a way as to get the prize (9:24). Track events were the key element in any set of Greek games. The original event was the *stadion*, which was the length of the track, about 630 feet (the equivalent of 192 meters). The prestige of winning the event was such that the winner's name was often attached to the set of games; Greek historians refer to the year in which "x" won the *stadion* at the Olympic Games. Other foot-races were developed, including the *diaulos*, consisting of two lengths of the running track, as well as the *dolichos*, or long-distance race. In A.D. 69 Polites won all three of these running events at Olympia.

Everyone who competes in the games goes into strict training (9:25). The "games" to which Paul alludes are probably those of the Isthmian Festival, held in the nearby sanctuary of Poseidon at Isthmia.[98] This was one of a number of so-called Panhellenic games — others were held at Olympia, Delphi ("Pythian Games"), and Nemea — where competitors from all over the Greek world competed. Training was taken seriously. Philostratos the Elder (2d century A.D.) comments, "If you have worked hard enough to render yourself worthy of going to Olympia, if you have not been idle or ill-disciplined, then go with confidence; but those who have not trained in this fashion, let them go where they will."[99] Olympic athletes had to reside at Elis (the town that controlled Olympia) for a month before the games.

A crown that will not last (9:25). The crowns for the Panhellenic games were often no more than wreaths. At Olympia

▶ **Athletics at Corinth**

The sanctuary of Poseidon at Isthmia was located within the territory of the city of Corinth. This was located at the Isthmus of Corinth, some 8 miles (12 km) away. Attached to the sanctuary were athletic games held every two years. These were one of the Panhellenic festivals, which drew competitors from all over the Greek world; other similar festivals were held at Delphi and in the Peloponnese at Olympia and Nemea. The games continued into the Roman period, and in A.D. 67 the emperor Nero used the games as the moment to proclaim the freedom of Greece, a privilege repealed by the subsequent emperor Vespasian.

Excavations at Isthmia have revealed remains of the sanctuary as well as parts of the stadium. One of the most important discoveries, though dating from the classical city rather than the Roman period, was a specially designed starting gate for the runners.

Inscriptions from Corinth give the names of the magistrates or *agōnothetai* responsible for holding the games. Monuments recording specific victors as well as victor lists are also known.[A-24] These show that there were three main groups of events at the Isthmian festival: cultural, including music, equestrian, and athletic. There were separate events for boys and men. The winning victors had originally been given a garland of celery, which was replaced by one of pine.[A-25]

In the Roman period the games were expanded to include events linked to the imperial cult. The Caesarean games were established under Tiberius and held every four years. When these Caesarean games coincided with the Isthmian festival, they were known as the Great Isthmia; in the intervening years the local games were known as the Lesser Isthmia.

it was an olive wreath, at Isthmia one of pine.[100] The individual was often honored with a statue at Olympia as well as in his own city.

No, I beat my body and make it my slave so that after I have preached to others, I myself will not be disqualified for the prize (9:27). The integrity of the gospel is at stake if Paul does not follow his own advice. It might be possible for Paul to offer encouraging teaching to the Christian community at Corinth but then succumb to the same temptations they faced.

Eating Food Offered to Idols in the Idol Temple (10:1 – 22)

Paul finished the last section looking at the way in which a competitor in an athletic event might be disqualified as an illustration for Christian ministry. The next section, linked with "for" (10:1), develops the argument. It addresses the key issue in a Roman colony of how the Christian can take part in civic life, yet remain untainted by the pagan beliefs of his or her fellow-citizens.

For I do not want you to be ignorant of the fact, brothers, that our forefathers were all under the cloud and that they all passed through the sea (10:1). Any members of the Corinthian church from a Gentile background would be ignorant about Jewish history. Thus, Paul takes the trouble to explain that the God of the Jews leaving Egypt is the same as the God of the church of Corinth. Therefore, the Old Testament provides lessons for them. The "cloud" refers to the pillar of cloud that led the Jews out from Egypt (e.g., Ex. 13:21), and the "sea" refers to the parting of the waters (14:21 – 22). Notice how our Christian heritage lies in our Jewish past by the way Paul presents the Jews of the Exodus as "our forefathers." The condensed story of the Exodus that Paul relates is similar to that found in Psalm 78:13 – 16, which in its original context reminded God's people of the dangers of disobedience. The emphasis on "all" in this and subsequent verses contrasts with the "some" within the Christian community at Corinth (4:18; 6:11).

REFLECTIONS

THERE IS A THRILL WHEN A STUDENT works hard and obtains a prize for achievement. Any Christian minister has a sense of thanksgiving and joy when individuals are converted and start to grow in their faith. There would be something suspect if we paid our pastors on the basis of a head count — or even worse, withheld payment for lack of apparent progress! Yet as members of the Christian community, we must support our pastors in a practical way so that they can minister the gospel of Jesus Christ among us.

COMPETING IN THE GAMES

The starting grid for the runners in the games held at Isthmia. ▼

They were all baptized into Moses in the cloud and in the sea (10:2). The "cloud" led the people (Ex. 13:21; 14:19 – 20) and the "sea" parted to allow them to leave Egypt (14:21 – 31), but it was placing their trust in Moses that was important.

They all ate the same spiritual food (10:3). In the desert of Zin — the great desert of the Negev — the people of Israel started to grumble about the food they had been able to eat in Egypt (Ex. 16:3). In response God provided first quail and then manna (16:13 – 15). This manna was to be their sustenance for the duration of the forty years in the desert (16:35).

They drank from the spiritual rock that accompanied them, and that rock was Christ (10:4). There are two incidents in the wandering in the desert that refer to rocks being struck. The first was at Rephidim before the people of Israel reached Mount Sinai (Ex. 17:1 – 7). The second was in the Desert of Zin, a place that became known as the waters of Meribah (or quarrelling) (Num. 20:2 – 13). The people grumbled about the lack of water and their departure from the "benefits" of Egypt, and the Lord commanded Moses to strike the rock with his staff.

Their bodies were scattered over the desert (10:5). The language evokes the prayer used by Moses to God where he anticipates what the nations will say if God punishes the people for their disobedience: "The LORD was not able to bring these people into the land he promised them on oath; so he slaughtered them in the desert" (Num. 14:16). Although all had passed through the waters of the Red Sea and all had been sustained by the bread, God's displeasure

fell on "most of them" because they had not followed his commands.

Now these things occurred as examples to keep us from setting our hearts on evil things as they did (10:6). The events of Jewish history may seem irrelevant to those brought up in a Roman (or Greek) culture. Yet the issues of idolatry, sexual immorality, putting God to the test, and grumbling are all issues that the Corinthians are facing.

Do not be idolaters, as some of them were; as it is written: "The people sat down to eat and drink and got up to indulge in pagan revelry" (10:7). Paul quotes here from Exodus 32:6. While the people were camped at the foot of Mount Sinai, they became disenchanted, created a golden calf, and made offerings before it. As a result Moses, when he had come down from the mountain, instructed certain Levites to kill those who had rebelled against the Lord (32:25 – 29). The application for this lesson from history is for those Corinthian Christians who feel that they can still attend festivals in the sanctuaries and precincts of the colony, including the sanctuary of Poseidon at Isthmia, and yet be loyal to the Lord. In Corinth, pagan festivals included the sacrifice of animals, and parts of the offerings were consumed by the participants.

We should not commit sexual immorality, as some of them did — and in one day twenty-three thousand of them died (10:8). The allusion here is to the incident when the people of Israel were staying at Shittim (Num. 25:1 – 9). The Moabite women seduced the Israelite men and then encouraged them to worship Baal of Peor. Moses dealt with

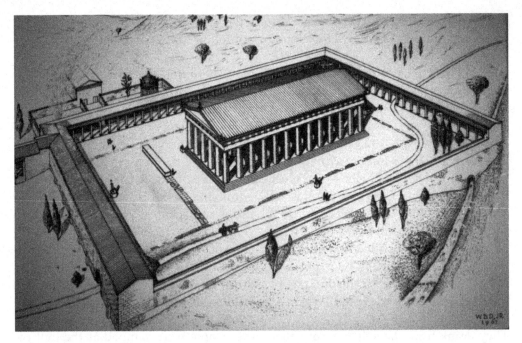

▶

SANCTUARY OF POSEIDON AT ISTHMIA

An artistic recon-
struction of this
famous temple.

this immorality, and the plague that decimated the Israelites was brought to a halt. In the Roman world, prostitutes were frequently present at banquets. Dio Chrysostom mentions prostitutes being taken from festival to festival to satisfy the sexual needs of the participants and those attending.[101] Paul was no doubt concerned that indulgence with prostitutes might lead people into engagement with the pagan festivals of the colony.

We should not test the Lord, as some of them did — and were killed by snakes (10:9). This refers to another incident during Israel's desert wandering. When the people "spoke against God and against Moses" (Num. 21:5), God sent poisonous snakes, which killed a number of the Israelites. People were only saved when a bronze snake was erected in their midst for them to look upon (21:6 – 9). Some of the Corinthian Christians may have felt that since nothing seemed to have happened to them as they contin-ued to attend festivals in pagan sanctu-

aries, they might as well continue. Paul views such an attitude as tempting God.

And do not grumble, as some of them did — and were killed by the destroying angel (10:10). When the spies returned from exploring Canaan, the Promised Land, the people were frightened at the report the majority of them brought (Num. 13); this led to grumbling against Moses and Aaron and an attempt to choose a new leader (14:1 – 4). Conse-quently, God promised that not one of the adults who left Egypt would enter the Promised Land (except Caleb and Joshua, 14:30). The men who had spread the depressing reports about Canaan were "struck down and died of a plague before the Lord" (14:37).

Examples and . . . warnings for us, on whom the fulfillment of the ages has come (10:11). These lessons from Jewish history are applicable to Gentiles because of God's promise to Abram, "All peoples on earth will be blessed through you" (Gen. 12:3).

If you think you are standing firm, be careful that you don't fall! (10:12). Some in the church seem to be using the argument, "We know that an idol is nothing at all in the world and that there is no God but one" (8:4). Some may even be "eating in an idol's temple" (8:10). The lesson from Israel's history is that such people may be in for a fall.

No temptation has seized you except what is common to man. And God is faithful (10:13). The Corinthian Christians may be faced by the general temptations Paul has been rehearsing. They would be foolish to pretend that such temptations do not face them. They also are presented with specific temptations or possible compromises because of the nature of their involvement in the life of the ancient city, with its emphasis on religious cults and activities.

Flee from idolatry (10:14). Corinthian Christians can flee from idolatry by making sure they take no part in the pagan life of the colony. This would create tensions for those perhaps holding civic magistracies, who are expected to attend festivals and make sacrifices.

I speak to sensible people (10:15). Paul has used the same Greek word for "sensible" (*phronimos*) in an ironic way earlier in the letter (4:10). Here he recognizes that the Corinthian Christians have obtained wisdom in the way they relate to their pagan world.

Is not the cup of thanksgiving for which we give thanks a participation in the blood of Christ? (10:16). At the Passover meal, celebrating the Exodus from Egypt and thus picking up on the thrust of Paul's earlier illustrations, four cups of wine were drunk during the course of the meal. The cup of thanksgiving was the third cup.

Is not the bread that we break a participation in the body of Christ? (10:16). When animals were sacrificed in pagan sanctuaries, meat was offered to the participants, something that did not form part of a regular diet in the ancient world. Yet the use of bread reminded the Christians of the sacrifice Jesus Christ had made on the cross on their behalf.

People of Israel (10:18). The Greek phrase here (lit., "Israel according to the flesh") refers to the Jews of Paul's day who continued to offer sacrifices in the temple at Jerusalem.

Participate in the altar (10:18). The Jewish writer Philo saw that those who took part in the sacrifice were "partners in the altar."[102] The imagery goes back to the days of Moses when the priests were required to eat the food together by the altar, "for it is most holy" (Lev. 10:12). The parts of the offerings that were not consumed by fire on the altar of God could be consumed by the priests and Levites (Num. 17:8 – 10; Deut. 18:1 – 5). However others could also consume by the altar part of what had been offered to God (e.g., Deut. 12:4 – 7).

Do I mean then that a sacrifice offered to an idol is anything, or that an idol is anything? (10:19). Paul clarifies the three strands of his argument: those who take part in the Lord's Supper, those who participate in Jewish sacrifices, and those who have engaged with pagan practices. Paul has already reminded them that "an idol is nothing at all and that there is no God but one" (8:4). The language used for the idol meat (*eidōlothyton*) is derived from the Jewish background.

The sacrifices of pagans are offered to demons, not to God, and I do not want you to be participants with demons (10:20). This theme of sacrificing to demons picks up on the Song of Moses in Deuteronomy (32:17): "They sacrificed to demons, which are not God." This picks up on the themes from the desert wandering earlier in the chapter.

You cannot drink the cup of the Lord and the cup of demons too; you cannot have a part in both the Lord's table and the table of demons (10:21). Paul makes it clear that participation in any form of pagan worship, whether festivals or the imperial cult, is prohibited to the Christian. Metal and ceramic vessels were often inscribed in antiquity with the name of a deity to which they had been dedicated.

Are we trying to arouse the Lord's jealousy? Are we stronger than he? (10:22). The Jews remembered that when in the desert they had worshiped other gods, "they made [God] jealous by what is no god and angered [God] with their worthless idols" (Deut. 32:21).

Eating Food Offered to Idols in Private Gatherings (10:23 – 11:1)

"Everything is permissible " — but not everything is beneficial. "Everything is permissible " — but not everything is constructive (10:23). The slogan "everything is permissible" has a link with the rights asserted by the Corinthian Christians (8:9). Thus this phrase can be translated "Everything is lawful" or "Everything is allowed."[103] But Paul's main point is to urge the Corinthian Christians to seek what is "beneficial" for their city and society[104] and what "is constructive"; this latter phrase can also be translated as "builds up" or "edifies," indicating the way that the Christian life develops like a building.

Nobody should seek his own good, but the good of others (10:24). The colony of Corinth, like virtually any other city in the Roman world, gave opportunity for the social elite to display their status. Buildings prominently displayed details of their benefactors; portrait statues were erected in public places. For example, the dedication by the city magistrate Erastus of a piazza next to the theater at Corinth had bronze letters (see "Paul Quotes an Athenian Playwright" at 15:33). By contrast, the Christian is to serve others rather than promote himself or herself.

Eat anything sold in the meat market without raising questions of conscience (10:25). The meat market (*makellon*)

lay near to the forum in Corinth and has been partially excavated.[105] Similar markets of roughly the same date have been recognized at Pompeii and in North Africa. Food for sale in a *makellon* may have been initially sacrificed in a temple or sanctuary.

"The earth is the Lord's, and everything in it" (10:26). The quotation from Psalm 24:1 was used in Jewish society as a means of giving thanks for food.[106]

If some unbeliever invites you to a meal and you want to go, eat whatever is put before you (10:27). The context for this meal is clearly in the private home rather than in the temple. The Christian community does not have to separate itself from fellow Corinthians. The word used for "invites" is found in papyri from Egypt relating to both secular and religious meals.

If anyone says to you, "This has been offered in sacrifice," then do not eat it (10:28). The "anyone" need not be another Christian. It may be the non-Christian host at the meal or a fellow diner who is puzzled how a Christian can eat something offered to a pagan god. The phrase in quotation marks can be translated, "This is sacred meat" (*hierothyton*), using language that might be more appropriate for somebody from a non-Jewish background; it contrasts with the Jewish expression "idol meat" used earlier in 10:19.

The other man's conscience (10:29). If the person who pointed out the origin of the meat was a pagan, then "conscience" may be better translated as "moral consciousness."[107] Thus the person who has made the statement at the dinner was concerned that the Christian might follow Jewish dietary regulations.

If I take part in the meal with thankfulness, why am I denounced because of something I thank God for? (10:30). The thanksgiving at the Jewish meal would be Psalm 24:1 (quoted in 10:26), endorsing that God is the origin of all things.

So whether you eat or drink or whatever you do, do it all for the glory of God (10:31). God touches every corner of the Christian life, even aspects not regularly thought of as "sacred" in the ancient world.

Do not cause anyone to stumble, whether Jews, Greeks or the church of God (10:32). The Jews and the Greeks reflect the cultural composition of the church at Corinth. Consideration must be given to the backgrounds and perceptions of the members of the church.

I am not seeking my own good but the good of many, so that they may be saved (10:33). The good mentioned here is the "welfare" or "benefit" mentioned in 10:23 (see comments).

Follow my example (11:1). "Follow" is better translated as "imitate." The Corinthian Christians are urged to follow Paul's model as he has had to work out his response to the pagan backdrop of civic life in the Greek East.

Veiling the Head (11:2 – 16)

After talking about the way Christians relate to the pagan festivals and cult practices of the Roman colony, Paul now turns to how Christian fellowship operates; in particular, he emphasizes points that will make it distinctive as a community.

I praise you for remembering me in everything and for holding to the teachings, just as I passed them on to you (11:2). Praise was a feature of elite society, and so Paul is using language to which the Corinthians can respond. He refers to teachings that have been "passed . . . on" (lit., "handed down"), that is to say, "traditions." They are, of course, traditions that carry the weight of an apostle. Presumably some of the issues Paul goes on to address in chapter 11 are ones that had not arisen during his time in the colony.

The head of every man is Christ, and the head of the woman is man, and the head of Christ is God (11:3). The words "man" and "woman" can also be translated as "husband" and "wife." The choice of the word "head" (*kephalē*) seems to indicate that Paul has a hierarchical structure in mind. Although the Liddell, Scott, and Jones' *Greek Lexicon* allows the possibility of the translation "source," this has been disputed.[108] The thinking behind Paul's metaphor is not obvious.

Every man who prays or prophesies with his head covered dishonors his head (11:4). The covering of the man's head — called the *capite velato* — was commonplace in a Roman religious cult. One explanation was that it helped to reduce the noise of the animals being sacrificed (see "Roman Portraits"). The statue of Augustus displayed at Corinth showed the emperor with his head covered; similar iconography is found on the frieze of the Ara Pacis ("Altar of Peace") that he dedicated at Rome. The social elite took an active part in the religious cults of the city by serving as priests, and thus those who had joined the church may have introduced this Roman cultural norm into Christian worship. Thus, Christian worship was expressing not that all were one in Christ but the social divisions of secular society. Praying with a covered head drew attention to the man's place in Roman society, whereas in Christian worship the focus should be on Christ.

REFLECTIONS

IN CORINTH, SOME CHRISTIANS were offended when they saw other members of their church community eating meat that had been offered as a sacrifice to the pagan gods. Those eating could come up with a theological argument to allow them to enjoy the festivities — but they may not have thought through the practical pastoral considerations. What sort of things do we do that might become stumbling blocks to other Christians?

ARA PACIS IN ROME
▼

Every woman who prays or prophesies with her head uncovered dishonors her head (11:5). Notice that Paul clearly envisages that women should be involved in prayer and prophecy in the fellowship. The hairstyles of the women in the imperial family at Rome tended to set the trends for women in the rest of the empire. It is clear from portraits on coins and in sculpture that women's hair in the middle of the first century A.D. tended to be worn longer than under Augustus. Agrippina the Younger, the wife of the emperor Claudius, and the mother of the future emperor Nero (from a previous marriage), adopted a hairstyle where "the hair is braided and gathered into a long loop; two long strands of curled hair fall at either side of the neck."[109] The covering of the head is an emblem found in sculptural representation in the late republic and under Augustus, where the palla is pulled up over the top of the head. This became an emblem for modesty and chastity.[110] Presumably women who felt able to uncover their heads were considered immodest, unchaste, and therefore by definition un-Roman.

It is just as though her head were shaved (11:5). A shaved head could be equated with shame for a women. There is some evidence that shaving was a punishment for adultery.[111]

If a woman does not cover her head, she should have her hair cut off; and if it is a disgrace for a woman to have her hair cut or shaved off, she should cover her head (11:6). Failing to cover a woman's

---

▶ Roman Portraits

The covering and uncovering of heads, which is a feature of this letter, needs to be considered against the norms of Roman dress. A major insight is provided by the discovery of a number of imperial and private portrait statues in Corinth.[A-26] For example, the statue of Augustus from the Julian basilica at Corinth (though probably originally displayed elsewhere as it is earlier than that particular building) shows the emperor dressed in a toga.[A-27] A fold of the cloth is pulled over his head in the so-called *capite velato*. Plutarch tells us that a priest pulled the cloth over his head in this way to exclude the noise of the animal being sacrificed.[A-28] This portrait was a standard image of the emperor and of a type found elsewhere in the empire. In contrast, portrait statues of Augustus' adopted heirs, Gaius and Lucius, found in the same basilica were shown naked like athletes. Because they died young, they could be presented unclothed as athletes. In the Julian basilica other imperial statues were also displayed, such as that of the emperor

Nero, also shown with his toga pulled over his head.[A-29]

Coin portraits of the emperor's wife (e.g., Livia) could show her either with her head covered or bare. These coin portraits show how hairstyles developed during the first century into elaborate creations; no doubt the women of the imperial elite in colonies such as Corinth followed the fashion of the imperial court. An early first century A.D. portrait of a woman found at Corinth shows her with her head uncovered and with the hair braided and brought together above the forehead.[A-30]

◀ _____

BRAIDED HAIR

IN THE ROMAN WORLD THE TYPE of dress worn by women could indicate status. A toga, for example, would indicate coveted Roman citizenship. In the church in Corinth there was tension. Some men were adopting a dress code that tried to make a statement about their "high" status in the church community. Some women were dressed in a way that might have led to critical comment from outside the church. How does the dress we adopt for worship reflect Christian values to those outside the church? Do we dress up? Or dress down?

head was dishonoring to her husband. A woman would cover her head when she was married.[112] Thus if "woman" is translated as "wife" (see comments on 11:3), immodest dress would reflect badly on her marriage and therefore her husband.

A man ought not to cover his head, since he is the image and glory of God; but the woman is the glory of man (11:7). Paul uses an illustration from creation to discuss the role of the man (or husband): "So God created man in his own image, in the image of God he created him" (Gen. 1:27a). The woman's role is seen in relation to her husband: "A wife of noble character is her husband's crown" (Prov. 12:4a).

For man did not come from woman, but woman from man; neither was man created for woman, but woman for man (11:8 – 9). Paul follows the order of creation in Genesis 2:23b: "She shall be called 'woman,' for she was taken out of man." Paul has moved away from social

conventions to a theological reason for the wife to reflect respect for her husband.

Because of the angels (11:10). It is not immediately clear what Paul means here. He may be developing an idea, noted at Qumran, that angels participated in worship. Perhaps Paul has in mind that Christians, men and women, will one day "judge angels" (6:3).

The woman ought to have a sign of authority on her head (11:10). The sign of authority may be an allusion to the veil a Roman woman might use to cover her head.

In the Lord, however, woman is not independent of man, nor is man independent of woman (11:11). This develops the idea in Christian marriage that there is mutual respect (see comments on 7:4). This is in contrast with the status of a Roman wife, whose identity was entirely bound up with that of her husband.

As woman came from man, so also man is born of woman. But everything comes from God (11:12). Paul states an important principle that both men and women ultimately come from God.

right ▶

CAESAR AUGUSTUS

A bust of the emperor from the Corinth museum.

Does not the very nature of things teach you that if a man has long hair, it is a disgrace to him (11:14). Nature (*physis*) was thought to be the determining factor in the way society expressed itself. Long hair for men was unusual in ancient society. It was common in the representation of the deities Apollo and Dionysos (Bacchus), but not for other gods. Men were expected to wear their hair short.

If a woman has long hair, it is her glory? For long hair is given to her as a covering (11:15). Portraits of women, and in particular female members of the imperial family, show that their hair was carefully braided and arranged.[113]

Divisions at the Lord's Supper (11:17 – 34)

Paul moves from issues of dress and status in the gatherings of the people of God at Corinth to issues of much more pressing importance.

In the following directives I have no praise for you, for your meetings do more harm than good (11:17). Paul contrasts the praise for the Corinthian Christians

▸ Women in Corinth

A number of women from the Roman colony are known by name, either in their own right or because they wished to honor their husbands by erecting some monument. For example, a possible Augustan marble statue base from the southeastern part of the forum recorded the erection of a (now lost) portrait statue of Sextus Olius Secundus by his son Sextus and by his wife Cornelia.[A-31] A first century A.D. inscription also from the southeastern part of the forum honored Cornelius Pulcher, who had helped to organize the Isthmian games, by his wife.[A-32]

Archaeology has also revealed inscriptions relating to women who were prominent in their own right. A statue base from Corinth was inscribed with this text:

> To Polyaena, daughter of Marcus, priestess of Victory. The high priest [Publius] Licinius Priscus Juventianus, [while still living, (set up this monument)] with the official sanction of the city council to (this) excellent woman.[A-33]

Polyaena held a specific religious role within the life of the colony. Perhaps one of the most extensive documents for women in the Greek east during the first century was found on a stele that had been used in a late antique tomb near Corinth.[A-34] The

text consists of a transcript of a number of decrees from the Lycian confederation, the cities of Myra, Patara, and Telmessos, and a letter to the Corinthians from the Lycian confederation. They relate to Iunia Theodora,

> living in Corinth, a fine and worthy woman, and devoted to the nation, [who] continuously shows her zeal and her munificence towards the nation and being full of goodwill both to individual Lycians and to all in general has gained for the nation the friendship of many of the authorities, employing her assistance in all areas which most directly interest all the Lycians.[A-35]

Iunia Theodora was specifically praised "since . . . very many of our people in exile were welcomed by her with magnificence."[A-36] These Lycian exiles were probably linked either to the civil strife in Lycia when it became a Roman province in A.D. 43,[A-37] or perhaps in A.D. 57, when the Lycian federation unsuccessfully prosecuted the governor, Titus Clodius Eprius Marcellus.[A-38] Iunia Theodora's residence at Corinth, though her family came from Lycia, may have had a commercial reason, and this may explain why individual cities of Lycia were grateful to her for looking after their interests in one of the major ports of the Mediterranean.

over holding onto the teaching he has communicated to them (11:2) with a refusal to praise them for their actions at the Lord's Supper.

When you come together as a church, there are divisions among you (11:18). Paul has already noted the divisions within the church (1:10), but here they are manifest when the church comes together. The word Paul uses to describe the church (*ekklēsia*) is the same one that was commonly used in Greek cities for describing the political body.[114] The political assembly was where oratorical skills could be displayed, sometimes with the goal of creating factions and divisions to further civic or political ends. Perhaps the Corinthian Christians thought that the politicking of the citizen body in Corinth was a role model for their own assembly. The church met as a body in a house of one of its members, such as the house of Gaius (Rom. 16:23).

To some extent I believe it (11:18). Earlier in the letter Paul made it clear that he knows about the divisions because of the reports he received from "Chloe's household" (1:11). Now it appears that Paul is only partially informed. The clause can in fact also be translated as "and I believe a certain report."[115] This "report" (translating the Greek word *meros*) would be the one from Chloe's household.

There have to be differences among you to show which of you have God's approval (11:19). Those who wave "God's approval" are in fact those who have passed the "examination" or "test." Such a "test" reappears in 2 Corinthians 2:9: "The reason I wrote you was to see if you would stand the test and be obedient in everything." The "test," and thereby

"God's approval," is adherence to Paul's teaching as an apostle. The implication is that within the Corinthian church there are some who do not accept Paul's apostolic authority. It has been argued that the group separating themselves from the rest may in fact be the social elite.[116]

When you come together, it is not the Lord's Supper you eat, for as you eat, each of you goes ahead without waiting for anybody else (11:20–21). The Greek phrase implies that either some at the Lord's Supper start eating before anybody has had a chance, or that some have brought their own meals along and do not share them. The implication for the Lord's Supper is that while some members of the Christian community dine rather well — some even get drunk — others have nothing to eat. Clearly there are some who have brought food and others who have none to bring.

The "Lord's Supper" refers to the meal that commemorates the supper Jesus ate with his disciples in the Upper Room in Jerusalem before his arrest. Luke refers to the Christians at Troas (Troy) in northwestern Turkey coming together "to break bread" on the first day of the week (i.e., Sunday) (Acts 20:7). The fact that Jesus asked his disciples to have such a meal "in remembrance of me" (Luke 22:19) seems to have led to the creation of a regular gathering of Christian disciples that included a meal known as "the Lord's Supper," where the events and significance of Christ's death on the cross could be recalled.[117]

Don't you have homes to eat and drink in? Or do you despise the church of God and humiliate those who have nothing? What shall I say to you? Shall

I praise you for this? Certainly not! (11:22). Paul now asks some searching questions of the Corinthian Christians. Those bringing their own food (and wine) to the Lord's Supper and treating it like one of the banquets common in the city[118] have their own homes. The Greek word *oikia* ("house, home") can be translated "household"; it may reflect the fact that those abusing the Lord's Supper are part of the social elite of the colony who are accustomed to hosting lavish banquets in their villas. Paul is critical of those who have been despising those who "have nothing" (lit., the "have nots"). These "have nots" may represent the urban poor of the Roman colony who had not fallen under the patronage of the leading families of the city. Such patronage was a common feature of Roman society. If Paul was writing at a time of food shortage in the colony — "the present crisis" (7:26) — some in the church may have been facing starvation. In contrast, some of the wealthy may have had estates across Greece — some of the wealthy Corinthians came from Sparta, and another is recorded as having grazing rights on the Methana peninsula in the Saronic gulf — and would have been cushioned from crop failures or drought in a specific area.

For I received from the Lord what I also passed on to you (11:23). Paul now recounts the story of the Last Supper on the night of Jesus' arrest in Jerusalem. It affirms that at this early stage the Christian church had formulated an account of the events of that night as it gave meaning to the act of holding a Lord's Supper as a commemoration of that event. Paul's version of the events is similar to that which appears in Luke's account:

The Lord Jesus, on the night he was betrayed, took bread, and when he had given thanks, he broke it and said, "This is my body, which is for you; do this in remembrance of me." In the same way, after supper he took the cup, saying, "This cup is the new covenant in my blood; do this, whenever you drink it, in remembrance of me." (1 Cor. 11:23 – 25)

And he took bread, gave thanks and broke it, and gave it to them, saying, "This is my body given for you; do this in remembrance of me." In the same way, after the supper he took the cup, saying, "This cup is the new covenant in my blood, which is poured out for you." (Luke 22:19 – 20)

The covenant recalls the Exodus of the people of Israel from Egypt, marked by the Passover and the sprinkling of the blood of the lambs (Ex. 12), but it also looks back to the original covenant made with Abraham, who would be a blessing for all people (Gen. 12:2 – 3). The "new covenant" picks up on the prophecy of Jeremiah (Jer. 31:31), when the Lord says that he "will put my law in their minds and write it on their hearts" (31:33). This "new covenant" was important to the early church as seen by the discussion in the letter to the Hebrews (Heb. 8:8).

For I received from the Lord what I also passed on to you (11:23). Paul is alluding either to receiving this teaching as part of the revelation of Jesus Christ as he made his way to Damascus, or through subsequent teaching (by the apostles) at Jerusalem.

The Lord Jesus . . . took bread, when he had given thanks (11:23 – 24). The common Jewish form of blessing was,

"Blessed are you, O Lord our God, king of the universe, who brings forth bread from the earth."[119]

This is my body, which is for you; do this in remembrance of me (11:24). During the Passover meal, the person presiding at the meal would take up the unleavened bread — the "bread of affliction" (Deut. 16:3) — and make a statement about it, recalling the Exodus from Egypt. Although the words used at the Passover in the first century A.D. are not known, a later common formula was, "This is the bread of affliction which our fathers ate in the land of Egypt; let all who are hungry come and eat."[120] Jesus as president of this Passover meal thus transformed the words and applied them to himself. The act of remembrance at the Passover of the Exodus was now applied to the *exodus* of Jesus, "which he was about to bring to fulfillment at Jerusalem" (Luke 9:31).

This cup is the new covenant in my blood; do this, whenever you drink it, in remembrance of me (11:25). The cup referred to here is likely the "cup of blessing" that came in the Passover meal. The words used evoked the words of Moses: "This is the blood of the covenant that the Lord has made with you" (Ex. 24:8).

For whenever you eat this bread and drink this cup, you proclaim the Lord's death until he comes (11:26). Christ's death on the cross was a selfless act. Those members of the Corinthian church who abuse the Lord's Supper by bringing their own food and allow fellow Christians to starve in their very presence can be considered as selfish.

Whoever eats the bread or drinks the cup of the Lord in an unworthy manner will be guilty of sinning against the body and blood of the Lord (11:27). Paul places the focus of the actions of the Lord's Supper on our attitudes toward those who share the meal together. The wealthy elite, who place such an emphasis on worth and status, are being accused of having the unenviable attribute of being "unworthy."

A man ought to examine himself before he eats of the bread and drinks of the cup (11:28). The examination looks back to attitudes toward divisions within the church and toward those less well off in the Christian community.

Anyone who eats and drinks without recognizing the body of the Lord eats and drinks judgment on himself (11:29). The "judgment" is in fact the (guilty) verdict passed down by a judge at a trial. This emphasizes the seriousness with which believers should treat the celebration of the Lord's Supper.

That is why many among you are weak and sick, and a number of you have fallen asleep (11:30). Illness in the Chris-

CORINTH

The Propylaia in the Roman forum with the Acrocorinth in the background.

tian community is seen here as perhaps a consequence of wrongdoing, in the way that the Jews were judged during their exodus from Egypt. This may indicate the presence of a number of people familiar with the Old Testament in the Christian community at Corinth. "Fallen asleep" refers to the death of believing Christians (cf. 1 Thess. 4:14 – 15).

But if we judged ourselves, we would not come under judgment. When we are judged by the Lord, we are being disciplined so that we will not be condemned with the world (11:31 – 32). The gods of the pagan world had to be appeased in order to avert evil; the Roman writer Pausanias noted a temple in the agora at Athens dedicated to Apollo Alexikakos ("Averter of Evil"), the god perceived as bringing the late fifth-century B.C. plague in the city under control (Pausanias, *Descr.* 1.3.4). Piety toward the gods was a possible route to an untroubled life; Paul presents the Lord's judgement in contrast to that generally accepted in the ancient world.

When you come together to eat, wait for each other (11:33). The phrase "wait for each other" can also mean that the Corinthian Christians should share their food together, thus avoiding the situation of some who eat well and some who have no food at all.

If anyone is hungry, he should eat at home, so that when you meet together it may not result in judgment (11:34). Food shortages, not famines, were a major feature of the ancient world.[121] This was especially true of large urban populations, and a number of riots are known at Rome. Emperor Claudius is even said to have been pelted with hunks

of bread in the Forum at Rome.[122] Such a food shortage may lie behind the "present crisis" mentioned in 7:26.

When I come I will give further directions (11:34). Paul anticipates his own visit, which is briefly described in Acts 20:2 – 3. His stay in "Greece" (i.e., the province of Achaia as opposed to Macedonia) lasted three months, and Corinth is likely to have been one of the main centers.

Now About Spiritual Gifts (12:1 – 13)

Paul now turns from the Lord's Supper to the way that meetings of the Christian fellowship are conducted. One of the key issues is the use of the gift of "tongues," which is referred to throughout the next three chapters (12:10, 28, 30; 13:1, 8; 14:5, 6, 18, 22, 23, 39).

Now about spiritual gifts, brothers (12:1). "Spiritual gifts" can in fact also be translated "spiritual people." Such a view would develop Paul's arguments from earlier in the letter (2:15; 3:1), to which he will again turn (14:37). The emphasis he places on these issues is the same as he placed on the lessons from Israel's past (10:1).

You know that when you were pagans, somehow or other you were influenced and led astray to mute idols (12:2). "Pagans" identifies the members of the church at Corinth as coming from the Gentile, that is to say, the non-Jewish, world (though see comments on 1:8; "Jews at Corinth" at 1:23). The city of Corinth was dominated by a range of cults, from the temple of Aphrodite on the top of Akrocorinth overlooking the city to the archaic temple above the forum and various temples dedicated to the imperial cult. Within each sanctuary was a representation of its deity, often created by famous craftsmen. Yet these idols, with all their costly art, were unable to speak, just as is stated in the Old Testament times about idols (e.g., Hab. 2:18 – 19).

Paul presents a similar idea in Romans 1:23, where he notes that some have "exchanged the glory of the immortal God for images made to look like mortal man and birds and animals and reptiles." Such "mute idols" or deities were viewed as making utterances through oracles, the most famous of which was the oracle of Pythian Apollo at Delphi, which continued to be active in the Roman period (see comments on 14:28).

No one who is speaking by the Spirit of God says, "Jesus be cursed," and no one can say, "Jesus is Lord," except by the Holy Spirit (12:3). Curses were part of Roman cult practice, and adherents of a particular god might leave a short note in a temple or sanctuary, asking him or her to act on their behalf. Some of these have survived, most commonly on lead tablets. One from the sanctuary of Demeter at Corinth reads, "Hermes of the underworld [grant] heavy curses."[123] The curse that some in Corinth seem to have been using is "Jesus [is] a curse [*anathema*]." Members of the church may have been adopting the normal Corinthian practice of using the gods to forward their cause by casting a curse on those opposing them. Paul encourages the Corinthians to make the statement that "Jesus [is] Lord." Paul later calls down an *anathema* on those who do "not love the Lord" (16:22).

There are different kinds of gifts, but the same Spirit . . . the same Lord . . . the same God works all of them in all men (12:4 – 6). From the same "Spirit," "Lord," and "God" come the means for the church to carry out its function through gifts, service, and working. Pagans might consider what they could do for the deity concerned through offering sacrifices and making dedications in a sanctuary, but in Christian terms it is God, through the Holy Spirit and through Jesus Christ, who equips his church.

ACROCORINTH

(left) The Acrocorinth with some of the ruins of ancient Corinth in the foreground.

(right) Roman, Byzantine, and Turkish walls on the top of the Acrocorinth.

▼

To each one the manifestation of the Spirit is given for the common good (12:7). The Corinthian community was used to rich individuals in the colony providing benefactions of food, festivals, or buildings for the "common good" or "welfare of the community." Thus by the theater in Corinth the magistrate Erastus laid a piazza from his own money as a benefaction to the city (see "Paul Quotes an Athenian Playwright" at 15:33).[124] Such benefactions gave status to the individual, especially if the new building or facility carried a Latin inscription, sometimes with the letters fitted with bronze. Paul is reminding the Corinthian Christians that the Holy Spirit is given for the benefit or welfare of the community, not for personal glorification.

To one there is given through the Spirit the message of wisdom, to another . . . to another speaking in different kinds of tongues (12:8 – 10). Paul draws attention to the diversity of gifts. Notice how the gifts are not given to the same person but are spread throughout the Christian community ("another"). "Tongues" can also be translated as "languages."

All these are the work of one and the same Spirit, and he gives them to each one, just as he determines (12:11). The diversity of gifts is derived from one Spirit. Some may have thought that different gifts reflected a diversity of belief.

The body is a unit . . . and though all its parts are many, they form one body. So it is with Christ (12:12). The use of the body as an image of diversity but unity was well used in the ancient world. The Roman philosopher Seneca, the brother of the Corinthian governor Gallio, noted: "All that you behold, that which comprises both god and man, is one — we are the parts of one great body."[125]

For we were all baptized by one Spirit into one body — whether Jews or Greeks, slave or free — and we were all given the one Spirit to drink (12:13). Paul has moved from the Old Testament parallel drawn from Exodus where the people of God "drank the same spiritual drink" (10:4) to the New Testament experience of the Holy Spirit.

The Body of the Church (12:14 – 31)

This discussion of body parts recalls the way that in the ancient world small models of parts of the body were dedicated in sanctuaries of the healing god Asklepios.[126] One of the most famous sanctuaries of the god was at Epidauros in the Argolid, some forty kilometers (twenty-five miles) southeast of Corinth. Corinth itself had a sanctuary of Asklepios, called the Asklepieion.[127] It is perhaps not coincidental that Paul links the body parts to gifts of healing.

If the foot should say . . . if the ear should say (12:15 – 16). Paul uses a series of rhetorical questions to make his point.

God has arranged the parts in the body . . . just as he wanted them to be (12:18). As God created the body, so God has initiated the church with all its diversity.

The eye cannot say to the hand, "I don't need you!" And the head cannot say to the feet, "I don't need you!" (12:21). The idea of speaking eyes and listening hands and feet might amuse, but one suspects that some of the elite members may have been formulating these phrases when confronted with poorer members of the Christian community as they met together to celebrate the Lord's Supper.

On the contrary, those parts of the body that seem to be weaker are indispensable (12:22). No part of the body is redundant, in the sense that the diversity of the Christian community reinforces the fact that Christ died for all people.

The parts that we think are less honorable we treat with special honor. And the parts that are unpresentable are treated with special modesty (12:23 – 24). In the Roman colony of Corinth, the norm was to show individuals draped.[128] This was in marked contrast to the Greek honorific statues, especially of victorious athletes, erected in sanctuaries such as Olympia or Isthmia or in public spaces of their home towns, where an individual might be shown naked. An exception at Corinth was the pair of statues to Gaius and Lucius, the intended heirs of the emperor Augustus, who were shown naked. However, nakedness was also linked to divinity and hinted at the cult of the imperial family. One of the scandals in the Jewish world was the introduction of Greek games to Jerusalem, where male individuals were expected to compete naked.

There should be no division in the body, but . . . its parts should have equal concern for each other (12:25). Once again Paul refers to the division within the Christian community at Corinth (see 1:10; 3:3; 11:18).

If one part suffers, every part suffers with it; if one part is honored, every part rejoices with it (12:26). A similar lesson is found in the Jewish historian Josephus: "If one part suffers, all parts suffer together."[129]

You are the body of Christ, and each one of you is a part of it (12:27). Whereas it was only possible to take an active part in the life of a colony like Corinth if you were a male Roman citizen and had sufficient wealth to stand for public office, all could play a role in the life of the church. No one can say he or she does not have a part; passivity is not an option!

In the church God has appointed first of all apostles, second prophets, third teachers, then workers of miracles, also those having gifts of healing, those able to help others, those with gifts of administration, and those speaking in different kinds of tongues (12:28). Church order is ordained by God. The first three form a group consisting of specific individuals in the church, beginning with apostles (like Paul), who hold first place because of their special role as communicators of teaching. The appearance of "teachers" suggests that "teaching" (and with it learning and maturity) were integral to the life of the early church. The second group consists of those holding specific gifts, also mentioned in

PARTS OF THE BODY

People who claimed healing by Asclepius offered representations of their healed body part to the god. These are on display in the Corinth Museum.

▼

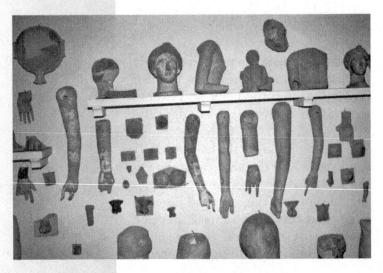

DO WE FEEL THAT WE HAVE SOME-
thing to offer the life of our local church?
Is there just scope for the confident, the
musicians, the public speakers? We need
to remember that God has equipped
each one of us for a role in the life of our
church community. Perhaps it is to give
that welcoming smile at the church door,
which helps to reassure the newcomer.
Or it may be to ensure that the building
is clean and fresh for a Sunday service.
All gifts enhance the body and life of the
church. What can I offer?

12:8 – 10. Paul mentions teachers and
leadership in Romans 12:6 – 8, written
from Corinth: "If your gift . . . is teaching, then teach; . . . if it is leadership,
then govern diligently."

**Eagerly desire the greater gifts. And now
I will show you the most excellent way
(12:31).** Paul does not want the Corinthians to rank their spiritual gifts but to
look at those that will build up their body
and bring a widespread understanding of
the good news that has been proclaimed
among them.

The Priority of Relationships over Achievements (13:1 – 13)

But have not love (13:1). The word Paul
uses for love here is *agapē*, a word used
in the LXX to translate God's love. The
Christian concept of love contrasts with
the two other Greek words: *erōs*, which
can be translated as a love of passion or
"desire," and *philia*, defined as "friendly
love" or "affection."[130] It is perhaps ironic
that Paul writes an essay on love to a city

whose patron deity was in fact Aphrodite, the goddess of love, whose temple
was situated on the Akrocorinth. Aphrodite (the Roman god Venus) was thought
to be the ancestor of Julius Caesar, and a
temple to her was a central feature of the
Julian Forum at Rome. Augustus, as the
adopted son of Julius, also promoted his
links with Aphrodite.

**I am only a resounding gong or a clang-
ing cymbal (13:1).** The "resounding
gong" is in fact literally "echoing bronze."
Corinth was famous in the ancient world
for a special bronze alloy (made of copper
and tin) that was even used on the doors
of the temple at Jerusalem.[131] The "cymbal" was an instrument that could be used
in pagan worship; reliefs of the cult of the
Anatolian deity Cybele show worshipers using cymbals.[132] The bronze gong
was the musical accompaniment to the
gods who are no gods (cf. 8:5), and the
tongues or languages of men and of angels
are equally meaningless in the worship of
the living God if love is absent.

**Can fathom all mysteries and all knowl-
edge (13:2).** "Mysteries" (*mystēria*)
and "knowledge" (*gnōsis*), echo Daniel
2:19 – 23, 28, especially in the LXX.

**If I have a faith that can move moun-
tains (13:2).** This may be a reference to
Jesus' own teaching: "I tell you the truth,
if anyone says to this mountain, 'Go,
throw yourself into the sea,' and does not
doubt in his heart but believes that what
he says will happen, it will be done for
him" (Mark 11:23; see also Matt. 17:20).

If I give all I possess to the poor (13:3).
This phrase may pick up on the teaching
of Jesus: "If you want to be perfect, go,
sell your possessions and give to the poor,

and you will have treasure in heaven. Then come, follow me" (Matt. 19:21; cf. Luke 12:33). The Greek word for "property" is the same in Jesus' teaching and Paul's writing.

Surrender my body to the flames (13:3). This may refer to the persecution of Jews by fire, such as Daniel's three friends in the fiery furnace (Dan. 3), or it may allude to Christian martyrdom. In the 60s, Nero persecuted Christians in Rome by igniting them as burning torches.[133]

Love . . . does not boast (13:4). This is the first instance of the verb *perpere-uomai* in Greek literature, though the adjective is found in Polybius relating to "wind-bags."[134]

[Love] is not proud (13:4). The pride addressed here was characteristic of parts of the Corinthian church (4:6, 18 – 19 ["arrogance"]; 5:2). Literally the Greek means "puffed up"; earlier Paul contrasted knowledge and love by using the two verbs "to puff up" and "to build up": "Knowledge puffs up, but love builds up" (8:1).

REFLECTIONS

IN THE ANDREW LLOYD-WEBBER musical *Aspects of Love* this line occurs: "Love, love changes everything." Paul sees love as providing the most excellent way for the life of the church. Yet so often our emphasis is on biblical teaching (important though that is!) or on social concern (vital though that is!); we forget to concentrate on encouraging each other to allow love to permeate our Christian ministry and service. Where can I start?

[Love] is not rude (13:5). Paul uses a verb that carries with it the concept of shame; the same verb in his section on virgins ("acting improperly" in 7:36). Such shaming was unacceptable in Roman elite society and should not be allowed to become acceptable in the Christian community.

[Love] is not self-seeking (13:5). Earlier Paul used this phrase when discussing the freedom of the Christian in the context of attending pagan festivals (10:24) — in particular of his own ministry: "For I am not seeking my own good but the good of many" (10:33).

[Love] keeps no record of wrongs (13:5). The record-keeping of wrongs uses a Greek phrase that resonates with the LXX of Zechariah 8:17, which is translated (from the Hebrew) as "do not plot evil against your neighbor."

Love never fails (13:8). The Greek sense implies "to fall" or "to fall short."

Prophecies . . . will cease . . . tongues . . . will be stilled . . . knowledge . . . will pass away (13:8). Paul returns to the group of issues he addressed earlier (12:8, 10; 13:2).

For we know in part and we prophesy in part, but when perfection comes, the imperfect disappears (13:9 – 10). The gifts familiar to the church will no longer be important when the end time comes. Gifts for edification will no longer be required.

When I was a child, I talked like a child, I thought like a child, I reasoned like a child. When I became a man, I put childish ways behind me (13:11). Paul is perhaps alluding to the classical form of education that placed an emphasis on clear thinking processes and public oratory. Children were expected to learn how to develop arguments and to present sophisticated cases.

Now we see but a poor reflection as in a mirror; then we shall see face to face (13:12). Mirrors in the Roman world were formed by a disc of polished metal, perhaps silver or bronze, placed on a handle. The viewing side might be convex and the reverse patterned.[135] The cult statue of Aphrodite on the Akrocorinth showed the deity, who in the Greek period had had a military role in protecting the city, admiring herself in the reflection of a shield.

Now these three remain: faith, hope and love. But the greatest of these is love (13:13). The combination of faith, hope, and love may have been a feature of the Christian gospel; see, for example, Paul's use of these three characteristics in Romans 5:1 – 5, written from Corinth. Love needs to be worked out in the life of believers, as Paul has tried to explain through this chapter.

Functioning in the Secular and Christian Ekklēsia (14:1 – 25)

Paul now develops how the concept of love will apply to the use of individual gifts in the life of the church community.

Eagerly desire spiritual gifts (14:1). This picks up on the argument from 12:31: "But eagerly desire the greater gifts."

Everyone who prophesies speaks to men for their strengthening, encouragement and comfort (14:3). Paul clearly sees

prophecy as a ministry focusing on the people of God, with the result that they are strengthened, encouraged, and comforted. Such a role was unusual in the religious framework of the ancient world. The word for "strengthening" (*oikodomē*) is drawn from architecture, where it means a "building." Thus the New Testament prophet is envisaged as the architect who lays the foundation and builds his structure in a systematic way. The buildings given to the Roman colony by rich benefactors were a credit to the city; in the same way the "strengthening" of the church at Corinth was to the glory of God.

What good will I be to you, unless I bring you some revelation or knowledge or prophecy or word of instruction? (14:6). Knowledge here translates the Greek *gnōsis*, a word often used in Greek philosophy.

In the case of lifeless things that make sounds, such as the flute or harp, how will anyone know what tune is being played unless there is a distinction in the notes? (14:7). Musical events were one aspect of some of the cultural events that came to be attached to athletic events in the Greek cities of the east. Thus proficiency in these musical forms was expected. The word translated "harp" (*kithara*) denotes a stringed instrument, often depicted in classical art as played by the god Apollo.

If the trumpet does not sound a clear call, who will get ready for battle? (14:8). This military allusion is derived from the way troops were controlled in battle. A trumpet would need to be heard over the din of fighting. Trumpets were also part of athletic festivals, often forming the first event so that the winner could have the privilege of "announcing" or trumpeting subsequent actions.

Unless you speak intelligible words with your tongue (14:9). The emphasis in the Greek is on clearly distinct words uttered by individuals.

▶

KITHARA

A marble representation of a *kithara* on a statue of Apollo.

There are all sorts of languages in the world, yet none of them is without meaning (14:10). Corinth itself was at the very least a bilingual city, with Latin as the official language, but Greek was in common usage (even the graffiti cut on pottery from the first century A.D. uses Greek). Paul's letter was itself written in Greek. With the ports of Lechaeum and Cenchrea, languages from all over the Mediterranean were likely heard in the city. Paul may have in mind the Jewish view that languages were created at the time of the tower of Babel (Gen. 11:9).

I am a foreigner to the speaker, and he is a foreigner to me (14:11). The Greek word for "foreigner" (*barbaros*) is suggestive. To the Corinthians foreigners speak languages that sound like "bar-bar."

Since you are eager to have spiritual gifts, try to excel in gifts that build up the church (14:12). The Corinthian Christians are seen as (lit.) "zealots" in their eagerness to acquire spiritual gifts. Paul instructs them to direct the energy of their seeking to the building up of the church, just as those in the wider Corinthian society sought to promote themselves through the building projects in the colony.

Anyone who speaks in a tongue should pray that he may interpret what he says (14:13). Paul's emphasis is not on seeking for a different type of gift to build up the church, but rather clarity on the use of gifts in the worshiping life of the Christian community.

If I pray in a tongue, my spirit prays, but my mind is unfruitful (14:14). For some the working of the Spirit in their lives may lead to praying "in a tongue."

So what shall I do? I will pray with my spirit, but I will also pray with my mind; I will sing with my spirit, but I will also sing with my mind (14:15). We could paraphrase this question as, "What are the implications for me?" Although an individual may "pray in a tongue," the use of the "mind" suggests that Paul encourages those with the gift of tongues to use an intelligible language like Greek or Latin in the meetings so that all can understand.

How can one who finds himself among those who do not understand say "Amen" to your thanksgiving? (14:16). The Hebrew word "Amen" — meaning "that which is sure and valid"[136] — was one used by those gathered in a Jewish synagogue to give endorsement to what was said; it is used here in the context of Christian worship.

You may be giving thanks well enough, but the other man is not edified (14:17). Thanksgiving is an appropriate part to Christian worship, but the encouragement of fellow believers is more significant.

I speak in tongues more than all of you (14:18). Presumably this side of Paul was largely unknown to the Christian community in Corinth. While he was with them, he had emphasized building up the Corinthian church rather than using this special gift of tongues. If the apostle Paul can show restraint, so can members of the congregation.

In the church I would rather speak five intelligible words to instruct others than ten thousand words in a tongue (14:19). "Ten thousand" (*myrias*) was the largest number that could be expressed in Greek, so its use here implies innumerable — in today's language, "a trillion, trillion."

Stop thinking like children. In regard to evil be infants, but in your thinking be adults (14:20). Children (*paidia*) suggests young people in training. Paul is

◀

HARBOR AT LECHAEUM

The western port of Corinth.

suggesting that the believers in Corinth be more mature and developed in their thinking.

"Through men of strange tongues and through the lips of foreigners I will speak to this people, but even then they will not listen to me" (14:21). The quotation is an abridged form of Isaiah 28:11 – 12: "Very well then, with foreign lips and strange tongues God will speak to this people, to whom he said, 'This is the resting place, let the weary rest'; and, 'This is the place of repose' — but they would not listen." Paul may also have had in his mind a verse from Deuteronomy 28:49: "The LORD will bring a nation against you from far away, from the ends of the earth, like an eagle swooping down, a nation whose language you will not understand."

Tongues, then, are a sign, not for believers but for unbelievers; prophecy, however, is for believers, not for unbelievers (14:22). Paul's mature reading of the Jewish law and the Old Testament in general leads him to conclusions about the gifts of tongues and prophecy.

So if the whole church comes together and everyone speaks in tongues, and . . . some unbelievers come in, will they not say that you are out of your mind? (14:23). The verb translated "are out of your mind" (*mainomai*) is one that was used to describe the frenzy of mystery religions (see comments on 4:1), such as that of the Greek god of wine, Dionysos. Paul wants the church to be different from these mystery cults.

If an unbeliever . . . comes in while everybody is prophesying, he will be convinced by all that he is a sinner. . . . So he will fall down and worship God (14:24 – 25). The purpose of Christian worship is to include and to draw people to God. This is in marked contrast to mystery cults, such as that surrounding the worship of Demeter and Persephone at Eleusis in Attica, where the uninitiated were excluded from the events and those who participated were forbidden from speaking of what went on. This is well illustrated by the usually informative Pausanias, who was clearly an initiate: "My dream forbade the description of the things within the wall of the sanctuary [of Demeter at Eleusis], and the uninitiated are of course not permitted to learn that which they are prevented from seeing."[137]

Ordering Corporate Worship (14:26 – 40)

The Corinthian Christians needed to think about the implications of meeting together in worship on a regular basis. How can they strengthen the body of the church?

When you come together, everyone has a hymn, or a word of instruction, a revelation, a tongue or an interpretation. All of these must be done for the strengthening of the church (14:26). Paul returns to the architectural image of building the

▶

DIONYSUS

A mosaic of the god at the Corinth museum.

church. The buildings of the Roman colony could be placed on terraces or on podia, supported by columns, and roofed in marble. These elements created the building but would look odd standing without the others (as indeed a reconstructed column can look lost in the midst of an archaeological site). So each element of the worship needs to complement the other.

If anyone speaks in a tongue, two — or at the most three — should speak, one at a time, and someone must interpret (14:27). Some of the cults of antiquity allowed ecstatic utterances, which were incomprehensible to those attending the rites. If these utterances in the Christian worship are from God, they must be treated in an orderly way so that they can be understood.

If there is no interpreter, the speaker should keep quiet in the church and speak to himself and God (14:28). The oracles of antiquity were well-known for giving ambiguous messages, which could be misinterpreted by those who had sought advice from the gods (in particular, from Apollo at Delphi). Christians must ensure that any message from God is interpreted by somebody in the community so that the community can benefit.

You can all prophesy in turn so that everyone may be instructed and encouraged (14:31). Two key elements of Christian worship, instruction and encouragement, were largely absent from the worship of the pagan deities in the colony. This type of worship was new.

The spirits of prophets are subject to the control of prophets (14:32). Christian worship is subject to control and order by designated leaders.

For God is not a God of disorder but of peace (14:33). Disorder was one of the negative characteristics of the church at Corinth, which Paul addresses in 2 Corinthians 12:20.

Women should remain silent in the churches. They are not allowed to speak (14:34). This verse needs to be balanced with what Paul has said earlier, where he expects women to be praying and prophesying in the fellowship (11:6).

Women . . . must be in submission . . . as the Law says (14:34). Paul is clearly alluding to the Garden of Eden, where God tells Eve, "Your desire will be for your husband, and he will rule over you" (Gen. 3:16b). The Greek word *gynē* can be translated as "woman" or "wife." Thus, Paul is most likely addressing the proper function of wives in the Christian assembly, where proper respect for their husbands needed to be shown. It should be noted that the specific context for these comments comes from Paul's addressing the issue of public prophecy for the edification of the church.

REFLECTIONS

AN UNBELIEVER MIGHT BE EXPECTED to walk into the worshiping Christian community at Corinth and exclaim, "God is really among you" (14:25). What would Paul's advice be to us if we are expecting unbelievers to be touched in our church services? What things do we need to change? Which elements of the service must be more welcoming?

If they want to inquire about something, they should ask their own husbands at home; for it is disgraceful for a woman to speak in the church (14:35). If a husband were to make a prophecy, it would perhaps be inappropriate for the wife to question the prophecy in a public gathering; according to social expectations, the wife should ask questions at home. This makes sense if Paul does not want wives to prophesy when their husbands are present.

Did the word of God originate with you? Or are you the only people it has reached? (14:36). The balance for the Corinthian Christians is that they are one of a number of churches that now stretch across the cities of the eastern Roman empire. They may live in one of the most important cities of the province, but they need to learn humility.

What I am writing to you is the Lord's command (14:37). Paul the apostle (1:1) is writing these words to the Corinthians at God's command. He brings his apostolic authority to bear on this issue of order in the service of worship.

Be eager to prophesy, and do not forbid speaking in tongues (14:39). Public teaching needed to be encouraged ("be eager" is lit. "be zealous").

Everything should be done in a fitting and orderly way (14:40). The word "fitting" is a word with elite overtones and can be translated as seemly or honorable. Meetings of the *ekklēsia* needed to be conducted in a dignified fashion.

Evidence and Belief (15:1 – 11)

When Paul addressed the Areopagus at Athens, the pagan hearers sneered at the ridiculous suggestion of a bodily resurrection (Acts 17:32). But those Greeks and Romans trained in Greek, and especially Platonic philosophy, would understand about the immortality of the soul.

I want to remind you of the gospel I preached to you, which you received and on which you have taken your stand (15:1). Paul's starting point is to find the common belief that all Christians shared, especially in the light of the pagan world around them. Note also his similar message to Christians in Galatia: "I want you to know, brothers, that the gospel I preached is not something that man made up" (Gal. 1:11). The gospel of Jesus is not like the fantastic stories connected with the pagan gods. The Roman travel writer Pausanias, for example, later recounted the story of the miraculous preservation of the baby Kypselos — the future tyrant of Corinth — when his mother placed him in a chest at birth; a chest that supposedly could still be seen at Olympia in Pausanias's day.[138] The gospel of Jesus is based on fact, not fiction.

By this gospel you are saved, if you hold firmly to the word I preached to you. Otherwise, you have believed in vain (15:2). The Corinthian Christians had understood the vanity, the emptiness, of the pagan deities that filled their city and required acts of piety. Paul brings them back to the essentials of the Christian gospel through which they received salvation.

For what I received I passed on to you as of first importance (15:3). Paul's argument is parallel to an earlier one in the letter concerning the Lord's Supper: "For I received from the Lord what I also passed on to you" (11:23). This type of language probably reflects the Jewish form of instruction. What follows appears to be an early Christian creed that contains the "basic" Christian doctrines (15:3 – 5).

Christ died for our sins according to the Scriptures (15:3). The Scriptures Paul is alluding to are the books of the Old Testament; in other words, these books point to the need for the Messiah to die for our sins. Paul perhaps had in mind the picture of the Suffering Servant of Isaiah, who "was pierced for our transgressions, he was crushed for our iniquities" (Isa. 53:5). This language resonates with the words of Jesus at the Last Supper: "This is my body, which is for you" (1 Cor. 11:24). Paul emphasizes the fact that Jesus died for our sins as the Christ, the anointed Messiah.

He was buried . . . he was raised on the third day according to the Scriptures (15:4). The doctrine of the resurrection of Jesus Christ was central to the early Christians. Peter's speech in Jerusalem at Pentecost emphasized how the resurrection had been predicted by David in Psalm 16:10b (quoted in Acts 2:27). Similar to the present passage is 1 Thessalonians 4:14, probably written on Paul's first visit to Corinth: "We believe that Jesus died and rose again." "The third day" may be derived from Jesus' own teaching to his disciples about his resurrection in connection with the temple at Jerusalem: "Destroy this temple, and I will raise it again in three days" (John 2:19; see also Matt. 26:61; Mark 15:58). The "third day" may also pick up on Hosea 6:2: "After two days he will revive us; on the third day he will restore us, that we may live in his presence." Burial presupposes death and excludes misunderstanding about Jesus' physical death on the cross.

Matthew recalled the misleading story derived from the guards that Jesus' disciples "came during the night and stole him away while we were asleep," an account that "has been widely circulated among the Jews to this day" (Matt. 28:13, 15).

He appeared to Peter, and then to the Twelve (15:5). As burial presupposed death, so resurrection was confirmed by appearances to trustworthy witnesses. These were no vague appearances that formed part of a folklore or mythology about Jesus; at the time of writing, Peter and the other disciples could be pressed about what they had seen and witnessed. The appearance to Peter was a cry of the early disciples: "It is true! The Lord has risen and has appeared to Simon" (Luke 24:34). Paul's language here resembles Jesus' words when he appeared to the disciples: "This is what is written: 'The Christ will suffer and rise from the dead on the third day'" (24:46).

He appeared to more than five hundred of the brothers at the same time (15:6). This appearance is not recorded in any of the Gospel accounts of the post-resurrection appearances of the risen Jesus. There

REFLECTIONS

IF WE THINK BACK TO OUR FIRST SCHOOL, WE CAN probably recall (hopefully with affection!) our first teachers. They were the ones who set us off on the path of learning, on the way to adulthood. Paul takes the Corinthians back to the point when they first believed. It is so easy for people to forget why they first trusted Jesus Christ as their Lord and their Savior. Perhaps they want to look "mature" in the eyes of their friends. Yet our Christian life started when we realized what it meant for Jesus Christ to die on the cross for our sins: "By this gospel you are saved" (15:2).

were others available in the first century besides those recorded in the Gospels.

Then he appeared to James, then to all the apostles (15:7). Paul had met James, "the Lord's brother," at Jerusalem at the start of his ministry (Gal. 1:19). The "apostles" may be another way of referring to the "Twelve" (15:5), though it might include others who had seen their risen Lord.

Last of all he appeared to me also, as to one abnormally born (15:8). Paul has already referred to meeting Jesus on the road to Damascus (9:1; see Acts 9). "Abnormally born" translates a word that can denote either a miscarriage or an abortion. Perhaps some of the Christians at Corinth dismissed Paul's position as an apostle because he had not been one of the Twelve or questioned his becoming an apostle in an abnormal route after having been a chief persecutor of Christians.

For I am the least of the apostles and do not even deserve to be called an apostle (15:9). Paul had come to the Corinthians in "weakness and fear, and much trembling" (2:3), hardly what was considered to have been the stature for an apostle.

But by the grace of God I am what I am, and his grace to me was not without effect. No, I worked harder than all of them — yet not I, but the grace of God that was with me (15:10). Paul's earlier hard work had gone into pursuing the early followers of Jesus: "as for zeal, persecuting the church" (Phil. 3:6). Yet Paul was transformed by the grace of God.

Whether . . . I or they, this is what we preach, and this is what you believed (15:11). Paul's preaching on the resur-

rection was in keeping with other teachers of the church, presumably including Apollos and Cephas (cf. 1:12); the Corinthians are the ones who have moved away from that teaching.

Immortality (15:12 – 34)

Paul now develops a series of six "ifs" relating to the beliefs of some of the Corinthian Christians. This rebuffs the view held by some that there was no resurrection of the dead.

How can some of you say that there is no resurrection of the dead? (15:12). The resurrection was central to the preaching and teaching of the church from the earliest days. For example, Peter on Pentecost proclaimed that "God raised [Jesus of Nazareth] from the dead, freeing him from the agony of death, because it was impossible for death to keep its hold on him" (Acts 2:24). Both Jewish and Roman authorities had had ample opportunity to reject this teaching by presenting an alternative to the Christian message of the resurrection, but none had presented a convincing case to the contrary.

If there is no resurrection of the dead, then not even Christ has been raised (15:13). A commonly held view in the ancient world at the time, and in the province of Achaia in particular (see Acts 17:32a), was a disbelief in the possibility of dead people rising back to life. Paul uses this mistaken view to show that it was incompatible with Christian belief.

If Christ has not been raised, our preaching is useless and so is your faith (15:14). However eloquent the teaching, however vibrant the outworking of faith, the core of Christian belief and life is the resurrection of Jesus Christ.

More than that, we are then found to be false witnesses about God (15:15). The integrity of Paul and the apostles is now at stake. Paul sees the presentation of the resurrection in legal terms with witnesses bearing testimony.

If the dead are not raised, then Christ has not been raised either (15:16). The logical extension of the argument presented by some of the Christians at Corinth is that Christ in whom they had placed their trust had not been raised. The resurrected Christ and the general resurrection of the dead are linked.

If Christ has not been raised, your faith is futile; you are still in your sins (15:17). Without the resurrection, there is no forgiveness of sins.

Then those also who have fallen asleep in Christ are lost (15:18). Those who have abandoned the worship of pagan deities are now addressed. The (flawed) logic is that the gods that the Corinthian Christians have rejected in response to the good news of Jesus Christ would save them. Paul is reducing the argument to the absurd so that the Corinthians can see afresh the power of the Christian gospel.

If only for this life we have hope in Christ, we are to be pitied more than all men (15:19). The logical conclusion of the argument held by some of the Corinthian Christians means that the Christian faith has no place or relevance against the multiplicity of religious expression found in the colony; Paul wants the Christian community to see the error in their argument.

But Christ has indeed been raised from the dead, the firstfruits of those who have fallen asleep (15:20). The Christian view of death is in marked contrast to that held in the ancient world. The Christians perceived death as no more than sleep, whereas pagan society saw it was important to protect the dead in the next life by sometimes placing apotropaic images (i.e., images to ward off evil) above the grave. The "firstfruits" was a concept familiar to both Jews and Gentiles; they were often offered to the gods in the sanctuaries of the Greek world.

Since death came through a man, the resurrection of the dead comes also through a man (15:21). The allusion is to the fruit of "the tree of the knowledge of good and evil" in the Garden of Eden; "for when you eat of it you will surely die" (Gen. 2:17).

As in Adam all die, so in Christ all will be made alive (15:22). This alludes to the curse on Adam: "For dust you are and to dust you will return" (Gen. 3:19).

Then the end will come, when he hands over the kingdom to God the Father after he has destroyed all dominion, authority and power (15:24). Such words must have been disturbing when Paul wrote them to the Christians at Corinth. The familiar authority structures they are accustomed to — the emperor, the Roman senate, the provincial governor, the Roman army, the civic magistrates — will all disappear. These structures, which brought peace to the Mediterranean world in their lifetime, will be no more.

He must reign until he has put all his enemies under his feet (15:25). This view picks up on Psalm 110:1: "Sit at my right hand until I make your enemies a footstool for your feet." Residents of Corinth know how enemies of Rome are brought before the emperor in chains.

The last enemy to be destroyed is death (15:26). Roman emperors might look for new territory to acquire on the fringes of the existing empire. For the Christian the ultimate battle and victory is over death. The resurrection serves the same function as the triumphal arches at the city of Rome, which marked the final defeat of a foe.

For he "has put everything under his feet" (15:27). The quotation is from the Psalms (8:6) which affirms, "O LORD, our Lord, how majestic is your name in all the earth!" It is also a psalm that speaks of "the son of man," a title of the Messiah or Christ (see Heb. 5 – 9).

Then the Son himself will be made subject to him who put everything under him, so that God may be all in all (15:28). The Corinthian Christians are brought back to the Psalms: "You have made him ruler over the works of your hands; you

put everything under his feet" (Ps. 8:6). God's authority will be in force.

Now if there is no resurrection, what will those do who are baptized for the dead? (15:29). It seems as if members of the church at Corinth were conducting baptism services for those — probably members of their families — who had already died. The precise details are unclear and there is no obvious precedent from the pagan world.

As for us, why do we endanger ourselves every hour? (15:30). Travel in the ancient world was a dangerous thing, and Paul himself experienced shipwreck in his travels (cf. 2 Cor. 11:23 – 28; Acts 27). Yet it was dangerous to speak out against the beliefs and views of the ancient world, and Paul had faced arrest and a beating at Philippi and a trial at Athens before the Areopagus. Ultimately, he was to lose his life in speaking of his risen Lord.

I die every day — I mean that, brothers — just as surely as I glory over you in Christ Jesus our Lord (15:31). Paul imposes a firm discipline on him-

---

▶ Paul Quotes an Athenian Playwright

Paul's pithy observation, "Bad company corrupts good character" (15:33) is actually a quotation from a work of Menander, where the immediate context is prostitution.[A-39] Menander was an Athenian comic playwright, whose first play was produced in 321 B.C. He is known to have written at least a hundred plays. Thus, Paul is using a quotation that would be familiar to a Greek-speaking audience. Plays were an important part in the cultural life of the Roman colony at

Corinth. The theater lay to the northwest of the forum. It had been an integral part of the original Greek city and had been restored in the early part of the Roman settlement.[A-40] It has been estimated to hold some 15,000 people. One of the benefactions to enhance the theater was the donation by an *aedile* of the city, Erastus, who paved a piazza at the east entrance; his benefaction was recorded by an inscription cut into the slabs and filled with bronze letters.[A-41]

self rather than adopting an attitude, common in the ancient world, that self-indulgence was important.[139]

If I fought wild beasts in Ephesus for merely human reasons (15:32). Hunts were often a feature of games established in the Greek east on a Roman model. They were an unusual feature in the first century A.D., but an inscription from the Roman colony of Pisidian Antioch records the gift of such an event by Caius Albucius Firmus in his will.[140] Animal games are likely to have formed part of the civic life at Ephesus. Paul is writing this letter to the Corinthian church from Ephesus, and this imagery reflects the opposition that he is facing.

Let us eat and drink, for tomorrow we die (15:32). Paul quotes here from Isaiah 22:13. The belief in eating and drinking (i.e., self-indulgence) was part of Epicurean belief.

Come back to your senses as you ought, and stop sinning; for there are some who are ignorant of God (15:34). Paul may be suggesting here that those who deny

the bodily resurrection feel they can adopt the ethical standards of the pagans in the Roman colony.[141] But Christians will stand before the judgment throne of God, where they will be accountable for their actions. If they look ahead to this day, they will change their lifestyle.

Resurrection (15:35 – 58)

The emphasis in the chapter moves from the "dead" to the word "body." The Corinthian Christians are presented with questions and answers about death.

With what kind of body will they come? (15:35). The roads leading to the gates of cities in the ancient world were lined with cemeteries, often with images of the deceased. It was not uncommon for families to visit graves and leave offerings, and it must have troubled Corinthians who knew from firsthand experience that bodies decomposed. How could these bones be turned into bodies?

How foolish! (15:36). This translates the Greek word *aphrōn* ("foolish man"; lit., "without sense"). It was often used to

81

1 Corinthians

bottom left

CORINTH AND EPHESUS

Ephesus was just across the Aegean Sea from Corinth.

bottom right

THE MEDITERRANEAN WORLD

Paul would travel from Ephesus to Macedonia and on to Corinth as he gathered the collection to take to Jerusalem.

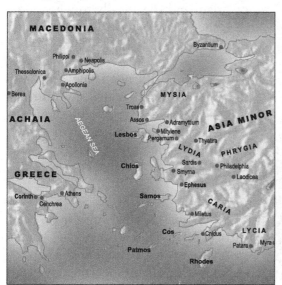

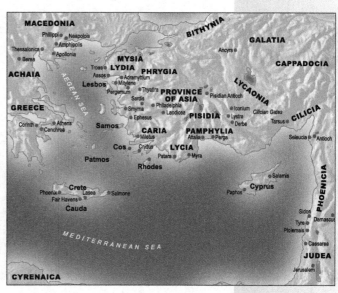

describe inanimate statues. But the word would also resonate with Greek-speaking Jews, who would recognize it as the one used in the LXX for "fool," especially in Proverbs.

When you sow, you do not plant the body that will be, but just a seed (15:37). Paul uses the agricultural imagery to explain the transformation. The Corinthia was an area suitable for growing large amounts of grain to support the large population of the colony.

But God gives it a body as he has determined, and to each kind of seed he gives its own body (15:38). God the Creator lies behind this resurrection, just as he lies behind the natural world.

All flesh is not the same: Men . . . animals . . . birds . . . fish (15:39). These four different types also appear in the created order in Genesis but in the reverse of how they appear in here: "Let the water teem with living creatures, and let birds fly above the earth" (Gen. 1:20); "let the land produce living creatures . . . livestock . . . and wild animals" (1:24); and

"let us make man in our image" (1:26). Such a view is derived from Paul's view of the Old Testament.

Heavenly bodies and . . . earthly bodies (15:40). Science was well developed in the ancient world. "Heavenly bodies" may relate the sun and other bodies.

The sun has one kind of splendor, the moon another and the stars another; and star differs from star in splendor (15:41). The Greek scientist Empedokles from Akragas in southern Sicily had written about the cosmos in the fifth century B.C. He attempted to explain night and day. Such views formed part of Roman education.[142]

The body that is sown is perishable, it is raised imperishable (15:42). The analogy of the transformed seed is used for the transformation of the body that decays in the grave but is transformed through the resurrection.

"The first man Adam became a living being"; the last Adam, a life-giving spirit (15:45). The allusion is to the creation of Adam and specifically to when God "breathed into his nostrils the breath of life" (Gen. 2:7).

The spiritual did not come first, but the natural, and after that the spiritual (15:46). The emphasis is on the sequence of the natural then the spiritual, rather than some philosophical idea that there is a spiritual state in conjunction with the physical.

The first man was of the dust of the earth (15:47). The earlier city of Corinth made use of the surrounding clay beds to produce fine figure-decorated pottery,

GREEK COUNTRYSIDE NEAR THE ACROCORINTH
▼

which is found in some quantity around the shores of the Mediterranean. Such an allusion to Adam made of clay may have had special significance to the Corinthian Christians.

As was the earthly man, so are those who are of the earth; and as is the man from heaven, so also are those who are of heaven (15:48). Ancestry was important in a city like Corinth, where status was valued; important ancestors meant high status. The ancestry that matters for the Corinthian Christians is that they are now descendants of Jesus Christ by faith.

Just as we have borne the likeness of the earthly man, so shall we bear the likeness of the man from heaven (15:49). If the Corinthians looked at the portraits of the Roman emperors, in particular those of Augustus and his heirs (Gaius and Lucius), they would see a family likeness in the treatment of the hair. No doubt Roman sculptors intended this so that people could be convinced by the legitimacy of rule. For Christians, they need to show the characteristics of Jesus Christ in their community to emphasize the validity of their professed faith.

I tell you a mystery (15:51). Unlike the mystery cults, such as Demeter and Kore at Eleusis in Attica at the other end of the isthmus of Corinth, where mysteries were kept quiet, the Christian gospel, the good news of the resurrection, must be told.

For the trumpet will sound, the dead will be raised imperishable, and we will be changed (15:52). Paul may have in mind Zechariah 9:14, a prophecy about the Lord's appearing: "The Sovereign LORD will sound the trumpet."

For the perishable must clothe itself with the imperishable, and the mortal with immortality (15:53). In the Greek east there was a philosophical belief about the immorality of the soul. For the Christian the resurrection of Christ allows the individual to be "clothed" with eternal life.

Then the saying ... will come true: "Death has been swallowed up in victory" (15:54). This appears to be an adapted form of Isaiah 25:8: "He will swallow up death forever," though the word "victory" does not appear.

"Where, O death, is your victory? Where, O death, is your sting?" (15:55). The context for this quotation is a modified version of Hosea 13:14: "I will ransom them from the power of the grave; I will redeem them from death."

The sting of death is sin (15:56). The result of Adam and Eve's disobeying God and eating the fruit from the tree of the knowledge of good and evil was death (Gen. 2:17).

God ... gives us the victory through our Lord Jesus Christ (15:57). Corinthian Christians would be familiar with the way the Roman emperor celebrated famous victories, especially when new provinces were acquired. Such secular celebrations — though with religious overtones, such as sacrifices — pale into insignificance with Christian rejoicing. The emperor Augustus passed through Corinth after the fall of Alexandria in 30 B.C. on his way to celebrate a triple triumph at Rome in August, 29 B.C.

Always give yourselves fully to the work of the Lord, because you know that your labor in the Lord is not in vain (15:58).

Paul develops this theme more completely in 2 Corinthians 5:8: "For we must all appear before the judgement seat of Christ, that each one may receive what is due to him for the things done while in the body, whether good or bad."

The Issue About the Collection for God's People (16:1 – 4)

In this closing section Paul focuses on Jerusalem, but he places his message within the Roman provincial structure; notice the stress on Galatia, Macedonia, and Asia.

Now about the collection for God's people: Do what I told the Galatian churches to do (16:1). Paul is picking up on the fifth of the issues put in the letter to him by the Corinthian church (see comments on 7:1). Under the Roman empire Jewish communities sent money to Jerusalem. Philo in his *Embassy to Gaius* records a letter of the proconsul Gaius Norbanus Flaccus to the magistrates at Ephesus: "Caesar has written to me saying that it is a special ancestral custom of the Jews, wherever they live, to meet and contribute money which they send to Jerusalem. He does not wish them to be prevented from doing this."[143] The difference with Corinth is that this is a Christian community with strong, though not exclusively, Gentile features. Paul is encouraging the Corinthian believers to identify with their Jewish-Christian fellow believers in Judea; the destination of Jerusalem for the collection is made clear (16:3).

The collection was a feature of Paul's third missionary journey. Starting from Antioch in Syria, Paul presumably took the Roman road up from Cilicia, which took him to such places as the key Roman colony of Pisidian Antioch in the Roman province of Galatia (Acts 18:23). If Paul wrote 1 Corinthians from Ephesus during the events described in Acts 19, he would have just passed through Galatia before entering Asia.

On the first day of every week, each one of you should set aside a sum of money in keeping with his income, saving it up (16:2). The calendar implies that the early Christians are following a Jewish pattern; the Roman calendar was dominated by feast days. The first day of the week was the day that Christ was found to have risen from the tomb — in other words, the day after the Jewish Sabbath. Note, for example, how the Christians in Troas met together "on the first day of the week . . . to break bread" (Acts 20:7). Presumably the Corinthian church follows a similar pattern of meeting on the day after the Jewish Sabbath, on what we now term Sunday. Paul is here advocating a planned and regular scheme of putting aside a sum of money (or perhaps even items in kind) for the benefit of the Christian community in Jerusalem. It is important to remember that the Corinthian church includes slaves and women, who probably do not have access to cash in their own right.

I will give letters of introduction to the men you approve (16:3). Few letters have survived from the ancient world because of their fragile nature. Some of the best examples written on papyri have been obtained from Egypt, though excavations at Vindolanda just south of Hadrian's Wall in northern England have revealed first century A.D. correspondence from the archive of the fort.[144] The gift Paul is collecting is to be accompanied to Jerusalem by members chosen by the Corinthian church; they will be responsible for the safety

PAUL ASKS THE CORINTHIAN CHURCH to respond to the needs in Jerusalem on a weekly basis. What Christian causes can we support in a regular and planned way? How can we develop our links with the bodies we support? How can we use our resources to help those of our Christian brothers and sisters in need?

of the gift, but they will also be able to carry personal messages between the two churches. It was common, even during the empire, for cities to send embassies to the emperor; this may be the model Paul has in mind for the delegation. The use of such messengers ensures Paul's integrity so that there will be no question whether he is acquiring the money for his own benefit.[145]

Your gift to Jerusalem (16:3). Paul describes this gift for Jerusalem and its purpose in Romans 15:25 – 28, where he notes that the provinces of Macedonia and Achaia (which includes Corinth) "were pleased to make a contribution for the poor among the saints in Jerusalem."

If it seems advisable for me to go also, they will accompany me (16:4). In 2 Corinthians 1:16 Paul records his intention for the Corinthian church to "send me on my way to Judea" with the collection.

Paul's Plans (16:5 – 9)

After I go through Macedonia, I will come to you — for I will be going through Macedonia (16:5). The journey that Paul is planning to make here is described in Acts 20:1 – 3. He deliberately chose the land route rather than sailing from Asia to Achaia. Macedonia was a Roman province in what is now northern Greece. It was a key province as its western frontier was defined by the Adriatic, and through the port of Dyrrachium gave access to Brundisium (modern Brindisi) and Italy. Macedonia also gave access to the Aegean on its south side. The whole province was traversed by the strategic Egnatian way, the Roman road that gave access to the eastern provinces. There is a possibility that Paul may have reached Corinth by sailing down the west coast of mainland Greece from Dyrrachium. In Romans 15:19, written from Corinth, perhaps during this intended stay, Paul notes that "from Jerusalem all the way around to Illyricum, I have fully proclaimed the gospel of Christ." Illyricum is the area to the north of Dyrrachium, and such a visit would make sense of the journey across Macedonia. Such a route would allow him to visit other important cities in the Peloponnese, such as the colony at Patras.

Perhaps I will stay with you awhile, or even spend the winter, so that you can help me on my journey (16:6). In Acts 20:3 Paul is recorded as staying three months in Greece (which presumably means the Roman province of Achaia). Most likely most of this time was spent in Corinth. Paul would avoid the dangerous winter season for sailing in the Mediterranean. The verb translated "help me on my journey" implies that the Corinthian Christians will provide Paul with the means to complete his journey, which may include traveling companions.[146]

I do not want to see you now and make only a passing visit; I hope to spend some time with you, if the Lord permits

(16:7). If Paul sails directly from Ephesus to Corinth, he will have to press on for Macedonia and will only be able to stay a short time in Corinth. If he goes by the land route, he will have opportunity for a longer stay at Corinth by wintering there.

I will stay on at Ephesus until Pentecost (16:8). This gives us the information that Paul is writing from the province of Asia in early spring, perhaps of A.D. 56. Pentecost was the Jewish festival, fifty days after Passover. (In the Christian calendar, Pentecost is calculated as fifty days from Easter and thus always falls on a Sunday.) Pentecost is also the time that the apostles were filled with the Holy Spirit (Acts 2:1), the day usually recognized as the birthday of the church. By Pentecost of the following year Paul planned on being in Jerusalem (Acts 20:16).

A great door for effective work has opened to me, and there are many who oppose me (16:9). The door is an image Paul uses elsewhere (2 Cor. 2:12; Col. 4:3). The effective work in Ephesus and the magnitude of the opposition is described in the account in Acts 19:23 – 41, where Demetrius the silversmith initiates a riot. Interestingly the account is placed between the dispatch of Timothy and Erastus for Macedonia and Paul's own departure (19:22; 20:1).

Timothy's Planned Visit (16:10 – 11)

If Timothy comes (16:10). Timothy's mission has been noted earlier in 4:17.

Send him on his way in peace so that he may return to me. I am expecting him along with the brothers (16:11). Peace may be an allusion to the Jewish *shalom*.

The "brothers" may include Erastus, who was sent with Timothy from Ephesus (Acts 19:22).

Apollos and the Appointment of Leaders in the Church (16:12 – 18)

Now about our brother Apollos: I strongly urged him to go to you with the brothers . . . he will go when he has the opportunity (16:12). This is the sixth issue raised by the Corinthian church. Apollos is clearly with Paul in Ephesus, and the Corinthian church has presumably requested his return. Paul is urging him to return to Corinth with the delegation from the church (presumably those mentioned in 16:17). Given the earlier tensions and perceived rivalries at Corinth (1:12), Paul's urging of Apollos demonstrates his confidence in his "brother" and coworker in the gospel of Jesus Christ.

The household of Stephanas were the first converts in Achaia, and they have devoted themselves to the service of the saints (16:15). "The household of Stephanas" (mentioned also in 1:16) were the "first converts" of Paul's ministry in the province of Achaia. Achaia was the name of the Roman province covering southern Greece and the Peloponnese; it was created in Augustus's reorganization of the provinces in 27 B.C. In A.D. 15 it was reunited with Macedonia (northern Greece), but in 44 it became a province again in its own right. The word translated "first converts" (*aparchē*) is in fact the word used in the Greco-Roman world for the "firstfruits" that were sacrificed to one of the gods or offered as a dedication in a sanctuary. For example, the famed king Kroisos made special offerings in the sanctuary of Apollo at Delphi, which were the *aparchē* of the wealth he inherited.[147] It may be that the household's ministry was a model for other Christians in the province. The "service [*diakonia*] for the saints" may allude to the use of the household for acts of worship, including hosting the Lord's Supper.

To submit to such as these and to everyone who joins in the work (16:16). This refers not to submission as recognized in the Roman colony, that is to say, by class or status, but rather to the Christian role in the ministry of the church.

I was glad when Stephanas, Fortunatus and Achaicus arrived, because they have supplied what was lacking from you (16:17). The three men are presumably the delegation with whom Apollos should return to Corinth (16:12). Fortunatus is a Latin name meaning "lucky." As a personal name it was often used of slaves, though it would be retained if freedom had been obtained. The name Achaicus is derived from the name of the province of Achaia, and it too may suggest a servile origin for this person. Both men may be connected to the household of Stephanas.

Greetings and Salutations (16:19 – 21)

The churches in the province of Asia send you greetings (16:19). The province of Asia consists of what today is western Turkey and included the city of Ephesus. It had become a province on the death of king Attalos III of Pergamon in 133 B.C. The churches of Asia may have included the communities at Miletus, Colosse, Smyrna, Sardis, Pergamum, and Troas.

Aquila and Priscilla greet you warmly in the Lord (16:19). Aquila was a native of Pontus; the province of Bithynia and Pontus was in northern Turkey on the shores of the Black Sea. He and his wife, Priscilla, had fled from Rome during the time of Claudius (Acts 18:2), perhaps c. A.D. 49, and had settled in Corinth. Shortly after Paul wrote this letter to Corinth, Aquila and Priscilla seem to have returned to Rome (Rom. 16:3). It should be noted that Paul uses the shorter form, Prisca, though some translations give the full form (Rom. 16:3; 1 Cor. 16:19; 2 Tim. 4:19), whereas in Acts 18:2, 18, 26 she is referred to as Priscilla. In most New Testament references, Priscilla's name occurs first.

The church that meets at their house (16:19). At this time the church usually met in a private house; it was not until Constantine that specific buildings tended to be built for holding services of worship. Plans of houses of this period suggest that the numbers who could come together at one time were quite limited.

Greet one another with a holy kiss (16:20). The kiss may have had its origins in Jewish culture, perhaps an allusion to the fact that members of the church needed to be reconciled with each other, just as Jacob was reconciled to Esau with a kiss (Gen. 33:4). Paul uses the same request in 2 Corinthians 13:12 as well as in Romans 16:16 and 1 Thessalonians 5:26.

I, Paul, write this greeting in my own hand (16:21). Although the beginning of the letter suggests that Paul and Sosthenes have jointly written the letter, this final valediction is in Paul's own hand. In

Romans 16:22 Paul's scribe Tertius adds his greetings at the end of the letter. Paul makes a similar point in Galatians 6:11 and Colossians 4:18. Some scholars have posited attempts to pass off other letters under Paul's name; thus, by adding his own postscript in his own handwriting, Paul gives this letter authenticity.

Cursings and Blessings (16:22 – 24)

Paul draws the letter to a close with the unusual feature of a curse followed by a blessing.

If anyone does not love the Lord (16:22). Paul uses the verb *phileō* ("to love") instead of *agapaō* (also "to love"), which he has used elsewhere in the letter (see comments on 13:1). One of the few other places where *phileō* occurs in Paul's letters is Titus 3:15: "Greet those who love us in the faith." The contrast between the two Greek words also recalls the conversation between the resurrected Jesus and Simon Peter by the Sea of Galilee (John 21:15 – 17).

A curse be on him (16:22). For the use of set curses see comments on 12:3.

Come, O Lord! (16:22). The phrase "Come, O Lord" translates the Greek form of the Aramaic phrase *Maran atha*.

The grace of the Lord Jesus be with you (16:23). These words are similar to those used at the end of other Pauline letters (e.g., Rom. 16:20; 2 Cor. 13:14; Phil. 4:23; Philem. 25). A more standard letter, concluding with a simple "Farewell," was sent by the Council of Jerusalem to the Christian believers in Antioch, Syria, and Cilicia (Acts 15:23 – 29).

My love to all of you in Christ Jesus (16:24). In a letter that includes Paul's essay on love (13:1 – 13), it is fitting that love (*agapē*) is the closing word.

ANNOTATED BIBLIOGRAPHY

Commentaries

Bruce, F. F. *1 and 2 Corinthians.* NCBC. London: Oliphants, 1971.

A commentary from a scholar sensitive to the classical texts of the Greek and Roman world.

Fee, Gordon D. *The First Epistle to the Corinthians.* NICNT. Grand Rapids: Eerdmans, 1987.

A comprehensive commentary on the letter complete with footnotes and discussion of the Greek text. His magisterial commentary remains one of the most useful works on this letter.

Green, Michael. *To Corinth With Love: The Vital Relevance Today of Paul's Advice to the Corinthian Church.* London: Hodder and Stoughton, 1982.

A popular discussion of the Corinthian correspondence, which draws on relevant background material.

Prior, David. *The Message of 1 Corinthians.* BST. Leicester: Inter-Varsity, 1985.

An exegetical commentary on the letter rooted in parish ministry in South Africa and Oxford, England.

Thiselton, Anthony C. *The First Epistle to the Corinthians.* NIGTC. Grand Rapids: Eerdmans, 2000.

The most comprehensive commentary available on 1 Corinthians.

Winter, Bruce W. "1 Corinthians." *New Bible Commentary: 21st Century Edition.* Eds. D. A. Carson, R. T. France, J. A. Motyer, and G. J. Wenham. Downers Grove, Ill.: InterVarsity, 1994.

Although this commentary lacks critical apparatus, there are some important windows on the relevant cultural background.

Special Studies

Clarke, Andrew D. *Secular and Christian Leadership in Corinth: A Socio-Historical and Exegetical Study of 1 Corinthians 1 – 6.* Leiden: E. J. Brill, 1993.

A sensitive and methodological discussion of Paul's letter against the background of the Roman colony.

Engels, Donald. *Roman Corinth: An Alternative Model for the Classical City.* Chicago: University of Chicago Press, 1990.

The only short discussion of the Roman colony, the study draws on the results of the excavations by the American School of Classical Studies at Athens.

Gill, David W. J., and Conrad Gempf, eds. BAFCS 2. *The Book of Acts in its Graeco-Roman Setting.* Grand Rapids: Eerdmans, 1994.

A series of essays that provides key discussions of the Roman provincial structure and religious background during the first century A.D.

Winter, Bruce W. *Philo and Paul Among the Sophists.* SNTSMS. Cambridge: Cambridge University Press, 1997.

This study includes important comments on the Corinthian material against the background of public oratory in the eastern Mediterranean during the first century A.D.

CHAPTER NOTES

Main Text Notes

1. For the most recent study of the colony, see D. Engels, *Roman Corinth: An Alternative Model for the Classical City* (Chicago: Univ. of Chicago Press, 1990). However, this work should be read alongside the searching reviews: A. J. S. Spawforth, *Classical Review* 42.1 (1992): 119 – 20; R. Saller, *Classical Philology* 86.4 (1991): 351 – 57. For a survey of the archaeology, see M. E. H. Walbank, "The Foundation and Planning of Early Roman Corinth," *Journal of Roman Archaeology* 10 (1997): 95 – 130. Results of the excavations appear in the *Excavations at Corinth* monograph series (see note 21).

2. Strabo, *Geography* 8.6.23 (trans. Loeb).

3. Cicero, *Fam.* 4.5.4.

4. Cicero, *Tusc.* 3.22.53.

5. L. Foxhall, D. Gill, and H. Forbes, "The Inscriptions of Methana," in C. B. Mee & H. Forbes (eds.), *A Rough and Rocky Place: The Landscape and Settlement History of the Methana Peninsula, Greece* (Liverpool: Liverpool Univ. Press, 1997), 273 – 74, no. 15; *IG* 4.853; *SEG* 37 (1987): 321. The dating of the inscription to the Actian era (commemorating Augustus's victory at Actium) is discussed by A. J. Gossage, "The Date of *IG* V (2) 516 (*SIG*³ 800)," *Annual of the British School at Athens* 49 (1954): 53, 56.

6. Favorinus's speech has been preserved by Dio Chrysostom (*Orations* 37.34).

7. Strabo, *Geography* 8.6.20.

8. Ibid., 8.6.20.

9. J. H. Kent, *The Inscriptions, 1926 – 1950* (Corinth: Results of Excavations Conducted by the American School of Classical Studies at Athens 8.3; Princeton, N.J.: American School of Classical Studies at Athens, 1966), pl. 8, no. 56.

10. Pausanias, *Descr.* 2.2.8.

11. M. E. H. Walbank, "Evidence for the Imperial Cult in Julio-Claudian Corinth," in Alastair Small (ed.), *Subject and Ruler: The Cult of the Ruling Power in Classical Antiquity. Papers Presented at a Conference Held in the University of Alberta on April 13 – 15, 1994, To Celebrate the 65th Anniversary of Duncan Fishwick* (Journal of Roman Archaeology Supplement 17; Ann Arbor, Mich.: Journal of Roman Archaeology, 1996), 201 – 12.

12. Suetonius, *Nero* 19.

13. Engels, *Roman Corinth*, 102 – 6. The sanctuary of Isis at Cenchreae has been excavated.

14. I. F. Saunders, *Roman Crete* (Warminster, U.K.: Aris & Phillips, 1992). Other cults of Isis are known around the Saronic Gulf.

15. In addition to the works cited in the bibliography, I am also indebted to Rev. David Holloway, who first opened the letter to me in a series of sermons at Jesmond Parish Church, Newcastle upon Tyne, UK.

16. The inscription is published by Kent, *Inscriptions*, no. 165.

17. Favorinus is generally considered to have been the author of *Oration* 37 attributed to Dio Chrysostom. This sophist is discussed in B. W. Winter, "Favorinus," in B. W. Winter and A. D. Clarke (eds.), *The Book of Acts in its Ancient Literary Setting* (BAFCS 1; Grand Rapids: Eerdmans, 1993), 296 – 305.

18. For the initial publication, see D. I. Pallas, S. Charitonidis, and J. Venencie, "Inscriptions lyciennes trouvées à Solômos près de Corinthe," *Bulletin de correspondance hellénique* 83 (1959): 496 – 508. For discussion, see L. Robert, "VII. Décret de la confédération lycienne à Corinthe," *Revue des études anciennes* 62 (1960): 324 – 42.

19. The inscription is conveniently illustrated in M. Lang, *Cure and Cult in Ancient Corinth: A Guide to the Asklepieion* (American Excavations in Old Corinth, Corinth Notes 1; Princeton, N.J.: American School of Classical Studies at Athens, 1977), 3, fig. 2.

20. This position is argued Winter, *Philo and Paul*, 186 – 94.

21. V. Ehrenberg and A. H. M. Jones, *Documents Illustrating the Reigns of Augustus and Tiberius* (2d ed., Oxford: Clarendon, 1955), no. 98a (Greek text); translated in N. Lewis and M. Reinhold, *Roman Civilization; I: The Republic and the Augustan Age* (New York: Columbia Univ. Press, 1990), 627.

22. Herodotus, *Histories* 4.77.1.

23. See, e.g., Pliny, *Letters* 10.96.

24. On the rhetorical construction, see Winter, *Philo and Paul*, 193.

25. For a full discussion, see Winter, *Philo and Paul*, 149 – 51.

26. Favorinus, *Orations* 37.1.

27. Dio Chrysostom, *Orations* 47.22. See Winter, *Philo and Paul*, 151.

28. These words feature in Aristotle's discussion of rhetoric (*Rhetoric* 2.2.7).

29. Ibid., 519. See Winter, *Philo and Paul*, 157 – 58.

30. Winter, *Philo and Paul*, 155, observes that "rhetoric is the art of persuasion."

31. Cicero, *Academica* 2.8.

32. Quintilian, 5.10.7. For a discussion of the oratorical setting of this word, see Winter, *Philo and Paul*, 154.

33. Dio Chrysostom, *Orations* 33.3. For further discussion on this, see Winter, *Philo and Paul*, 154–55.

34. Epictetus, 2.16.39.

35. Philo, *Agriculture* 9.

36. For an overview (with bibliography), see D. W.J. Gill, "Mines and Quarries," in G. Speake (ed.), *Encyclopedia of Greece and the Hellenic Tradition* (Chicago: Fitzroy Dearborn) 2.1059–61.

37. A convenient range of such building accounts in translation can be found in J. J. Pollitt, *The Art of Ancient Greece: Sources and Documents* (Cambridge: Cambridge Univ. Press, 1990), 190–93.

38. Dio Cassius, 57.10.1–3 (trans. Pollitt).

39. Pagan gods might appear to have several expressions in one city. They were differentiated by different epithets. Thus at Corinth there were several cult centers of the Greek god Apollo, one being Clarian Apollo (Pausanias, *Descr.* 2.1.8), named after the god's oracle center, not at Delphi, but at Claros in Anatolia.

40. For the description of this event, see the account by the Roman historian Livy, 29.14.10–14.

41. Philo, *Worse* 33. See further: Winter, *Philo and Paul*, 107.

42. The title was used from the late second century A.D., though the concept of the emperor having dominion across the empire and beyond is found in the *Res Gestae* ("Achievements") of the emperor Augustus, inscribed on columns outside his mausoleum at Rome. This inscription even notes contact with India.

43. For a summary of the archaeological issues, see M. B. Walbank, "The Foundation and Planning of Early Roman Corinth," *Journal of Roman Archaeology* 10 (1997): 115, fig. 9 (aerial photograph), 124–25, fig. 10.

44. Dio Chrysostom, *Orations* 31.121. Ancient cemeteries do in fact adjoin the amphitheater.

45. A. J. S. Spawforth, "Corinth, Argos, and the Imperial Cult: Pseudo-Julian, *Letters* 198," *Hesperia* 63 (1994): 211–32; with corrigendum, *Hesperia* 63 (1994): 522.

46. For a detailed consideration of this section of the letter see A. D. Clarke, *Secular and Christian Leadership in Corinth: A Socio-Historical and Exegetical Study of 1 Corinthians 1–6* (Leiden: Brill, 1993), ch. 6.

47. Philo, *Sacrifices* 32.

48. B. W. Winter, *Seek the Welfare of the City: Christians as Benefactors and Citizens* (Grand Rapids: Eerdmans, 1994), 105–21, provides a full discussion of this section of 1 Corinthians.

49. E.g., Dio Cassius, 52.7.5.

50. *SEG* 9.8, decree I (see also note 73, below).

51. Winter, *Seek the Welfare of the City*, 110. For the Augustus decree, see *SEG* 9.8, decree I; K. Chisholm and J. Ferguson (eds.), *Rome: The Augustan Age. A Source Book* (Oxford: Oxford Univ. Press/The Open Univ. Press, 1981), 128 no. C20: "There exist certain conspiracies to oppress the Greeks in trials on capital charges. . . . I myself have ascertained that some innocent people have in this way been oppressed and carried off to the supreme penalty."

52. E.g., Dio Chrysostom, *Orations* 8.9; Favorinus, *Orations* 37.16–17; Apuleius, *Metam.* 9.33.

53. Winter, *Seek the Welfare of the City*, 107 n. 7 provides a useful list of what was covered by criminal law.

54. Ibid., 107.

55. Winter, *Seek the Welfare of the City*, 116.

56. B. W. Winter, "Homosexual Terminology in 1 Corinthians 6:9: The Roman Context and the Greek Loan-word," in A. N. S. Lane (ed.), *Interpreting the Bible: Historical and Theological Studies in Honor of David F. Wright* (Leicester, U.K.: Apollos, 1997), 275–90 (ch. 14).

57. This law was passed by the tribune Scantinius c. 146 B.C. See S. Lilja, *Homosexuality in Republican and Augustan Rome* (Helsinki: Societas Scientiarum Fennica, 1982), 112–21.

58. For a selection of recipes from Apicius's cookbook, see J. Shelton, *As the Romans Did: A Sourcebook in Roman Social History* (New York: Oxford Univ. Press, 1988), 86–88, nos. 93, 94, 95, 96, and 97.

59. Winter, "Homosexual Terminology," 287; idem, "Gluttony and Immorality at Elitist Banquets: The Background to 1 Corinthians 6:12–20," *Jian Dao* 7 (1997): 55–67.

60. *CIL* 1.2.1221. A translation may be found in Shelton, *As the Romans Did*, 37, no. 47, 48, no. 57.

61. Winter, "1 Corinthians," 1171.

62. Soranus, *Gynecology* 1.60.4 (trans. Shelton). On contraception in the ancient world, see Shelton, *As the Romans Did*, 26, nos. 27–28.

63. Fee, *Corinthians*, 287–88.

64. Pliny the Younger, *Letters* 8.5.1–2.

65. *BGU* 1103 (A. S. Hunt and C. C. Edgar, *Select Papyri* [Loeb Classical Library; Cambridge,

Mass.: Harvard Univ. Press, 1956], 6). A translation may be found in Shelton, *As the Romans Did*, 50, no. 61; Lewis and Reinhold, *Roman Civilization*, 2:344.

66. *BGU* 1103 (*Select Papyri* 6). A translation may be found in Shelton, *As the Romans Did*, 50, no. 61.

67. For this section see Winter, *Seek the Welfare of the City*, 145–64.

68. See ibid., 160–61.

69. Celsus, *De Medicina* 7.25. Epispasm is discussed by Winter, *Seek the Welfare of the City*, 147–52.

70. See Winter, *Seek the Welfare of the City*, 155–57.

71. Part of the oath taken by the new slave was to the *genius* of the master (see Winter, *Seek the Welfare of the City*, 159).

72. S. Treggiari, *Roman Marriage: Iusti Coniuges from the Time of Cicero to the Time of Ulpian* (Oxford: Clarendon, 1991), 153–55.

73. B. Winter, " 'The Seasons' of This Life and Eschatology in 1 Corinthians 7:29–31," in K. E. Brower and M. W. Elliott (eds.), *"The Reader Must Understand": Eschatology in Bible and Theology* (Leicester, U.K.: Apollos, 1997), 331.

74. B. Winter, "Secular and Christian Responses to Corinthian Famines," *TynBul* 40.1 (1989): 86–106.

75. Peter Garnsey, *Famine and Food Supply in the Graeco-Roman World: Responses to Risk and Crisis* (Cambridge: Cambridge Univ. Press, 1988).

76. Tacitus, *Annals* 3.25.

77. *IG* IV. 853. See now L. Foxhall, D. Gill, and H. Forbes, "The Inscriptions of Methana," in C. Mee and H. Forbes, *A Rough and Rocky Place*, 273–74, no. 15.

78. See Winter, "Seasons of This Life," 323–34.

79. This follows the meaning in LSJ, ἀσχημονέω.

80. B. Winter, "Puberty or Passion? The Referent of ὑπέρακμος in 1 Corinthians 7:36," *TynBul* 49.1 (1998): 78–79.

81. Treggiari, *Roman Marriage*, 159.

82. See LSJ, ὑπέρακμος. For a discussion of this term, see Winter, "The Seasons of This Life," 333; idem, *After Paul Left Corinth: The Impact of Secular Ethics and Social Change* (Grand Rapids: Eerdmans, 2000), ch. 8. Winter suggests that the term "refers . . . to the growing sense of physical closeness and expectation of sexual intimacy naturally felt as the actual marriage grew closer."

83. Soranus, *Gynecology* 1.22. For the English translation see O. Temkin, *Soranus' Gynaecology* (Baltimore: Johns Hopkins Univ. Press, 1956). The passage is discussed by Winter, "Puberty or Passion?" 75.

84. Hesychius. For a discussion: Winter, "Puberty or Passion?" 76.

85. *Acta Divi Augusti* (Rome, 1945), 187. A convenient translation is found in Shelton, *As the Romans Did*, 29, no. 33.

86. Kent, *Inscriptions*, no. 153. For a convenient summary of his career, see Clarke, *Secular and Christian Leadership*, 143, no. 59.

87. Plutarch, *Quaest. Conviv.* 723A: "During the Isthmian games, the second time Sospis was president, I avoided the other banquets, at which he entertained a great many foreign visitors at one, and several times entertained all the citizens" (trans. Winter).

88. See Winter, *Seek the Welfare of the City*, 132, for the grammatical structure of this section.

89. Spawforth, "Corinth, Argos, and the Imperial Cult," 522. For its application to the Christian church at Corinth, see Winter, *Seek the Welfare of the City*, 126.

90. See Winter, *Seek the Welfare of the City*, 174.

91. Strabo, *Geography* 8.3.30.

92. See on this section Winter, *Seek the Welfare of the City*, 165–77.

93. Some of the best known dining rooms come from the sanctuary of Demeter and Kore on the lower slopes of Akrocorinth. However, archaeological evidence suggests that the rooms were not in use at this time. Equally impressive dining rooms come from the extramural sanctuary at Perachora at the northwestern end of the Isthmus. See R. A. Tomlinson, "Perachora: The Remains Outside the Two Sanctuaries," *Annual of the British School at Athens* 64 (1969): 155–258.

94. M. S. Kos, "A Latin Epitaph of a Roman Legionary from Corinth," *Journal of Roman Studies* 68 (1978): 22–25.

95. Another soldier known at Corinth is the *optio* Aurelius Nestor of the 4th Flavian legion; see A. B. West, *Latin Inscriptions, 1896–1926* (Corinth: Results of Excavations Conducted by the American School of Classical Studies at Athens 8.2; Princeton, N.J.: American School of Classical Studies at Athens, 1966), no. 10. See also R. K. Sherk, "Roman Imperial Troops in Macedonia and Achaia," *American Journal of Philology* 78 (1957): 52–62.

96. See the discussion in H. Bowden and D. Gill, "Roman Methana," in Mee and Forbes, *A Rough and Rocky Place*, 80–81, and Foxhall, Gill, and Forbes, "Inscriptions of Methana," ibid., 273–74, no. 15. The inscription is *IG* 4:853; *SEG* 37 (1987): 321. For an earlier discussion, see Gossage, "The Date of *IG* V (2) 516 (*SIG*[3] 800)," 53, 56.

97. Translation from Fee, *Corinthians*, 417.

98. E. R. Gebhard, "The Isthmian Games and the Sanctuary of Poseidon in the Early Empire,"

in T. E. Gregory (ed.), *The Corinthia in the Roman Period* (Journal of Roman Archaeology Supplement 8; Ann Arbor, Mich.: Journal of Roman Archaeology, 1994), 78 – 94. See also D. J. Geagen, "Notes on the Agonistic Institutions of Roman Corinth," *Greek, Roman and Byzantine Studies* 9 (1968): 69 – 80; W. R. Biers and D. J. Geagen, "A New List of Victors in the Caesarea at Isthmia," *Hesperia* 39.2 (1970): 79 – 93.

99. Philostratus the Elder, *Apollonius of Tyana* 5.43. Translation from J. Swaddling, *The Ancient Olympic Games* (London: British Museum Press, 1980), 35.

100. The pine wreath is shown on dedications from the sanctuary of Poseidon.

101. Dio Chrysostom, *Orations* 77/78.4.

102. Philo *Spec. Laws* 1.221.

103. See Winter, *Seek the Welfare of the City*, 168.

104. The term can be translated as "welfare"; see Winter, *Seek the Welfare of the City*, 174 – 75.

105. D. W. J. Gill, "The Meat-Market at Corinth (1 Corinthians 10:25)," *TynBul* 43.2 (1992): 389 – 93.

106. F. F. Bruce, *1 and 2 Corinthians* (NCB; Grand Rapids: Eerdmans, 1971), 99, cites *t. Ber.* 4.1 as endorsement of the use of Ps. 24 in the context of eating.

107. As suggested by Fee, *Corinthians*, 485.

108. See the two articles by W. Grudem: "Does κεφαλή ("Head") Mean 'Source' or 'Authority Over' in Greek Literature? A Survey of 2,336 Examples," *TrinJ* NS 6 (1985): 38 – 59; "Catherine Kroeger, IVP, Liddell-Scott, and Others on the Meaning of κεφαλή ('Head'): An Evaluation of New Evidence, Real and Alleged," *JETS* (forthcoming, 2001). However, see Fee, *Corinthians*, 502 – 3.

109. In a discussion of an aureus (gold coin) of Claudius (A.D. 51) showing the portrait of Agrippina the Younger: D. E. E. Kleiner and S. B. Matheson, *I Claudia: Women in Ancient Rome* (New Haven, Conn.: Yale Univ. Press, 1996), 65 no. 18.

110. For a funerary relief of the Augustan period showing Vesinia Iucunda flanked by two male freedmen, see Kleiner and Matheson, *I Claudia*, 199 – 200, no. 150; for a free-standing portrait statue possibly from the late republic or early Augustan period, see ibid., 197, no. 145.

111. Tacitus, *Germania* 19 (though the context regards Germanic tribes).

112. See R. MacMullen, "Women in Public in the Roman Empire," *Historia* 29 (1980): 208 – 18.

113. See Kleiner and Matheson, *I Claudia*.

114. A. H. M. Jones, *The Greek City from Alexander to Justinian* (Oxford: Clarendon, 1940), 176 – 78.

115. Winter, "1 Corinthians," 1179.

116. R. A. Campbell, "Does Paul Acquiesce in Divisions at the Lord's Supper?" *NovT* 33 (1991): 61 – 70. He suggests the translation: "For there actually has to be discrimination in your meetings, so that (if you please!) the elite may stand out from the rest."

117. For a helpful discussion, see I. H. Marshall, "Lord's Supper," *DPL*, 569 – 75.

118. The discovery of animal bones near the theater has suggested that food was being served for communal banquets, and that these may have been eaten in the theater itself.

119. Adapted from Bruce, *1 and 2 Corinthians*, 111.

120. Quoted by ibid., 113.

121. Garnsey, *Famine and Food Supply*.

122. Suetonius, *Claudius* 18 – 19.

123. Cited by Winter, "1 Corinthians," 1180.

124. See D. W. J. Gill, "Erastus the Aedile," *TynBul* 40 (1989): 293 – 301. The piazza was laid at the private expense of Erastus.

125. Seneca, *Epistles* 95.52.

126. See, e.g., A. E. Hill, "The Temple of Asclepius: An Alternative Source for Paul's Body Theology," *JBL* 99 (1980): 437 – 39; G. G. Garnier, "The Temple of Asklepius at Corinth and Paul's Theology," *Buried History* 18 (1982): 52 – 58. Fee, *Corinthians*, 602 n. 11, dismisses the Asklepieion as a possible source for this illustration.

127. C. Roebuck, *The Asklepieion and Lerna* (Corinth 14; Princeton, N.J.: American School of Classical Studies at Athens, 1951).

128. Winter, "Puberty or Passion?" 81.

129. Josephus, *J.W.* 4.7.2 §406.

130. The translation suggested by LSJ, φιλία.

131. D. M. Jacobson and M. P. Weitzman, "What Was Corinthian Bronze?" *American Journal of Archaeology* 96.2 (1992): 237 – 47.

132. See the marble container in the Fitzwilliam Museum, University of Cambridge, England, which is decorated with scenes of Cybele: L. Budde and R. Nicholls, *Catalogue of Greek and Roman Sculpture in the Fitzwilliam Museum, Cambridge* (Cambridge: Cambridge Univ. Press, 1964), 77 – 78, pl. 41, no. 125.

133. Fee, *Corinthians*, 634, suggests that there may have been a manuscript change that substituted the Greek word for "burning" instead of "boasting." The suggestion is in part based on similarities with the text of Clement of Rome in his letter to Corinth. For Nero's persecution of the Christians at Rome, see Tacitus, *Annals* 15.44.

134. See LSJ, περπερεύομαι.

135. For a silver mirror from the first century A.D., said to be from Egypt, see D. von Bothmer,

A Greek and Roman Treasury (New York: Metropolitan Museum of Art, 1984), 69, no. 129. The mirror was inscribed with the owner's name, "Iris."

136. See Fee, *Corinthians*, 672, esp. n. 37.

137. Pausanias, *Descr.* 1.38.7 (trans. Loeb).

138. For a description of the chest of Kypselos, which included many of the Greek myths, see ibid., 5.17.5 – 5.19.10.

139. A suggestion I owe to Bruce Winter ("1 Corinthians," 1184).

140. Further games were held at the extra-mural sanctuary of Mên Askaenos (a local deity often associated with the Roman deity Luna, the personification of the Moon) outside Pisidian Antioch at Kara Kuyu. For details of the games (though placing them much later than is necessary) see J. G. C. Anderson, "Festivals of Mên Askaênos in the Roman Colony at Antioch of Pisidia," *Journal of Roman Studies* 3 (1913): 267 – 300.

141. Winter, "1 Corinthians," 1184 – 85.

142. See, e.g., Quintilian's comments on the importance of Empedokles (*Inst. Or.* 1.4.1 – 5).

143. Philo, *Embassy* 40.314 (trans. Lewis and Reinhold, *Roman Civilization*, 2:314).

144. For a convenient overview, see P. G. Bahn, "Vindolanda: Letters from Rome," in P. G. Bahn (ed.), *Wonderful Things: Uncovering the World's Great Archaeological Treasures* (London: Weidenfeld & Nicolson, 1999), 182 – 85.

145. On this question of integrity, see Winter, *Philo and Paul*, 219.

146. See also, e.g., Rom. 15:24; 2 Cor. 1:16.

147. Herodotus, *Histories* 1.92.2.

Sidebar and Chart Notes

A-1. Strabo, *Geography* 8.5.21.

A-2. Ibid., 8.6.19.

A-3. A helpful discussion on Pausanias as a source is to be found in C. Habicht, *Pausanias' Guide to Ancient Greece* (Sather Classical Lectures 50; Berkeley: Univ. of California Press, 1985, 1998).

A-4. E.g., Pausanias, *Descr.* 5.13.7.

A-5. Ibid., 5.1.2.

A-6. Ibid., 2.2.6.

A-7. The excavations are published in the monograph series *Corinth: Results of Excavations Conducted by the American School of Classical Studies at Athens* (Cambridge, Mass., and Princeton, N.J.: American School of Classical Studies at Athens). Preliminary reports also appear in *Hesperia*, the journal of the American School. S. Dyson, *Ancient Marbles to American Shores: Classical Archaeology in the United States* (Philadelphia: Univ. of Pennsylania Press, 1998), 85, has observed that "Corinth's association with St. Paul's mission and the development of early Christianity provided another major incentive for raising financial support for what the School hoped would be long-term excavations."

A-8. The results have been published in the monograph series *Kenchreai: Eastern Port of Corinth* (Leiden: Brill, 1976 – 1981). For a color photograph of the harbor, see R. V. Schoder, *Ancient Greece from the Air* (London: Thames & Hudson, 1974), 111 – 13. For a history of the excavations, see L. S. Meritt, *History of the American School of Classical Studies at Athens 1939 – 1980* (Princeton, N.J.: American School of Classical Studies at Athens, 1984), 171.

A-9. E.g., D. I. Pallas, "Anaskaphai ereunai en Lechaio," *Praktika* (1965): 137 – 66; idem, "Anaskaphai Lechaiou," *Archaiologikon Deltion* 17.2 (1961 – 62): 69 – 78 (both in Greek).

A-10. The excavations appear in the monograph series *Isthmia Excavations* (Princeton, N.J.: American School of Classical Studies at Athens). Preliminary reports appeared in *Hesperia*. For a history of the excavation, see Meritt, *History of the American School*, 169 – 71.

A-11. Philo, *Embassy* 281.

A-12. The text of Favorinus's speech can be found in the Loeb edition of Dio Chrysostom (*Discourses* 4.37). For a discussion of Favorinus, see Winter, *Philo and Paul*, 132 – 37.

A-13. Favorinus, *Orations* 37.8 (trans. Loeb).

A-14. Philostratos, *Lives of the Sophists* 490 – 91.

A-15. Kent, *Inscriptions*, no. 322.

A-16. A. B. West, *Latin Inscriptions, 1896 – 1926*, nos. 2, 3, 98 – 101, 132; Kent, *Inscriptions*, no. 155.

A-17. A helpful table showing building activity at Corinth may be found in Engels, *Roman Corinth*, 169, table 11.

A-18. *SEG* 9.8, decree IV. The translation comes from Chisholm and Ferguson, *Rome: The Augustan Age*, 129 no. C20. For such juries operating within the context of a province see A. H. M. Jones, *The Greek City from Alexander to Justinian* (Oxford: Clarendon, 1940), 122.

A-19. Martial, 7.82.

A-20. See Winter, *Seek the Welfare of the City*, 149.

A-21. Agonistic festivals were established at Jerusalem in the Hellenistic period when Judea fell under the control of the Seleucids. This required the establishment of institutions such as a gymnasium, where the young men were trained as well as met for educational purposes. As yet we have no archaeological evidence for a gymnasium or for that matter a stadium at Jerusalem. For a convenient summary of the later evidence, see D. Sperber, *The City in Roman Palestine* (New York/Oxford: Oxford Univ. Press, 1998), 85 – 89.

A-22. West, *Corinth*, 8.2, nos. 86 – 90; Kent, *Inscriptions*, nos. 158 – 63.

A-23. E.g., Tacitus, *Annals* 12.43.1 (A.D. 51). See also Garnsey, *Famine and Food Supply*, 261.

A-24. Biers and Geagan, "A New List of Victors," 79 – 93 (dating to the early second century A.D.). For other lists, see Meritt, *History of the American School*, 8.1, nos. 14 (A.D. 3), 19 (Claudian), and 18 (early empire).

A-25. Plutarch, *Moralia* 675d – 677b.

A-26. F. P. Johnson, *Sculpture 1896 – 1923* (Corinth 9; Cambridge, Mass.: American School of Classical Studies at Athens, 1931). See also C. L. Thompson, "Hairstyles, Head-Coverings, and St Paul: Portraits from Roman Corinth," *BA* 51.2 (June 1988): 99 – 110.

A-27. Johnson, *Sculpture*, 72. For a helpful discussion of Roman portraiture, see S. Walker, *Greek and Roman Portraits* (London: British Museum Press, 1995).

A-28. Plutarch, *Quaest. Rom.* 266 D. For more on this, see D. J. Gill, "The Importance of Roman Portraiture for Head-Coverings in 1 Corinthians 11:2 – 16," *TynBul* 41.2 (1990): 246 – 51.

A-29. Johnson, *Sculpture*, 76 – 77. For a convenient overview of the portraiture of Nero, see D. E. E. Kleiner, *Roman Sculpture* (New Haven, Conn.: Yale Univ. Press, 1992), 135 – 39.

A-30. Johnson, *Sculpture*, 86, no. 160.

A-31. Kent, *Inscriptions*, no. 156.

A-32. Ibid., no. 173.

A-33. Ibid., no. 199.

A-34. Pallas, Charitonidis, and Venencie, "Inscriptions lyciennes trouvées à Solômos près de Corinthe," 496 – 508; L. Robert, "VII. Décret de la confédération lycienne à Corinthe," *Revue des Études Anciennes* 62 (1960): 324 – 42. For a convenient translation and discussion, see R. A. Kearsley, "Women in Public Life in the Roman East: Iunia Theodora, Claudia Metrodora and Phoibe, Benefactress of Paul," *Ancient Society* [Macquarie Ancient History Association] 15, 3 (1985): 124 – 37; idem, "Women in Public Life in the Roman East," *TynBul* 50.2 (1999): 189 – 211.

A-35. Decree 1, ll. 1 – 7 (trans. Kearsley).

A-36. Decree 4, ll. 57 – 58.

A-37. Suetonius, *Claudius* 25.9.

A-38. Tactius, *Annals* 13.33.4.

A-39. Menander, *Thais*. For the context of this citation see Winter, "Homosexual Terminology," 288.

A-40. R. Stillwell, *The Theater* (Corinth 2; Princeton, N.J.: American School of Classical Studies at Athens, 1965).

A-41. Gill, "Erastus the Aedile," 293 – 301.

2 CORINTHIANS

by Moyer Hubbard

Corinth and the Corinthians

See Introduction to 1 Corinthians.

Developments Between 1 and 2 Corinthians

When Paul wrote 1 Corinthians (probably from Ephesus), he promised to send Timothy to Corinth (1 Cor. 4:17; 16:11) to guide the struggling community through some difficult issues that had arisen since his departure. These included factionalism (1 Cor. 3), immorality (1 Cor. 5), continued participation in pagan religious feasts (1 Cor. 8; 10:14 – 22), and questions related to theology and church practice (1 Cor. 11 – 15). Although what happened next is not entirely clear, it seems likely that Timothy returned with news that the situation had worsened, which forced Paul to abandon the travel plans he announced in 1 Cor. 16 and make an abrupt visit to Corinth (cf. 2 Cor. 13:1 – 2). This was a painful experience for Paul (2:1), who found himself personally attacked by a member of the congregation (2:5 – 11; 7:12). Upon returning to Ephesus, Paul wrote an

THE SUMMIT OF THE ACROCORINTH

In the location of the notorious temple of Aphrodite.

◀

▶ 2 Corinthians
IMPORTANT FACTS:

- ▪ **AUTHOR:** Paul the apostle.
- ▪ **DATE:** A.D. 55.
- ▪ **OCCASION:** Written to reaffirm his affection for the Corinthians, to re-ignite enthusiasm for the collection, and to rebuff intruding opponents.
- ▪ **THEMES:**
  1. The new covenant ministry of the Spirit.
  2. Strength in weakness.
  3. The inner dynamic of the Christian life.

emotional letter, now lost, which he conveyed through Titus (2:4, 12 – 13; 7:6 – 7).

Titus eventually brought Paul news that the Corinthians had responded favorably to that letter written "with many tears" (2:4) and had taken disciplinary action against the offender (2:5 – 11; 7:5 – 12). However, Titus also reported a new threat: flamboyant missionaries from churches in Judea had arrived in Corinth and challenged Paul's legitimacy as an apostle (see "Paul's Opponents" at 11:6). Paul responded by dispatching Titus from Macedonia with the letter we now call 2 Corinthians (around A.D. 55), while he made preparations for his third visit to the troubled community (13:1 – 2).

Unity of 2 Corinthians

The historical reconstruction sketched above assumes that the canonical form of 2 Corinthians represents a single correspondence written by Paul, addressing a complex set of circumstances in Corinth. This is hardly universally accepted, however. In particular, the dramatic change of tone in chapters 10 – 13 seems to many impossible to reconcile with the confident and hopeful tenor of chapters 1 – 9. This has led some to propose that these later chapters are a portion of the earlier tear-

ful letter (2:4), or perhaps comprise a letter written subsequent to chapters 1 – 9, after Paul had been more fully appraised of the situation in Corinth. Many other partition theories have been offered, though it is beyond the scope and focus of this commentary to examine these in any detail. Recent discussions of this issue tend to favor the unity of 2 Corinthians.[1] The following arguments are especially pertinent:

1. **Lack of textual support.** There is no evidence that 2 Corinthians ever existed in any form other than its present canonical form.
2. **Unifying motifs.** Certain key themes occur throughout our canonical 2 Corinthians and suggest a rhetorically unified composition: *strength in weakness* (2:14 – 16; 4:7 – 18; 11:30 – 33; 12:10; 13:3); *Paul's style and philosophy of preaching* (2:17; 4:2 – 5; 5:11 – 13; 10:10 – 12; 11:5 – 6; 13:2 – 3); *testing one's faith* (2:9; 8:8; 13:5 – 6); *proper*

REMAINS OF
THE STADIUM AT
ISTHMIA

and improper boasting (1:12, 14; 5:12; 7:4, 14; 8:24; 9:2; 10:8 – 17; 11:10 – 30; 12:1 – 10); *commendation* (3:1 – 3; 4:2; 5:12; 7:11; 10:18; 12:11), and so on.

3. **Chapters 1 – 9 preparatory to 10 – 13.** In significant ways, chapters 10 – 13 presuppose the argumentation of 1 – 9.[2] In both sections Paul is defending himself before the Corinthians, and his direct confrontation of his opponents in 10 – 13 is almost expected, given his allusions to their activity in 1:12 – 13; 2:17; 4:2 – 4; 5:12. It is simply not true that chapters 1 – 9 contain no hint of simmering problems between Paul and the Corinthians.[3]

4. **Various contexts, various strategies.** From the Corinthian correspondence we know there were those in Corinth who questioned Paul's leadership (1 Cor. 3 – 4), some who were Paul's supporters (1:11; 16:15 – 17), at least one person who had openly attacked Paul (2 Cor. 2:5; 7:12), others who had a change of heart over their opposition to Paul (7:9 – 12), not to mention intruders who wished to undermine Paul's authority (2 Cor.

10 – 13). In other words, there was a variety of situations and groups to address. Thus, to evaluate the integrity of this letter on problematic notions of "restricted coherence, focused consistency, and unitary intentionality"[4] is to fail to grasp the complexity of the situation on the ground in Corinth.

Problems in Corinth

According to 1 Corinthians, the fundamental problem in Corinth was the Corinthians themselves. In Paul's view they were worldly, immature, and still not ready for the "solid food" of advanced discipleship (1 Cor. 3:1 – 4). Although some improvements are evident by the time of 2 Corinthians, it is clear that many of the same problems persist. Paul again has to confront those who continue to frequent pagan temples (2 Cor. 6:14 – 7:2; cf. 1 Cor. 8; 10:14 – 22), and again has to address Corinthian dissatisfaction with his oratory (2 Cor. 10:10; 11:6; cf. 1 Cor. 2:1 – 5). The Corinthians are also somewhat embarrassed by Paul's insistence on plying his trade as a tentmaker rather than accepting their patronage, thus elevating his social status. When Paul speaks of "lowering himself" through pursuing his craft (2 Cor. 11:7), he certainly echoes the Corinthian perspective on his trade, and the picture that begins to emerge is one of a superficial, status-conscious community that has failed to grasp the cruciform character of the Christian life.

The Purpose of 2 Corinthians

Given the problems outlined above, it is not surprising that most of Paul's theological argumentation in 2 Corinthians is aimed at correcting an inverted value system. In chapters 3 – 6 Paul emphasizes the transforming work of the Spirit (3:3 – 6, 7, 17 – 18; 5:4, 17), the priority of inner reality over outward display (3:1 – 3, 6; 4:6 – 7, 16, 18; 5:7, 12), and the radical newness of life in Christ: "You are a new creation" (5:17). In chapters 10 – 13 Paul takes this argument one step further by demonstrating that what the Corinthians regard as weakness is actually the very strength

of God (12:9 – 10). In short, what Paul attempts in this letter is nothing less than a theological program of re-enculturation.

There are, of course, other reasons for this lengthy letter. Paul's ever-changing travel plans have brought charges of indecision and suspicions of waning affection, and Paul is eager to set the record straight (1:15 – 2:4). He also needs to reignite enthusiasm for the collection, a beneficent gift on behalf of the Gentile churches to their brothers and sisters in Judea (chs. 8 – 9). The Corinthians had already pledged their support (1 Cor. 16:1 – 4), and Paul needs to act quickly in order to capitalize on the momentum of Titus's recent efforts on this front (2 Cor. 8:6). And then there are Paul's opponents — recently arrived emissaries from Judea who seem determined to undermine Paul's authority and presumptuously foist themselves on the vulnerable community (chs. 10 – 13). Their version of the gospel places themselves at the center, rather than Christ, and Paul exposes this anemic, truncated pseudo-gospel for the sham that it is.

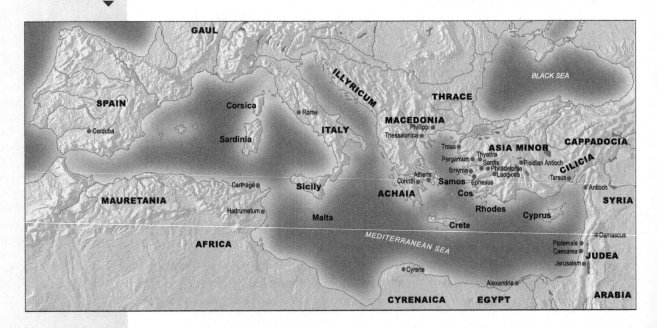

If we were to summarize these disparate interests under one rubric, we might identify *reconciliation* as the dominant concern of Paul in 2 Corinthians. In what may be his most personal letter (cf. 6:11 – 13), Paul aims to regain the support of key groups in Corinth in order that the community as a whole can grow to maturity in Christ. Although Paul's language is at times harsh and scolding, it issues from genuine parental affection: "I speak as to my children — open wide your hearts also" (6:13).

Greeting and Opening Blessing (1:1 – 7)

The opening paragraphs of Paul's letters usually set the tone for what follows and contain important clues to the main themes of the letter. In this introductory segment Paul emphasizes his *authority as an apostle* (1:1 – 2) and expresses his deep *relief and joy* (1:3 – 7) over the successful mission of reconciliation carried out by Titus (see 7:5 – 6).

To the church of God in Corinth (1:1). The earliest Christian groups met in private homes, and in this respect "the church" in Corinth was actually a collection of household assemblies. Acts 18:7 mentions Titius Justus as the first host of the fledgling community in Corinth, and later we learn that Gaius was able to accommodate "the whole church," apparently meaning all of the household assemblies (Rom. 16:23). We know from 1 Corinthians 14:23 that such gatherings did occur, though we can only speculate how often. Meeting in individual homes afforded privacy (though they were not closed gatherings; see 1 Cor. 14:23), and contributed to a sense of community, though there were some obvious drawbacks.

Recent excavations in Corinth have uncovered a number of elegant villas from the Roman era, but the maximum number of guests that an atrium (a formal reception room) and triclinium (the dining room) together could have held was not more than fifty.[5] According to common Roman practice, guests of higher social standing were given preferential treatment at mealtime, so that the Roman satirist Martial complains to his host, "Why is not the same dinner served to me as to you? You take oysters fattened in the Lucrine lake, I suck a mussel through a hole in the shell. . . . Why do I dine without you although, Ponticus, I am dining with you?"[6] One wonders if the divisions that arose in Corinth in connection with the Lord's Supper ("one remains hungry, another gets drunk," 1 Cor. 11:17 – 22) were not partially the result of the chosen mechanism of fellowship, the private home.

▶ **Corinth**
IMPORTANT FACTS:

- Population: About 100,000.
- Religion: Aphrodite, Poseidon, and the Imperial Family worshiped, along with many other deities.
- Society: Cosmopolitan, ethnically diverse, relatively prosperous.
- Politics: Roman form of government, capital city of the province of Achaia.
- Culture: Competitive, status conscious.
- Economy: Port city; host of the Isthmian Games, important center of trade and tourism.

Together with all the saints throughout Achaia (1:1). At the time of the writing of 2 Corinthians, the Roman province of Achaia extended well beyond Athens, but Paul's usage elsewhere suggests he has in mind here a smaller geographical region. His earlier ministry in Athens resulted in at least a few conversions (Acts 17:32 – 34), yet he refers to the household of Stephanas of Corinth as the "firstfruits of Achaia" (1 Cor. 16:15). Even so, the clear implication of this verse is that the gospel had not only taken root in Corinth, but had spread to some of the surrounding communities. Romans 16:1 names Phoebe as a deaconess of the church in nearby Cenchrea, and presumably this letter is to be copied and dispatched to other household assemblies in the area.

Grace and peace to you from God our Father and the Lord Jesus Christ (1:2). The standard opening salutation in Greek letters of this era was *chairein!* (Greetings!). In a clever play on words, Paul christianizes this formulaic greeting and changes it to *charis!* (Grace!). This is expanded by a wish of "peace" (Gk. *eirēnē*; Heb. *shalom*), which was the typical Hebrew/Aramaic greeting.[7] The Hellenistic form is filled with Christian/Jewish content, and this perfectly expresses the complexity of Paul's biography and thought.

The Father of compassion and God of all comfort (1:3). Paul's Jewish faith is especially evident in his designation of God as "Father." From his study of the Torah, the young Saul of Tarsus learned that God was "the Father and Creator" of Israel (Deut. 32:6; cf. 8:5, 14:1). With the prophets he called on God as "Lord, Father, Redeemer of old."[8] Reflecting the same intimacy that characterized the prayer of Jesus, Paul addressed his heavenly Father as "Abba."[9] Although such affectionate language was not widely used by Jewish writers in this era, the hymns from Qumran offer this heart-warming parallel:

> *Because you are Father to all the*
> *   sons of your truth.*
> *In them you rejoice,*
> *   like one full of gentleness for*
> *   her child,*
> *   and like a wet-nurse,*
> *you clutch to your chest all your crea-*
> *   tures.*[10]

It is important to remember, however, that the Roman conception of fatherhood was considerably more harsh and authoritarian than our modern Western ideal. As the head of his family, the Roman father held absolute legal authority (*patria potestas*) over his children as his property. Unwanted infants could be discarded, and older children could be sold as slaves. The Roman historian Tacitus regards as eccentric the Jewish conviction that it was criminal "to kill any newly-born infant."[11] Although the exposure of infants was held in check by

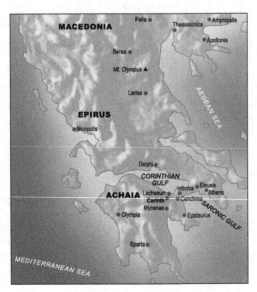

public opinion and eventually outlawed under Christian emperors, both pagan and Christian writers from this period protest against this act of cruelty, which confirms its widespread practice.[12] In describing God as a "compassionate Father," Paul is assuring the Corinthians that, whatever their earthly fathers may have been like, the head of the Christian family is a responsive and loving Father, who exercises his authority in the best interests of his children.

Who comforts us in all our troubles (1:4 – 7). Comfort in affliction is the dominant theme of Paul's introductory blessing and one that resonates throughout chapters 1 – 9 (see esp. 2:14 – 16; 4:8 – 12; 5:4 – 5; 6:2 – 12). The depth of emotion so obvious in 2 Corinthians renders it perhaps Paul's most personal letter. At one point in the letter Paul himself comments on his candid self-disclosure, "O Corinthians, we have poured out our hearts to you" (6:11).

Paul's Change of Plans (1:8 – 2:13)

Paul's change in his travel itinerary raised the accusation in Corinth of fickleness and worldliness (1:12 – 22). In order to correct this misperception, Paul explains that it was out of concern for them that he decided to postpone his third visit to Corinth (1:23 – 2:4), allowing them time to discipline the person who had offended Paul (2:5 – 13).

The province of Asia (1:8) The province of Asia, bordered on the west by the Aegean, and on the east by Galatia, included such towns as Colosse, Smyrna, Pergamum, Troas, and Ephesus. Paul visited these cities on his second and third missionary journeys. Ephesus, an important sea port in the province, became one of the strategic centers of his missionary endeavor.

The hardships we suffered in the province of Asia . . . in our heart we felt the sentence of death (1:8). As the hardship catalogs of 6:3 – 6 and 11:23 – 29 illustrate, there is much about Paul's biography that we do not know, and the precise nature of the hardship (the Greek is singular, indicating one specific hardship) mentioned here remains obscure. Paul may be referring to the Ephesian riot related in Acts 19, though there is no indication in Acts of a sentence of death. Because this official verdict (*apokrima*; NIV, "sentence") was experienced "within," some feel Paul is speaking figuratively of a personal distress or perhaps a physical illness (see 12:7). If this were the case, however, his use of first-person plural ("we," "our") is unusual.

In holiness and sincerity . . . not according to worldly wisdom (1:12). In contrasting

REFLECTIONS

IN PONDERING THE HARDSHIP HE EXPERIENCED IN Asia, Paul senses a divine purpose involved, which he relates in verse 9: "But this happened that we might not rely on ourselves, but on God." Paul recognizes that the painful experiences of life are not random, pointless happenings, but divinely intended opportunities for growth. The lesson Paul needed to learn is not to rely on his own strength, intelligence, or natural abilities, but to trust wholly on God (Zech. 4:6). Not only is this a lesson that we need to learn (and relearn) today, but Paul's candid admission of his own need for growth serves as an important reminder that spiritual leaders do not come preassembled from the factory. They are grown from saplings through seasons of heat, frost, and rain, and require years of cultivation and pruning to reach maturity.

his own "simplicity" (*haplotēs*; NIV, "holiness") and "sincerity" with the "fleshly" (*sarkikos*; NIV, "worldly") conduct of others, Paul alludes to the practice of many self-styled philosophers who were in fact charlatans out for their own interests. Many writers of the period heap contempt on this ever burgeoning throng of pretenders who, "in the guise of philosophers [operate] with a view to their own profit and reputation, and not to improve [their followers]"(see comments on 1:24; 2:17; 4:2, 5; 5:11; 10:5; 11:20).[13]

The day of the Lord Jesus (1:14). The "day of the LORD" was a prominent motif in Israel's prophetic traditions, where it usually connoted a dark and foreboding day of judgment (Isa. 2:12 – 21; Amos 5:18 – 20; Zech. 14:1 – 2). This day of judgment would lead to the vindication and restoration of Israel (Amos 9:11 – 15; Zech. 14:6 – 21). Both positive (Matt. 16:27) and negative (Rom. 2:5) aspects of "the day of the Lord" are present in the New Testament; in this verse the emphasis lies on the hopeful prospect of

receiving the approval of the Lord on the day of his visitation (see Phil. 2:16).

I planned to visit you. . . . do I make my plans in worldly manner? (1:16 – 17). Paul's change of plans provoked strong criticism in Corinth (see the introduction), which forces the apostle to give a detailed defense of his apparently fickle disposition (1:12 – 2:4). The strength of the reaction in Corinth may be due, in part, to fashionable Stoicism, which considered decisiveness a defining virtue of the wise man:

> Nor do [the Stoics] assume that a man with good sense changes his mind, for changing one's mind belongs to false assent, on the grounds of erring through haste. Nor does he change his mind in any way, nor alter his opinion, nor is he confused. For all these things are marks of those who waver in their beliefs, which is alien to the person with good sense.[14]

He anointed us (1:21). Although the Greek word for "anoint" could be used of lotion massaged into an athlete or of oils used after bathing, Paul's vocabulary here is drawn from the Greek Old Testament, where the word refers to consecration to sacred office. Kings, priests, prophets, and other leaders were commissioned to service through a ceremony involving anointing with oil.[15] This anointing set them apart from their peers and authorized them to carry out their divinely ordained task.

In the present context, Paul's claim that the anointing of the Spirit extends to *all* believers ("he anointed *us*") has both sociological and theological implications. Given the prominence of this imagery in the Old Testament, Jewish converts in Corinth like Crispus (Acts

PAUL'S INTENDED ITINERARY

▼

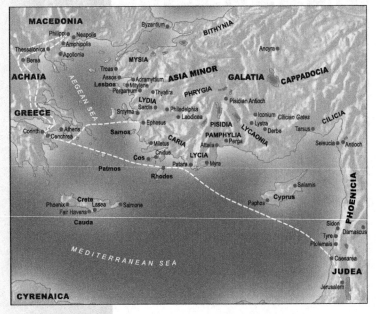

18:8) and God-fearers like Titius Justus (Acts 18:17) would have marveled at this bold democratization of a sacred rite once reserved for select individuals within the community of faith. This anointing, however, is not to a position of privilege, but to a position of service, as Paul himself modeled in Corinth (2 Cor. 4:4; 6:2 – 10; 11:23 – 29).

Set his seal of ownership on us (1:22). Unlike today, where seals are more decorative than functional, seals in antiquity were widely used and extremely important in commerce and everyday life. On a document, the seal serves as a signature, guaranteeing its authenticity. Parcels could be sealed to ensure that their contents were not disturbed in transit. The seal itself was made of stone, metal, or ivory, which was then pressed into soft wax or lead to make a distinctive impression. The imprint might bear the name of the owner, a unique symbol, or perhaps the image of a mythological figure or deity. Seals became objects of detailed craftsmanship in the Roman era and commonly imprinted the image of the one to whom they belonged.

In light of this, Paul's reference here to the divine seal of ownership impressed on every believer may include a subtle allusion to the believer's transformation into the image of God. The Corinthians were already familiar with this idea from Paul's previous correspondence (1 Cor. 15:42 – 49), and Paul will soon take up the issue explicitly (2 Cor. 3:18; 4:4 – 6). Philo, Paul's contemporary in Alexandria, was particularly fond of this analogy. Commenting on the creation of Adam in the divine image he writes, "He that was made according to the divine image was like . . . a seal."[16]

And put his Spirit in our hearts as a deposit, guaranteeing what is to come (1:22). Like the English word "deposit," the Greek term Paul employs here (*arrabōn*) is taken from the world of finance and denotes an initial down payment in promise of full payment at a later date. This precise phrase occurs again in 5:5, where we learn that the full payment involves being clothed with our "heavenly dwelling," when at last "what is mortal may be swallowed up by life" (5:4). In a parallel passage in Romans, Paul refers to the Spirit as "the firstfruits," guaranteeing our ultimate adoption and the redemption of our bodies (Rom. 8:23). For Paul, the Spirit was the power of the

ANCIENT SEALS

(left) Agate seal found in Mizpah (seventh century B.C.).

(right) Jasper seal bearing the inscription "Amos the Scribe" (seventh century B.C.).

future working in the present to renew, transform, and recreate God's people from the inside out (2 Cor. 3:3, 18; 4:6, 16, 5:5, 17).

I call God as my witness (1:23). Paul's Greek is more forceful than the NIV and can be accurately rendered, "I summon God as a witness *against me*."[17] This phraseology resembles the Old Testament oath formula, "May the LORD deal with me ever so severely if I do not do such and such. . ." (cf. Ruth 1:17; 2 Sam. 3:9). Oaths were more important in the ancient world than in modern Western societies and often carried the weight of a legally binding contract. In the Greco-Roman context, invoking the name of a deity added special gravity to the vow, and Zeus became known as "the god of oaths" among the ancients. The city of Assos (see Acts 20:13 – 14) in the province Asia publicly displayed this solemn oath of allegiance to the emperor Caligula on a bronze tablet: "We swear by Zeus the Savior and the God of Caesar Augustus . . . that we are loyally disposed to Gaius Caesar Augustus. . . . If we observe this oath, may all go well with us; if not, may the opposite befall."[18] Closer to Corinth, Pausanias tells of the oaths sworn before Palaemon, the mythological hero honored by the Isthmian Games: "Whosoever swears falsely here, whether Corinthian or stranger, can by no means escape from his oath."[19]

Paul's unusually strong language, subpoenaing God himself as a potential witness *against him*, indicates the seriousness of the issue in his mind. Far from being indecisive or unconcerned about the Corinthians (see 1:17), Paul's change of plans issued solely from his parental desire to spare his children another unpleasant confrontation.

Not that we lord it over your faith, but we work with you (1:24). Paul's determination to distance himself from those who would "lord it over" the Corinthians is rooted in his knowledge of the concrete reality of daily life in Corinth. Charlatans parading as philosophers and preying on the vanities of the populace blighted the cities of the Roman world during this period, so much so that the Emperor Vespasian felt justified in expelling all so-called philosophers from Rome in A.D. 71.[20] The sharp-tongued Roman satirist Lucian offers us this description:

> There is a class of men which made its appearance in the world not long ago, lazy, disputatious, vainglorious, quick-tempered, gluttonous, doltish, addle-pated, full of effrontery. . . . These people, dividing themselves into schools and inventing various word-mazes, have called themselves Stoics, Academics, Epicureans, Peripatetics, and other things much more laughable than these. . . . They amass biting phrases and school themselves in novel terms of abuse, and then they censure and reproach their fellow-men.[21]

Although Paul is not afraid to make use of his authority as an apostle when circumstances demand it, his preferred stance is that of a "coworker" (Gk. *synergos*; NIV, "we work with you"), working alongside his converts as a father with his son (cf. Phil. 2:22).

Another painful visit . . . through many tears I wrote to you (2:1 – 4). See "Developments Between the Letters" in the introduction.

The punishment inflicted on him by the majority is sufficient (2:6). A possible implication of Paul's wording is that there remains a minority who are not in agreement with the decision of "the majority" regarding the sentence passed on the offender, even though this person has admitted guilt and is grieved by his sin (2:7). Equally likely, however, is that the term *pleiones* (NIV, "majority") means simply "the rest of the community" as opposed to the one offender.[22] This seems to be the meaning of *pleiones* in 9:2 and Philippians 1:14; a similar idiom was also employed by the Qumran community, where "the Many" is equivalent to the entire congregation: "And to any in Israel who freely volunteers to enroll in the council of the Community, the Instructor who is at the head of the Many shall test him with regard to his insight and his deeds."[23]

In order that Satan might not outwit us. For we are not unaware of his schemes (2:11). In keeping with his Jewish contemporaries and unlike most moderns, Paul is acutely aware of Satan's intrigues and of the influence of the demonic realm on human affairs. Jewish literature of the pre-Christian era reveals an increased sensitivity to the activities of Satan and his cohorts, and in some quarters this heightened awareness led to a kind of demonic paranoia.

The author of the book of *Jubilees* (ca. 150 B.C.) went so far as to rewrite the book of Genesis in an attempt to iron out its theological wrinkles while implicating the demonic realm. According to this Jewish writer it was Satan, not Yahweh or his angel, who was responsible for the near sacrifice of Isaac, who planned to slay Moses on his way to confront Pharaoh, who killed the firstborn of Egypt, and who hardened Pharaoh's heart.[24] While Paul avoids this extreme, his Jewish heritage has endowed him with a deeper understanding of the spiritual nature of the conflict between good and evil, and it is this broader perspective that surfaces here (see comments on 2 Cor. 4:4).

Now when I went to Troas . . . I still had no peace of mind. . . . So I said good-by to them (2:12 – 13). Acts records that Paul's departure from Ephesus and journey to Greece occurred after a serious riot in that city, instigated by the guild of silversmiths, whose financial livelihood was threatened by the advance of the gospel (Acts 19:1 – 20:3). Paul probably journeyed to Troas by ship, and after the tumult in Ephesus he must have been pleased to find that "the Lord had opened a door" for the gospel in Troas. Yet Paul's concern for the Corinthians and how they had responded to his strongly worded letter carried by Titus compelled him to move on when Titus did not arrive in Troas on schedule. Paul was unwilling to foster a new family in Troas at the expense of his children in Corinth, and his decision to leave behind a potentially fruitful ministry in Troas is a poignant testimony to the genuineness of his words in 1 Corinthians 4:15:

REFLECTIONS

ACCORDING TO THE BOOK OF JOB, SATAN ROAMS ALL over the earth looking for those he can ruin (Job 1:6 – 12), and according to 1 Peter 5:8 he is like a lion continually on the prowl. Paul shares this conviction, and so he enjoins the Corinthians to reaffirm their love for the unnamed brother who sinned. In Paul's view, failure on the part of the Corinthians to make every effort to restore this penitent sinner would render them unwitting participants in the schemes of the enemy. The estrangement of a fallen saint is the victory of Satan, and the first line of defense for the believing community is to become aware of the enemy's designs.

"For in Christ Jesus *I became your father* through the Gospel" (italics added).

Ministers of the New Covenant (2:14 – 3:6)

The anxiety of verse 13 breaks into thanksgiving in verse 14 ("Thanks be to God"), as Paul is reminded of the good news that Titus brought of the Corinthians' reconciliation (7:5 – 16). This line of thought will be resumed in 7:5. The intervening material (2:14 – 7:4) constitutes a profound theological excursus on the nature of Paul's life, ministry, and message, as one of strength displayed through weakness, life revealed through death, and hope in the midst of despair.

▶ The Triumphal Procession

In 2:14 – 16 Paul alludes to one of the most spectacular and important celebrations in antiquity, the Roman triumph. Awarded by the senate to honor a victorious general, the triumph was essentially an enormous parade through the heart of Rome. It was designed to display the glory of the Roman general and offer thanks to Jupiter, the chief deity of the Roman pantheon, for granting the victory.[A-1] The festivities could last several days, and not only did the entire populace of Rome turn out to view the spectacle, but Rome itself was copiously adorned to embrace her conquering hero.

Josephus, an eye-witness to one such Triumph, remarks, "It is impossible to describe the multitude of the shows as they deserve, and the magnificence of them all."[A-2] The pageant would include all manner of plunder taken from the enemy, the victorious soldiers, and also captured soldiers and leading officers of the enemy. The captives would be led before the chariot of the conquering general, to the mockery and taunts of the onlookers. In recounting the events of his reign, Augustus boasted, "I waged wars on land and on sea. . . . In my Triumphs nine kings or children of kings were led before my chariot."[A-3] The climax of the procession involved a sacrifice to the Roman deities and the execution of any eminent captives in the Forum, as Josephus recounts:

Now the last part of this pompous show was at the temple of Jupiter Capitolinus, whither when they were come, they stood still; for it was the Romans' ancient custom to stay, till somebody brought the news that the general of the enemy was slain. This general was Simon, the son of Gioras, who had then been led in this triumph among the captives; a rope had also been put upon his head, and he had been drawn into a proper place in the forum, and had withal been tormented by those that drew him along, and the law of the Romans required that malefactors condemned to die should be slain there.[A-4]

Although the triumphal procession itself was confined to Rome, the imagery of the conquest and the triumph was disseminated throughout the empire on coinage, which depicted vanquished foes, victorious generals, triumphal arches, and so on. Triumphal arches, which served as veritable billboards advertising the conquest, were also scattered throughout the provinces. The first-century visitor to Corinth would have entered its main market through a magnificent triumphal-style arch.[A-5] By the second century A.D. (and perhaps earlier), the adjoining basilica was supported by columns carved in the shape of captured barbarian soldiers.[A-6]

◀

COIN DEPICTING CAPTIVES OF JULIUS CAESAR

Who always leads us in triumphal procession (2:14 – 16). While some translations of verse 14 give the impression that Paul is portraying himself as one of the victors marching in a triumphal procession, this rendering is linguistically impossible. If we were to fill out the NIV translation above in light of the triumphal imagery (see "The Triumphal Procession") and in accordance with the only attested meaning of this Greek construction, we would render this clause, "Thanks be to God who always leads us *as conquered foes* in his triumphal procession."[25] Paul makes a similar statement in 1 Corinthians 4:9: "For it seems to me that God has put us apostles on display at the end of the procession, like men condemned to die in the arena." Although formerly an "enemy of the cross" (Phil. 3:18; see Gal. 1:13; 1 Tim. 1:13), Paul now sees himself as Christ's slave (Rom. 1:1; 2 Cor. 4:5), whose suffering and ministry are offered as a continuous testimony to the glory of Christ and as a fragrant sacrifice (see below) of thanks to God.

And through us spreads everywhere the fragrance of the knowledge of him (2:14). One of the standard features of religious or civic rituals in antiquity was the use of incense and other fragrant materials. Religious processions, the arrival of an important dignitary, the triumphal return of a Roman general, and so on, were all occasions on which such aromatics might be used. In describing the triumphal procession of Aemelius Paulus, Plutarch tells us that "every temple was open and filled with garlands and incense."[26] Continuing the image of the Roman triumph, Paul portrays his crushed and vanquished apostolic existence as the means through which the aroma of the crucified Christ is mediated to those around him. Paradoxically, God's strength is most potently displayed through Paul's weakness. Already the apostle is preparing the ground for his startling declaration in 12:10, "For when I am weak, then I am strong."

For we are to God the aroma of Christ among those who are being saved and those who are perishing (2:15). Embedded within the imagery of the triumphal procession is an allusion to the Levitical sacrifices of the Old Testament, where the terms *euōdia* (NIV "fragrance") and *osmē* (NIV "aroma") combine to refer to a sacrificial "aroma pleasing to the LORD" (Lev. 2:2, 12; 6:14, etc.). As elsewhere (e.g., Col. 1:24), Paul portrays his apostolic suffering as an extension of the suffering of Christ, and he will make this point more explicitly in 4:10: "We always carry around in our body the death of Jesus."

To the one we are the smell of death; to the other, the fragrance of life (2:16).

Although the transitions between metaphors is abrupt, Paul returns to the spectacle of the triumph and notes the differing effects the aroma-filled parade route would have on those involved. For the cheering crowds, the victorious soldiers, and the gloating general, this was the sweet fragrance of victory. But to the unfortunate captives destined for the auctioneer's block or execution in the forum, this was the scent of death itself.

Unlike so many, we do not peddle the word of God for profit (2:17). Preaching the gospel for mere financial gain has been a problem from the earliest days of the Christian movement. Already by the time of the *Didache* (ca. A.D. 80 – 150) Christian communities were exhorted to judge itinerant Christian teachers with reference to their desire for monetary gain: "And when the apostle leaves, he is to take nothing except bread until he finds his next night's lodging. But if he asks for money he is a false prophet."[27] Paul may have in mind the intruders addressed in chapters 10 – 13, or he may be referring more generally to that familiar brand of itinerant philosopher who would peddle his teaching for a hefty profit.

The Greek verb Paul uses for "peddle for profit" (*kapēleuō*) was regularly used as an indictment against the Sophists, the popular rhetoricians of Paul's day. As early as Socrates we find the Sophists described as those who "take their doctrines the round of our cities, hawking them about (*kapēleuō*) to any odd purchaser."[28] Philo, Paul's contemporary in Alexandria, makes a similar disparaging assessment of the Sophists: "And the wisdom must not be that of the systems hatched by the word-catchers and Sophists who sell their tenets and

arguments like any bit of merchandise in the market."[29] Dio Chrysostom describes this lot as those who come "in the guise of philosophers," yet whose pretentious oratory was displayed solely "with a view to their own profit and reputation."[30]

But the charge of avarice was leveled against a variety of schools of philosophy whose practitioners earned their livelihood from attracting a crowd and then gaining a following. Indeed, the Cynics sometimes fared little better than the Sophists:

> These Cynics, posting themselves at street-corners, in alleyways, and at temple-gates, pass around the hat and play upon the credulity of lads and sailors and crowds of that sort, stringing together rough jokes and much tittle-tattle and that low bandage that smacks of the market-place.[31]

Paul's point is that unlike so many who proclaim their "religion" for a price, he and his companions preach Christ for altruistic reasons.

Are we beginning to commend ourselves again? . . . You yourselves are our letter . . . written not with ink . . . not on tablets of stone (3:1 – 3). No doubt Paul's initial ministry in Corinth involved a sincere effort to win the trust of these new believers, to "commend" himself to them. Paul's denial of any need for continual self-commendation is grounded in the obvious reality of their transformed lives: "You show that you are a letter from Christ" (3:3).

To the Corinthians, surrounded on all sides by monuments of self-commendation, Paul's words may have been heard as a friendly barb. Many of Corinth's civic structures were donated by wealthy patrons, and inscriptions of self-commendation, engraved in stone and proudly heralding the name of the benefactor, have been found on monuments, temples, market stalls, and pavements (see "The Erastus Inscription"). Although slightly later than Paul, an inscription on a statue that the orator Herodes Atticus allowed to be erected in his honor bears witness to the indulgent nature of some of these self-commendations: "Given by great Herodes Atticus, pre-eminent above others, who had attained the peak of every kind of excellence . . . famous among Hellenes and furthermore a son [of Greece] greater than them all, the flower of Achaia."[32]

Do we need, like some people, letters of recommendation to you or from you (3:1)? Although letters of reference are common enough today, they played a far more important role in ancient Roman society. Travelers, wishing to avoid the grubby and often sordid environment of roadside inns, relied on local hospitality. To help them obtain it, they carried letters of recommendation from people familiar with the region being traversed. Letters of reference were also written to introduce one party to another, frequently with a view to social advancement or to other practical assistance.[33]

Such letters presume a relationship of friendship or authority, or perhaps both (cf. the letter to Philemon, written by Paul on behalf of the runaway slave Onesimus). Most commentators see here a veiled reference to certain Christian missionaries who arrived in Corinth with letters of recommendation, perhaps from prominent members of the church in Jerusalem, and who subsequently caused trouble for Paul (see "Paul's Opponents in Corinth" at 11:6). This is plausible, but the additional phrase "to you or from you" may indicate simply an innocent reference to the familiar practice of sending and receiving letters of recommendation.

Ministers of a new covenant (3:6). The clear allusions to Jeremiah and Ezekiel in

REFLECTIONS

A MISSIONARY IN A PREDOMINATELY HINDU COUNTRY once related the story of a devout Hindu who admired Christ and studied the Gospels, and who frankly admitted to her, "I would become a Christian if it were not for Christians." This person's experience of Christians had left a bitter taste in his mouth and had led him to reject the faith he sensed, deep within, to be true. In telling the Corinthians that they are "a letter from Christ" read by all (3:2 – 3), Paul reminds us that our personal conduct and daily witness should authenticate the faith we proclaim. Any disjunction between our faith and our practice will cause our message to fall on deaf ears. Seeing is believing.

▶ The Erastus Inscription

One of the most remarkable discoveries from the excavations in Corinth is the Erastus inscription. Engraved on the pavement between the theatre and the market, the inscription reads, "Erastus in return for his aedileship laid [this pavement] at his own expense." This same Erastus is mentioned by Paul in Rom. 16:23 and is called the "city treasurer."

Both the Greek term used by Paul (*oikonomos*), and the Latin term found in the inscription (*aedile*) refer to one of the chief administrators of Roman Corinth. Elected magistrates were expected to make public benefactions in gratitude for their election, and Erastus's pavement was an appropriate token of appreciation to the local citizenry.

3:3 (see Jer. 17:1; 31:33; Ezek. 36:26 – 27) lead to a direct citation of Jeremiah's memorable "new covenant" (Jer. 31:31), as Paul explains that his ministry is the fulfillment of the prophetic expectation of the inner renewal of God's people. The newness of Jeremiah's "new covenant" and Ezekiel's "everlasting covenant" (Ezek. 37:26) was its inwardness: "I will write my law on their hearts" (Jer. 31:33); "I will give you a new heart and put a new spirit in you" (Ezek. 36:26). The scrolls from Qumran similarly describe entrance into that community as entering into the "new covenant," though membership in this sect entailed full and complete obedience to the Mosaic law and the rules of the community:[34]

> All who enter the council of holiness of those walking in perfect behavior as he commanded, anyone of them who breaks a word of the law of Moses impertinently or through carelessness will be banished.[35]

The new covenant Paul announces, however, is not of "the letter," which is unable to produce obedience, but of the life-giving Spirit, who energizes from within.

CORINTHIAN *BĒMA*

The judgment seat in the forum at Corinth.

▼

Not of the letter but of the Spirit; for the letter kills, but the Spirit gives life (3:6). In Jewish thought, the connection between "spirit" and "life" was as ancient as Genesis itself (Gen. 1:2; 2:7; 6:17), and Jewish writers regularly linked "spirit" with "life" as the substance that animates humanity: " 'Spirit' is the most life-giving, and God is the author of life."[36] But the life Paul describes here is not biological, but ethical, spiritual life, and the roots of the idea go back to the prophet Ezekiel: "I will put my Spirit in you *and you will live*" (Ezek. 37:14). Moral renewal through the infusion of God's Spirit was the hope of the prophets and is the reality of the new covenant community.

The Transforming Glory of the New Covenant (3:7 – 18)

The letter/Spirit antithesis of 3:6 (see also Rom. 2:29; 7:6) requires elaboration. Thus, in 3:7 – 18 Paul reflects on the inadequacies of the old covenant in contrast to the transforming power of the new covenant.

The ministry that brought death . . . the ministry that condemns (3:7 – 9). Paul begins with a description of the Mosaic era that surely must have startled and angered his Jewish contemporaries. Far from a "ministry of death," Jews of the period thought of the Torah as an "eternal law," "made for the sake of righteousness to aid the quest for virtue and the perfecting of character."[37] A common prayer in the ancient synagogue, which Paul himself may have recited, blesses "the Torah of life."[38] It is no wonder that Paul's message encountered fierce opposition from his Jewish kinsmen, including those in Corinth (Acts 18:12 – 17).

For what was glorious has no glory now in comparison with the surpassing glory ... how much greater is the glory of that which lasts (3:10 – 11). Paul is careful to affirm that the Mosaic law did possess a kind of glory. When viewed from the perspective of its origin and purpose, Paul can describe the law as "holy, righteous and good" (Rom. 7:12). Yet when viewed from the standpoint of its efficacy, Paul calls it "the law of sin and death" (8:2). From his post-Damascus vantage point Paul now sees that the glory of the new covenant surpasses the glory of the old in the same way as the sun outshines a candle.

Once again, this is entirely at odds with the views of his fellow-Jews, who described the law as "an eternal light," "a lamp that will abide forever."[39] Paul is consciously rejecting the cherished Jewish notion of the abiding and perpetual glory of the law: "For we who have received the law and sinned will perish ... the Law, however, does not perish but remains in its glory."[40]

We are very bold ... not like Moses, who would put a veil over his face (3:12 – 13). Moses' practice of veiling himself (Ex. 34:29 – 35) is contrasted with Paul's candid, open proclamation, which Paul is seeking to defend in 2 Corinthians. The Greek word *parrēsia* (NIV, "very bold") is usually associated with speech and denotes frank and candid expression, especially in contrast to duplicitous flattery. The swelling ranks of disingenuous Sophists prompted a renewed concern for sincerity in word and deed, and *parrēsia* became a popular topic for discourses during this period of Roman history:

> But to find a man who in plain terms and without guile speaks his mind with *frankness* (*parrēsia*), and

neither for the sake of reputation nor for gain makes false pretensions, but out of good will and concern for his fellow-man stands ready, if need be, to submit to ridicule and to the disorder of the mob — to find such a man is not easy, but rather the good fortune of every great city, so great is the dearth of noble, independent souls and such is the abundance of toadies, mountebanks and sophists.[41]

Paul's spoken proclamation was heavily criticized in Corinth (1 Cor. 2:1 – 5; 10:10; 11:6; 13:3), and this verse echoes his introductory statement in 2:17: "We speak before God with sincerity."

For to this day the same veil remains when the old covenant is read (3:14 – 15). Paul coins the phrase "old covenant" in deliberate antithesis to the new covenant prophesied by Jeremiah (Jer. 31:33), inaugurated by Christ (Luke 22:20; 1 Cor. 11:25), and heralded by

Paul (2 Cor. 3:6). The context indicates that the apostle is thinking of the Mosaic law in particular, as verse 15 confirms, "Even to this day when Moses is read, a veil covers their hearts." The primary setting for the reading of the Jewish Scriptures was the local synagogue, and Philo provides an illuminating description of a first-century synagogue gathering:

> [When the Jewish community gathers in the synagogue] they sit according to their age in classes, the younger sitting under the elder, and listening with eager attention in becoming order. Then one, indeed, takes up the holy volume and reads it, and another of the men of greatest experience comes forward and explains what is not very intelligible, for a great many precepts are delivered in enigmatical modes of expression.[42]

Especially prominent in the synagogue was the reading of the law, as this inscription, dated to the first century and found in Jerusalem, illustrates: "Theodotus Vattanus, priest and synagogue leader . . . built this synagogue for the purpose of the reading of the Law and for instruction of the commandments of the Law."[43]

And we, who with unveiled faces all reflect the Lord's glory (3:18). The Greek term behind the NIV's "reflect" (*katoptrizō*) means literally "to gaze upon as in a mirror"; in this passage it denotes studied contemplation of a something — in this case God's glory. Mirrors in antiquity were made of polished metal and did not produce the kind of clear and vivid reflection of modern mirrors. More than a casual glance was needed for personal grooming, and Paul's words here seem carefully chosen to emphasize the believer's steady, transforming contemplation of the glory of the Lord.

▶

SEAT OF MOSES

Stone-carved seat from the Chorazim synagogue in lower Galilee.

right ▶

SYNAGOGUE OF THE HEBREWS INSCRIPTION

▶ Synagogue of the Hebrews

The presence of a Jewish community in Corinth is noted by Philo, and a synagogue is explicitly mentioned in Acts 18.[A-7] A broken inscription found in Corinth and dated to the third century A.D. reads, "Synagogue of the Hebrews." Another fragmentary inscription has been reconstructed to refer possibly to "The teacher and ruler of the synagogue of Corinth."[A-8] According to Acts 18:8, Crispus, the ruler of the synagogue in Corinth, was converted under Paul's ministry.

We are being transformed into his likeness with ever-increasing glory, which comes from the Lord, who is the Spirit (3:18). Paul describes two transformative events in his letters: a present, progressive, moral transformation (Rom. 12:1 – 2; 2 Cor. 3:18; 4:16 – 17), and an instantaneous, eschatological, physical transformation (Rom. 8:21 – 25; 1 Cor. 15:51 – 54; 2 Cor. 5:1 – 5; Phil. 3:20 – 22). Jewish writers of the period looked forward to a glorious transformation in the future, but true parallels to what Paul describes here are hard to find.[44] Paul's new covenant conviction that the life-giving Spirit was presently operative in the believing community led him to use language that would have sounded odd to many of his contemporaries. According to Paul, the renewing Spirit was, even now, restoring the divine image (NIV, "likeness"), marred by Adam's transgression (see comments on 4:4 – 6).

Glorious Treasure in Jars of Clay (4:1 – 18)

Continuing his discussion of the transforming power of the new covenant ministry of the Spirit, Paul reflects on the paradox of the Christian life: inner renewal in the midst of outer decay and life concealed in death.

We have renounced secret and shameful ways; we do not use deception (4:2). The accusation of trickery and deceit was commonly leveled against Sophists and certain philosophers; thus, Paul's words here may not reflect an accusation leveled against him by his detractors in Corinth. Paul is probably trying to distinguish himself and his colleagues from these other itinerant preachers, because on the surface they looked similar: traveling from city to city, speaking on moral themes, gathering a following, soliciting funds, and so on. Using the same terminology as Paul, Lucian (c. A.D. 120 – 180) describes this brand of philosophers as those who "sell their lessons as wine merchants . . . most of them adulterating and cheating and giving false measure."[45] Both Paul and Lucian use the word *doloō* (to "distort, adulterate, water down"), and the image evoked is of a crafty wine merchant selling a pathetic and diluted concoction.

The god of this age (4:4). Canonical and extracanonical literature reveals a wide variety of designations for Satan (devil, Mastema, Azael, Samael, prince of error, angel of light, etc.), though only here is the evil one referred to with the word "god" (Gk. *theos*). The contrast between

◀

ISIS

Terracota statue of Isis with Harpocrates and Anubis.

this present evil age and the age to come was rooted in the eschatology of the prophets, where phrases such as "in that [coming] day" are commonplace.[46] This antithesis became part of the eschatological idiom of Paul's day and was particularly popular in apocalyptic writings, where the present evil age of foreign domination was contrasted with the day when Israel would throw off the yoke of Gentile oppression and finally "be the head, and not the tail."[47]

Has blinded the minds of unbelievers (4:4). Paul's deep-seated conviction of the power of Satan and his cohorts is echoed throughout Jewish literature of the period, where prayers for protection are common:

- And Abram prayed, "Save me from the hands of evil spirits which rule over the thought of the heart of man."[48]

PAUL'S ANALYSIS OF THE HUMAN DILEMMA IS BOTH similar to and different from other Jewish thinkers of his day. Jewish literature of the period accounts for the presence of evil in three primary ways: Satan, the Gentiles, and the evil inclination (i.e., the flesh). Especially important was the influence of the demonic realm, and in the early apocalypses of *1 Enoch* and *Jubilees*, it is the evil angelic host that is held responsible for the entrance of sin, not Adam.

In contrast to these, Paul reserves his most poignant, gripping analysis of the human predicament for his discussion of *the flesh* (Rom. 6 – 8; Gal 5 – 6). In his view, it is the life-giving presence of the Spirit (Rom. 8; 2 Cor. 3) that enables believers to successfully resist both the temptations of the flesh and the enticement of the evil one. To be sure, Satan represents an ever-present threat to the believer (2 Cor. 1:11; 1 Thess. 1:18). Those outside of Christ, however, remain helpless pawns in the clutches of these dark powers, blinded by "the god of this age."

- Strengthen your servant against fiendish spirits so that he can walk in all that you love, and loathe all that you hate.[49]
- Let not Satan rule over me, nor an evil spirit.[50]

Yet while Paul was keenly aware of the spiritual battle, he was also confident of the believer's victory in Christ (Rom. 8:38 – 39; Col. 1:13), and it is this sober optimism that separates him from many of his contemporaries.

The light of the gospel of the glory of Christ, who is the image of God (4:4). In 3:18 Paul spoke of transformation into the "likeness" of the Lord; here he identifies Christ as the "image of God." This motif is rooted in Genesis, where Adam is said to have been created in God's image (Gen. 1:26 – 27). As 1 Corinthians 15:14 – 49 demonstrates, Paul thought of Christ as a kind of second Adam, rectifying the failure of the first.

Many of Paul's Jewish contemporaries longed for the eschatological restoration of Adam's prefall glory, and the scrolls from Qumran document this sect's intense expectation of inheriting "all the glory of Adam."[51] Paul, however, leaves no room for the veneration of Adam: "In Adam all die . . . in Christ all will be made alive" (1 Cor. 15:22; cf. Rom. 5:12 – 21). Christ has supplanted Adam in the apostle's eschatology. Paul does not look back to the garden, but ahead to Christ's return and the complete conformation of the believer to the image of Christ (Phil. 3:21).

For we do not preach ourselves, but Jesus Christ as Lord (4:5). Once again Paul is carefully distinguishing himself from many of the popular teachers of his day, whose pretentious oratory served mainly as an exercise in vanity. Dio Chrysostom

(c. A.D. 40 – 120), who also struggled to distance himself from the Sophists, voices the same complaint to the Athenians: "Now the great majority of those styled philosophers proclaim themselves."[52] According to Epictetus (c. A.D. 50 – 120), the Sophist implores his listeners, "But praise me! . . . Cry out to me 'Bravo!' or 'Marvelous!' "[53] Seneca (4 B.C.-A.D. 65) is equally scornful of those orators whose "ostentatious gate" and "desire to show off" rendered their trivial discourses useless for the common good: "But speech that deals with the truth should be unadorned and plain. This popular style has nothing to do with the truth; its aim is to impress the common herd."[54]

Your servants for Jesus' sake (4:5). Paul refers to himself in a variety of ways in 2 Corinthians (apostle, minister/servant, ambassador, coworker with God); the term he uses here, *doulos*, is better

translated "slave" than "servant." While the duties of Roman slaves ranged from farm laborer to physician, the slave was regarded as the lowest order of the social class, "a tool that speaks" (*instrumentum vocale*), with none of the rights of citizens or freedmen. Paul's willingness to wear this label, even metaphorically, is illustrative of his indifference to such distinctions of social rank (1 Cor. 7:20 – 24; Gal. 3:28) and his readiness to spend and expend himself (2 Cor. 12:15) on behalf of his churches. The qualifying phrase "for Jesus' sake" delimits the sphere of Paul's servitude.

For God . . . made his light shine in our hearts to give us the light of the knowledge of the glory of God in the face of Christ (4:6). Most New Testament scholars rightly believe that Paul's description of a shining light that revealed the glory of God on the face of Christ betrays the apostle's vivid memory of his encounter with the risen Christ on the road to Damascus. In reflecting on his own conversion and applying it to believers generally, Paul strips his story of its nonparadigmatic elements (external light, a voice from heaven, blindness; see Acts 9:3 – 6; 22:6 – 18) in order to highlight its most crucial feature: "God . . . made his light shine *in our hearts*." Although the external phenomena associated with Paul's conversion were indeed striking, he presents the significance of this momentous revelation not in terms of what happened *around* him, but in terms of what happened *within* him, which constitutes the true miracle of authentic conversion.

Treasure in jars of clay (4:7). Jars and other kinds of containers were manufactured from a wide variety of materials,

◀ *left*

EMPEROR HADRIAN

This emperor, who reigned A.D. 117 – 138, was often acclaimed to be a "god."

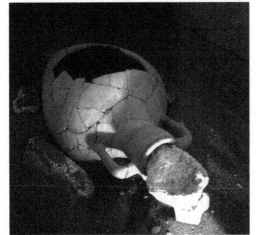

▶ "WE HAVE THIS TREASURE IN JARS OF CLAY..."

though clay was by far the most common. Archaeological digs at ancient sites, including Corinth, unearth vast amounts of pottery fragments, providing a contemporary illustration of Paul's point: the fragile, ephemeral character of earthenware contrasts sharply with the eternal nature of the treasure within. Also implicit in this word picture is the irony of an inestimable fortune concealed in a common clay jar. Corinth had a widespread reputation for the production of exquisite bronze vessels,[55] and this metaphor may have had a

▶ Jesus Christ as Lord: Paul's Counter-Imperial Gospel

"Why, what harm is there in saying 'Caesar is Lord,' and offering incense, and thereby saving yourself?"[A-9] This question, addressed to the aged bishop Polycarp by the local magistrates in Smyrna (c. A.D. 155), is a question that many believers faced during the first three hundred years of the Christian movement. The followers of Jesus proclaimed him as Lord, Savior, and Son of God, yet each of these titles was also claimed by another sovereign, the Roman emperor.

Emperor worship began in earnest sometime after the posthumous deification of Julius Caesar (42 B.C.), and by the middle of the first century the imperial cult was firmly established in Rome and the provinces. By the late A.D. 80s the emperor Domitian was demanding to be addressed as *dominus et deus*, "Lord and God."[A-10]

The veneration of the emperor and the imperial family was not undertaken solely for religious purposes. Significant economic and political benefits accrued to a city with a strong imperial cult, which left municipalities and the upwardly mobile citizenry competing to display their devotion to Caesar.[A-11] Corinth itself had a vibrant imperial cult, with an impressive temple above the forum and an active priesthood.[A-12] Statues of the emperors were scattered throughout the city, as were portraits and honorific inscriptions. All manner of deific titles are found on these dedications, and the following may be regarded as typical:

The Achaeans erected this monument in honor of the Emperor Caesar Trajan Hadrian Augustus, son of the deified Trajan Parthicus, grandson of the deified Nerva Pontifex Maximus, holder of the tribune power for the eighth time, Consul for the third time, Restorer and Savior and Benefactor of Greece.[A-13]

The epigraphic evidence indicates that the imperial cult was particularly popular with the upper class in Corinth,[A-14] which is not surprising considering the enormous debt the aristocracy owed Julius Caesar for establishing, populating, and supporting the colony. Although Paul instructed his churches to respect Roman authority (Rom. 13:1 – 7), his message of the impending epiphany from heaven of the Lord Jesus was ultimately deemed politically subversive.

By the first decade of the second century, Christians were routinely executed for failing to pay homage to the Roman gods and the Roman emperor.[A-15] As for Polycarp, after repeatedly being urged to "revile Christ," he finally replied to his inquisitors: "For eighty-six years I have been his servant and he has done me no wrong. How can I blaspheme my King who saved me?" He was subsequently burned at the stake.[A-16]

special poignancy for the proud makers of famed Corinthian bronze.

We are hard pressed on every side, but not crushed; perplexed, but not in despair; persecuted, but not abandoned; struck down, but not destroyed (4:8 – 9). In Paul's day this style of argumentation was in vogue among the Stoics and Cynics, and the Corinthians would have certainly recognized this antithetical formulation. Plutarch's essays on Stoicism contain the following caricature of the Stoic, who, "being mutilated, is not injured, and taking a fall in wrestling, is unconquerable, and under siege, is impregnable, and being sold into slavery by his enemies, is not taken captive."[56] In each instance, the anticipated negative outcome is unexpectedly truncated, and the intent is to create empathy and respect for the one undergoing such trials. Although similar in form, the presuppositions behind Paul's hardship catalogs are very different from those of the Stoics and Cynics, as 6:3 – 10 and 11:23 – 33 will reveal.

We always carry around in our body the death of Jesus. . . . For we who are alive are always being given over to death for Jesus' sake, so that his life may be revealed in our mortal body (4:10 – 11). In other contexts, Paul forcefully emphasizes the past, completed nature of the believer's death with Christ (Rom. 6:1 – 11), though here he depicts this event as one that continues to characterize his daily experience. A passage with verbal similarities to 4:10 – 11 comes from Seneca's "On Despising Death":

> I remember one day you [Lucilius] were handling the well known commonplace — that we do not suddenly fall on death, but advance towards it by slight degrees; *we die every day*. For every day a little of our life is taken from us; even when we are growing, our life is on the wane. We lose our childhood, then our boyhood, and then our youth . . . the final hour when we cease to exist does not of itself bring death; it merely of itself completes the death-process. We reach death at that moment, but we have been a long time on the way.[57]

Seneca refers to the "commonplace" notion that death is a daily experience of life. Paul, however, far from viewing his temporal pilgrimage and sacrificial ministry as the gradual ebbing of life, believed his apostolic suffering to be the means of experiencing and mediating true life — the life of the risen Jesus — in fullest form. For Paul, dying not only *initiates* the believer's new life (Rom. 6:1 – 11), it also *sustains* the believer's new life and has a redemptive effect on the believing community: "So then, death is at work in us, but life is at work in you" (4:12).

It is written: "I believed; therefore I have spoken." . . . We also believe and therefore speak (4:13). In this verse Paul offers a profound theological rationale for his spoken proclamation, which was under attack in Corinth (cf. 10:10; 12:19; 13:3). While placing himself in continuity with his Old Testament predecessors, Paul explains that his speech issues from the same Spirit that inspired the psalmist and is rooted in faith. Introduced in 2:17 ("we speak in Christ"), this theme will be taken up in 5:11 ("We persuade people").

Though outwardly we are wasting away, yet inwardly we are being renewed day by day (4:16). The distinction between the "outer person" and the "inner person" (NIV, "outwardly," "inwardly") was commonly made in Greco-Roman literature, especially as a means of disparaging humanity's physical component (see comments on 5:1 – 5). Marcus Aurelius (A.D. 121 – 180), for example, describes the body as "this dead thing" and exhorts his readers, "Remember that this which pulls the strings is the thing which is hidden within . . . this is life, this, if one may so say, is man."[58] While affirming the priority of the inner over the outer (4:16 – 17) and the eternal over the transitory (4:17), Paul offers no denigration of the decaying physical body. By means of this familiar language, Paul begins the process of reshaping his readers' anthropology, which will be continued in the verses that follow.

Our Eternal Dwelling (5:1 – 10)

Paul's confidence in an unseen eternal reality (4:18) leads him to elaborate on the transitory nature of our present earthly condition and the certainty of a transformed physical existence that will come (5:1 – 5). The apostle's assurances of a future, bodily, immortal existence inspire perseverance and good works (5:6 – 10), but are at odds with much of the popular eschatology of the period.

Earthly tent . . . eternal house (5:1 – 4). Paul depicts the temporary status of our present bodily condition through the imagery of a tent. Tents were commonly used by soldiers, herdsmen, and other nomadic tradesmen camping in the open field, but also by attendees at religious feasts and athletic games. As the host of the pan-Hellenic Isthmian games, the environs of Corinth swelled with these temporary dwellings every

two years, and the image in verse 1 of a tent suddenly collapsing (Gk. *katalyō*) would have been familiar to the Corinthians. Equally appropriate is the contrast with a permanent edifice, "a building from God . . . an eternal house" (vv. 1 – 2). The impressive stone structures of Roman Corinth, some of which are still visible, served as an imposing and daily reminder to the Corinthians of the incorruptible nature of the eternal state, when "mortality is swallowed up by life" (v. 4). Paul's confident present tense in verse 1, "*we have* a building from God," is not intended to indicate the *immediacy* of the new physical state upon death, but its *certainty* (see vv. 6 – 8).

Longing to be clothed with our heavenly dwelling (5:2). A more precise rendering of this verse might be, "longing to put on our heavenly dwelling as an overgarment." The Greek word Paul uses (*ependysasthai*) indicates a type of clothing that is put on *in addition to* something already being worn. Clothing styles varied only slightly in the Mediterranean basin in the period, consisting of outer garments and inner garments.[59] The outer garments were draped over or wrapped around the inner garment, and it is this layered manner of attire that Paul envisions. The apostle indicates his desire to survive until the second coming of Christ and so to put on his heavenly garment *over* his earthly garment, his physical body.

When we are clothed, we will not be found naked (5:3). Nakedness was more distasteful to Jews than to Gentiles, for both theological and historical reasons. Theologically, it was associated with Adam's transgression and the shame that followed (Gen. 3:7). Historically, Jews of the period viewed nakedness as one of the defining features of Hellenistic culture, and the construction of a gymnasium in Jerusalem — where Jewish men exercised naked like their Greek counterparts — prompted a violent reaction from Jews of the Maccabean era (1 Macc. 1:10 – 14; 2 Macc. 4:7 – 20). The (Jewish) author of the book of *Jubilees*, writing around 140 B.C., concludes from the judgment imposed on Adam and Eve in the Garden of Eden: "Therefore it is commanded in the heavenly tablets to all who know the Law that they should cover their shame and not go about naked as do the Gentiles" (*Jub.* 1:31).

Paul, in contrast to the popular dualism of Greek thinking (see "The After-Life"), feels a strong aversion to the separation of the material and immaterial components of personhood, and thus he chooses a word with a negative connotation to describe this condition, "naked." Yet the full force of his point would not have been felt by many of his readers in Corinth, who probably did not share his Jewish scruples on this subject. Nude figures graced the pottery, sculptures, artwork, and coinage of Roman Corinth, and nakedness per se was not considered objectionable. The public baths, the gymnasiums (from the Gk. word *gymnos*, "naked"), and the athletic events were important features of everyday life in Corinth, and in all these venues nudity was taken for granted.

In this tent, we groan and are burdened (5:4). Greek writers often described the body as a prison or tomb of the soul, which would be finally discarded upon death. Popular Greek philosophy viewed the physical component of human existence with contempt, believing it to be a lower nature, capable of only base desires and instincts. Although writing later than Paul, Plotinus perfectly summarizes this significant strand of Greek thought: "The body is brute beast touched to life. The true man is the other . . . the Soul which even in its dwelling here may be kept apart."[60]

In contrast to his pagan contemporaries, Paul's view of humanity is rooted in Genesis and affirms the goodness of the material creation, including humanity's

THE TABERNACLE

This is a model of the "tent" where the people of Israel worshiped God in their desert wanderings.

physical component. Paul's "groaning" is not for release from the shackles of bodily existence, but for the transformed physical state that will occur at Christ's second coming (Phil. 3:20 – 21) or the resurrection (1 Cor. 15:35 – 49). As Paul's encounter with the council of the Areopagus illustrates (Acts 17:16 – 34), this was not an easy proposition for the philosophically trained Greek mind to accept.

The Spirit as a deposit (5:5). See comments on 1:22.

Away from the body and at home with the Lord (5:8 – 9). Although Paul prefers to bypass the intermediate "naked" state, when the soul and/or spirit is temporarily separated from the body, he comforts himself with the knowledge that during this period he will be "at home" with the Lord. Paul chooses two picturesque words to describe this dilemma, both drawn from the vocabulary of the traveler. The Greek word *ekdēmeō* (NIV "away from") was used of a person who journeyed abroad, be it voluntarily or even in exile. In view of civic duties, the conscientious citizen might notify the proper authorities of an impending journey: "If we change our residence, or go abroad [*ekdēmeō*], we shall give notice."[61]

Its antonym, *endēmeō* (NIV, "at home"), describes someone living in his or her homeland, among friends and family. At this point in his missionary career, Paul has traversed innumerable miles of Roman roads, endured harrowing shipwrecks, spent countless months in foreign lands, and even experienced rejection from his own people (Gal. 5:11; 1 Thess. 2:14 – 16). It is no surprise that he should come to see the Christian life as a journey toward a home as yet unseen: "for we walk by faith, not by sight" (2 Cor. 5:7).

The judgment seat of Christ (5:10). Of Corinth's many impressive structures,

GRECO-ROMAN ATTIRE

Terracotta fiture of a woman wearing a *chitōn* (tunic) and *himation* (cloak).

right ▶

GREEK ATHLETE

Statue of an athlete stooping to throw the discus.

its *bēma* (NIV, "judgment seat") was certainly one of the finest. Located in the center of the large marketplace, Corinth's *bēma* was modeled after the *bēma* built by Caesar Augustus in Rome and was originally covered in marble with elaborately carved molding.[62] The *bēma* had two primary functions in the civic life of Corinth: It served as the seat for judicial pronouncements and, more commonly, as the platform for public oration.

During his initial ministry in Corinth, Paul was forced to stand before the Roman Governor Gallio seated on the *bēma* and face accusations from his fellow Jews (Acts 18:12 – 17). No doubt both Paul and the Corinthians had vivid memories of this event, and it may be that Paul is purposefully drawing on this shared recollection. Paul's concern, however, is with the *bēma* of Christ, not that of Gallio. In employing this image, the apostle invests this important municipal structure with a new significance, making it an object lesson for the judgment to come. The thoughtful Corinthian believer would probably be reminded of these words on his or her next visit to the marketplace.

Paul's Ministry of Reconciliation (5:11 – 6:2)

In 5:11 – 21 Paul offers a summary of his message and ministry, and the pivotal word in this ten-verse synopsis is "reconciliation" (vv. 18 – 20). Paul relates *his motives*, which include both fear (v. 11) and love (v. 14), and also explains *the results* of his ministry: inwardly transformed people ("a new creation," v. 17)

▶ The After-Life

The average citizen of first-century Corinth was familiar with a wide variety of views concerning the after-life. The popular Homeric legends spoke of the dreary underworld of Hades, to which all mortals are destined (*Odyssey* 11). Plato reasoned that the soul of the noble philosopher would survive death and attain perfect knowledge (*Phaedo*). Epicureans and Stoics were skeptical about *any* post-mortem existence (Epicurus, *Principal Doctrines;* Marcus Aurelius, *Meditations*), while the mystery religions (like the Isis cult in nearby Isthmia) promised their initiates a blissful celestial immortality.

One of the more common inscriptions on grave markers in this period is the epitaph: "I was not, I was, I am not, I care not." Funerary reliefs and artifacts also reveal the primitive but enduring notion that the spirit of the deceased lived on in the tomb. In defense of his plans for an elaborate funerary monument, one wealthy Roman reasons, "It is quite wrong for a man to decorate his house while he is alive, and not to trouble about the house where he must make a longer stay."[A-17]

With no clear conception of the after-life, it is no wonder that Paul could refer to unbelievers in Thessalonica as "those who have no hope" (1 Thess. 4:13). While vastly different, these pagan belief systems were united in their rejection of a bodily resurrection. But neither was first-century Judaism in complete agreement on this issue (Matt. 22; Acts 23). Some Jewish thinkers of the period, influenced by Hellenistic ideas, affirmed the immortality of the soul apart from any physical resurrection.[A-18] Others, including Jesus, Paul, and the Pharisees, vigorously defended the notion of a bodily resurrection.[A-19] Amidst this cacophony of voices, Paul's clear instructions to the Corinthians on the resurrection (1 Cor. 15) and the intermediate state (2 Cor. 5:1 – 10) provided hope for the discouraged ("Take courage!," 2 Cor. 5:6) and motivation for all toward godly living: "for we must all appear before the judgment seat of Christ" (v. 10).

▶

**GALLIO
INSCRIPTION**

The text mentions
Gallio, the Roman
governor of Achaia,
before whom Paul
stood at the
Corinthian *bēma*.

with a new orientation ("no longer living
for ourselves," vv. 15 – 16). *The basis* of
Paul's new covenant ministry of reconciliation is expressed in terms of the cen-
tripetal event of human history: the death
and resurrection of Christ (vv. 15, 21).

We try to persuade [people] (5:11). The
art of "persuasion" was deeply rooted in
Greek society, and the Greek term *peithō*
(NIV, "persuade") enjoyed a cultural and
literary heritage in the Greco-Roman
world that few other words can rival.[63] So
important was *persuasion* to the Greeks
that she was deified as a goddess and
worshiped. Writing around A.D. 175,
Pausanius describes the "Sanctuary of
Persuasion" located in the center of the
marketplace in Corinth.[64] The Roman
orator Cicero (106 – 43 BC) articulates
the ideal to which so many aspired:

> I mean the kind of eloquence
> which rushes along with the roar of
> a mighty stream, which all look up to
> and admire, and which they despair of
> attaining. This eloquence has power to
> sway men's minds and move them in
> every possible way. Now it storms the
> feelings, now it creeps in; it implants
> new ideas and uproots the old.[65]

Especially prominent in the first and
second centuries were the Sophists,
whose persuasive oratory dazzled the
crowds while lining their own pockets.
Not only was Corinth familiar with this
class of high-powered rhetoricians, they
also erected statues to their favorite
Sophists and became the beneficiaries
of public buildings from the wealthier
practitioners of the art. Although some
scholars have wondered about the connection between verses 10 and 11, from
the perspective of the Corinthians the
link between the *bēma* and Paul's "persuasion" would have seemed natural. In a
speech in Tarsus, the philosopher-Soph-
ist Dio Chrysostom (A.D. 40 – 120)
asked his audience why they wanted so
much to hear "sweet-voiced songbirds"
like himself, and concluded:

> Do you believe that we possess a
> different power in word and thought
> alike, a power of *persuasion* [*peithō*]
> that is keener and truly formidable,
> which you call rhetoric, a power that
> holds sway both in the market place
> and on the *bēma*?[66]

Compared to the crowd-pleasers the
Corinthians are so accustomed to, Paul
receives poor marks: "For some [of you]
say, 'His letters are forceful . . . but his
speaking amounts to nothing' " (10:10;
cf. 11:6; 12:19; 13:3). Paul has already
defended his unadorned style in a previous letter to the Corinthians, where
he explains that he did not come with
"eloquence" or "persuasive words" lest
their faith rest on mere human ingenuity
(1 Cor. 2:1 – 5). As we will see, however,
he does not succeed in silencing his critics.

An opportunity to take pride in us (5:12).
Seen in the context of Paul's continuing
dialogue with the Corinthians over his

unimpressive public speaking,[67] his concern to give them a reason to be proud of him is easily understood. In the typical Greco-Roman city, the local Sophist was an object of civic pride, as were buildings, coinage, canals, and other municipal achievements. Not unlike professional sports today, vicious rivalries sometimes developed between cities over whose representative was superior, as illustrated by the famous dispute between Polemo, hero of Smyrna, and Favorinius, spokesman for Ephesus.[68] Philostratus, the historian of the sophistic movement, goes to great lengths to recount the various exploits and entrepreneurial acts of the Sophists, all in service of one essential point: "For not only does a city give a man renown, but the city itself gains it from the man."[69]

Those who take pride in what is seen rather than in what is in the heart (5:12). A more exact translation of this phrase is "those who boast in externals." Again, it is the arrogant, self-commending Sophists Paul has in mind. Boasting, in fact, was a prime characteristic of the Sophists, and in a rare moment of unpartisan candor, Philostratus labels the entire Sophistic vocation "a profession prone to egotism and arrogance."[70] Particularly relevant is the speech of self-commendation that the Sophist Favorinus (A.D. 80 – 150) delivered in Corinth after he discovered that a statue the Corinthians had erected in honor of his eloquence had been removed. Given his superior lineage, athletic prowess, wisdom, and eloquence, Favorinus concludes, "Ought [I] not have a bronze statue here in Corinth? Yes! And in every city!"[71]

If we are out of our mind (5:13). The way Paul has constructed this sentence (in Greek) indicates he is responding to an accusation, and scholars have long puzzled over what activity could possibly warrant the charge that Paul has been "out of his mind." Is it his untiring zeal (2 Cor. 6:3 – 10)? His ecstatic experiences (1 Cor. 14:18; 2 Cor. 12:1 – 10)? His alleged fondness for self-commendation (2 Cor. 3:1; 5:12)? In all likelihood Paul's terminology reflects the language of his detractors in Corinth, those whose rhetorical sensitivities are easily offended.[72]

Indeed, Paul's unusual word for being out of his mind (*existēmi*) is found in popular rhetorical handbooks to describe an orator who fails to persuade because of his unpolished delivery.[73] Paul knows, as the Corinthians do not, that when form dominates over content, the result is misplaced faith. Thus, he is determined not to pattern his ministry after the self-serving style of the Sophists. Yet his straightforward, no-frills oratory does not sit well with some in Corinth and has become a running joke among this group (2 Cor. 10:10).

New creation (5:17). Although Paul introduces the phrase "new creation" into Christian vocabulary in his letter to the Galatians (Gal. 6:15), it was already current in the Judaism of his day. The apocalyptic visionaries spoke of a "new creation" in which Gentile oppression would end and Israel herself would finally be vindicated over the nations.[74] Somewhat later, the rabbis became fond of referring to a convert to Judaism as "a new creature," and this language probably had first-century antecedents.[75] Particularly illuminating, and contemporary with Paul, is the imagery found in *Joseph and Aseneth*, a Hellenistic romance of Diaspora Judaism. In this fictitious work, the patriarch Joseph prays for the conversion of Aseneth, a pagan priestess who had fallen hopelessly in love with him, and whom he later marries (cf. Gen. 41:45):

You, O Lord, bless this virgin,
make her new through your Spirit
re-create her by your hidden hand
give her new life through your life . . .
and number her with your people.[76]

Given the emphasis in 2 Corinthians 3 – 5 on *the Spirit*, *newness*, and *life*, this text offers an illuminating parallel to 2 Corinthians 5:17. Depicting conversion as a dramatic *new creation* underscores a complete and irrevocable break with the past, and so is an ideal expression to apply to converts from a pagan environment like Corinth. Paul's point is to remind the Corinthians who they are in Christ: a renewed humanity, already being transformed into the image of Christ through the Spirit (3:17 – 18).

The ministry of reconciliation (5:18 – 19). What Paul earlier refers to as the "ministry of the Spirit" (3:8) and the "ministry of righteousness" (3:9), he calls here "the ministry of reconciliation." The word group *katallagē* (NIV, "reconciliation") is drawn from the Greco-Roman political arena, where it referred to removal of enmity between two aggrieved parties.[77] Diplomatic envoys ("ambassadors," see below) between warring nations or communities in conflict hoped to achieve reconciliation and so gain a reputation for successful arbitration.

After a crushing defeat by the Romans, the first-century B.C. historian Dionysius of Halicarnassus records how the Sabines "sent ambassadors to the consul to sue for peace . . . and with difficulty obtained a reconciliation."[78] The reconciliation Paul describes, however, is initiated and accomplished by only one party, God, who has appointed his apostles (and ultimately all believers) as his emissaries in the task of reconciliation.

Christ's ambassadors (5:20). Continuing the imagery of Greco-Roman diplomacy, Paul explains that he and his coworkers are Christ's "ambassadors, as though God were making his appeal through us." The task of ambassador in Roman society fell, naturally, to the educated and eloquent, the *literati* who could best represent the interests of the polis. By the first and second century A.D. these prestigious assignments had become so monopolized by Sophists that historians today regularly identify this movement of Paul's day with ambassadorial service.

According to Philostratus, the crowning achievement of a Sophist's career

REFLECTIONS

IN THE LAST TWO CHAPTERS WE HAVE SEEN PAUL using common imagery in the Greco-Roman world ("inner man/outer man," "reconciliation," "ambassadorial service"), in order to more effectively communicate the gospel in this context. Each of these themes could have been articulated using Jewish categories and symbols, yet Paul purposefully chooses concepts familiar to the Corinthians so that the good news of Christ may take root more easily in the Greek soil of the Peloponnese. While the substance of the gospel remains unchanged, Paul's shrewd use of culturally appropriate symbolism gives his message an indigenous quality crucial for it to truly flourish.

Theologians and missiologists call this "contextualization," and it is just as important today as it was in the first century. The message of God's love and saving work in Christ is for all humanity, and it is our task as "ambassadors for Christ" to translate this message into culturally sensitive forms, without allowing the content of the message to be shaped by the culture. This translation is important not only for our neighbors across the globe, but also for our neighbors across the street.

was to be chosen as an ambassador, especially in making a petition to the emperor. The ancient historian recounts famous embassies by Sophists to Domitian (81 – 96 A.D.), Trajan (98 – 117), and Hadrian (117 – 138),[79] revealing the influence and power of these individuals in Greco-Roman society. According to Favorinus, Corinth's strategic position as "the promenade of Hellas" meant that "every year crowds of travelers, pilgrims, merchants, and *ambassadors*" passed through its gates.[80]

Heard within this context — as it would have been in Corinth — the polemical edge to Paul's argument is considerably sharpened. Unlike so many who aspired to represent the Corinthian community as its spokesman before the emperor, Paul turns this venerated tradition upside down and claims to represent the Great Emperor to the Corinthians — "as if God himself were making his appeal through us" (5:20). Indeed, in appropriating the terminology of Greek diplomacy and employing it as a vehicle for the Gospel, we see Paul the missionary at his finest.

Paul's Hardships (6:3 – 13)

Having summarized the *nature* of his message and ministry (5:10 – 6:2), Paul now focuses on the *character* of the minister. By means of the familiar hardship catalog, he demonstrates his altruistic motives and self-sacrificing labor.

As servants of God we commend ourselves in every way: in great endurance; in troubles, hardships and distresses (6:4). In 4:8 – 9, 6:3 – 10, and 11:23 – 33 Paul presents the Corinthians with his apostolic credentials, a partial list of hardships he has endured on their behalf. These "hardship catalogs," as they are called, were part of the standard repertoire of Stoic and Cynic instruction and served to demonstrate the moral character of the teacher. Through these inventories of adversity the teacher sought to

CORINTH

The Lechaeon Road leading into the Roman city with the Acrocorinth in the background.

exemplify three primary virtues: fortitude, self-sufficiency, and indifference to external circumstances.

In using this form of argument Paul also offers himself as a model to emulate, but he qualifies these virtues in significant ways. Fortitude and strength, perhaps; but more important, weakness (11:30; 12:10). Dependence on self? Absolutely not! Rather, dependence on God (6:6 – 7; 12:9). Unaffected by circumstances? Not really. While patiently enduring pain, Paul is not ashamed to admit profound emotion (1:8 – 9; 6:9; 11:28). Most of the following hardships are repeated in 11:23 – 33, and the details of each ordeal will be discussed there. At the present we will focus on comparing the perspective of Paul's hardship catalogs with some of his Greco-Roman contemporaries.

In beatings, imprisonments and riots; in hard work, sleepless nights and hunger (6:5). "Hardships . . . put virtue to the test" and successfully enduring hazardous trials demonstrated the philosopher's strength and superiority.[81] According to the *Epitome of Stoic Ethics* compiled by Arius Didymus (first century B.C.), the noble Stoic is "great, powerful, eminent and strong . . . because he has possession of the strength which befalls such a man, being invincible and unconquerable" (11g). In language similar to Paul, Epictetus refers to "exile and imprisonment, and bonds and death and disrepute" as matters of no concern.[82]

Like the Stoics, Paul believes physical hardships are of some value (1 Cor. 9:27; 1 Tim. 4:8), though his concern is not to parade Stoic bravado and claim "invincibility." Rather, he needs to make the Corinthians aware — especially those who question his leadership — of his tireless labor on their behalf. Contrary to the Stoic emphasis on invulnerable strength, Paul focuses his attention on his weakness (see comments on 12:10).

In purity, understanding, patience and kindness; in the Holy Spirit and in sincere love; in truthful speech and in the power of God (6:6 – 7a). The ideal sage, according to popular Stoic (and Cynic) representation, is one who relies solely on his own inner resources to face the deprivations and calamities that fortune supplies. According to Stoic doctrine, "he makes the whole matter [of happiness] depend upon himself" and is enjoined by God, "If you wish any good thing, get it from yourself."[83] Paul, by contrast, is adamant that his strength rests in "the Holy Spirit . . . and in the power of God" (cf. 3:1 – 6; 12:9 – 10); this is the most fundamental difference between the valiant Stoic and the follower of Christ.

With weapons of righteousness in the right hand and in the left (6:7b). Military imagery occurs frequently in Paul's letters, and the description here is of a well-equipped Roman legionary.[84] The offensive weapon in the right hand is either a medium-length javelin (infantrymen carried two) or a short thrusting

sword, while the left hand holds the defensive weapon, a sturdy shield. Roman field tactics called for both javelins to be discharged from a short distance, whereupon the soldier rushed upon the wounded enemy to finish him off with a quick thrust of his sword.

Through glory and dishonor, bad report and good report; genuine, yet regarded as impostors; known, yet regarded as unknown; dying, and yet we live on; beaten, and yet not killed (6:8 – 9). In the ancient Mediterranean world, honor and shame were core values, and within the highly stratified social structure of Roman society a great deal of daily energy was expended avoiding shame and accumulating honor. As a group value, honor was gained through public recognition (formally or informally) of personal worth. In expressing his indifference to public opinion, Paul dons the mantle of the suffering sage willing to endure contempt for the good of the community. Such a role was actually honored in Mediterranean society, and contemporary philosophers often adopted this posture:

- Hunger, exile, loss of reputation, and the like have no terrors for [the noble sage]; nay he holds them as mere trifles.[85]
- These are examples of indifferent things: life, death, reputation, lack of reputation, toil, pleasure, riches, poverty, sickness, health.[86]

Sorrowful, yet always rejoicing; poor, yet making many rich; having nothing, and yet possessing everything (6:10). Once again, Paul's argument reflects both continuity and discontinuity with his Greco-Roman contemporaries. Unlike the Stoic, who strove to "view with unconcern

pains and losses, sores and wounds . . . wholly unchanged amid the diversities of fortune," Paul freely admits his sorrow (cf. 1:8 – 9; 7:5; 11:28 – 29).[87] The display of emotion during hardship was considered an indication of moral weakness, hence Epictetus extols the man "who though sick is happy, though in danger is happy, though dying is happy, though condemned to exile is happy, though in disrepute, is happy."[88] Yet Paul does advocate contentment in all circumstances (Phil. 4:11 – 13), and the final words of 2 Corinthians 2:10, "having nothing, and yet possessing all things" echo an important Stoic principle:

Alone and old, and seeing the enemy in possession of everything around me, I, nevertheless, declare that all my holdings are intact and unharmed. I still possess them; whatever I have had as my own, I have. . . . So far as my [true] possessions are concerned, they are with me, and ever will be with me.[89]

The Temple of God and the Temple of Idols (6:14 – 7:1)

The plea of 6:1 not to receive God's grace in vain is now given concrete expression in a prohibition against nurturing harmful relationships with unbelievers. Paul treated this topic in 1 Corinthians 8; 10:14 – 22, but apparently his advice was treated too lightly.

Do not be yoked together with unbelievers (6:14). The scene evoked by Paul's words is less obvious to those living in industrialized Western societies, where a team of oxen plowing a field is an unimaginable sight. The term *heterozygeō*, to yoke differently, refers to placing two animals of different species under the same yoke (e.g., an ox and a donkey). The obvious difference in strength, height, and disposition could lead to disastrous consequences. Although one *application* of this verse relates to believers marrying unbelievers, Paul's purview is much broader and includes all manner of spiritually detrimental social intercourse, especially pertaining to the practice of frequenting pagan temples (see below).

What harmony is there between Christ and Belial? . . . between the temple of God and idols? . . . Dear friends, let us purify ourselves from everything that contaminates body and spirit (6:15 – 7:1). In 1 Corinthians 8:1 – 13 and 10:14 – 30, Paul dealt extensively with problems relating to dining in pagan temples and eating meat sacrificed to idols. These activities were not simply a function of pagan religiosity from which the new believer could easily abstain. Rather, they were an integral part of the social fabric of Roman society and were often associated with the fulfillment of civic responsibilities. Since only the well-to-do had homes large enough for a formal dining room, the abundant temples of Corinth

▶

THE TEMPLE OF GOD AND THE TEMPLE OF AN IDOL

(right) The Apollo temple in Corinth.

(bottom right) A model of the Jerusalem temple.

R E F L E C T I O N S

FOR JEWS OF PAUL'S DAY, THE TEMPLE IN JERUSALEM was a symbol of God's favor, of his choice of Israel, and a visual reminder of God's presence with his people. In line with the perspective of the prophets (Jer. 7, Mic. 3:9 – 12), Jesus (John 4:20 – 24), and other New Testament writers (Heb. 8:1 – 6; 1 Peter 2:4 – 10), Paul undermines the significance of this physical structure by claiming that the Christian community now constitutes the true dwelling place of God: "We are the temple of the living God" (2 Cor. 6:16). As with the temple of old, the sacredness of the Christian assembly issues from the presence of the Holy One — a continual testimony of God's amazing grace.

provided facilities for entertaining dinner parties. The related fees were naturally used for the support of the temple and cult. Numerous invitations to these ancient cocktail parties survive:

> Herais asks you to dine in the (dining-)room of the Serapeion at a banquet of the Lord Serapis tomorrow, the 11th from the 9th hour.[90]

Drunkenness, gluttony, and sexual promiscuity were part and parcel of such affairs, and against this backdrop Paul's harsh warning against the "contamination of body and spirit" (7:1) becomes more comprehensible.[91] Also understandable is Paul's insistence that Christ and Belial (Satan) cannot consort. Not only were offerings and toasts made to the god, but the deity was believed to be present at the meal and sometimes even sent the invitation: "The god calls you to a banquet being held in the Thoereion tomorrow from the 9th hour."[92] Given Paul's conviction that the worship of pagan deities is actually the worship of demons (1 Cor. 10:20 – 22), no participation in such rituals could be tolerated. But in a culture where religion and the social order walked hand in hand, such separation was a delicate and dangerous task. It is not surprising that Christians were later charged with misanthropy, antisocial behavior.[93]

Paul's Joyful Reunion with Titus (7:2 – 16)

Paul now returns to the thought he left dangling in 2:13 and expresses his great joy at the good news Titus brought him in Macedonia of the Corinthians' reaffirmation of their affection for Paul and their commitment to his leadership. The momentum of this positive memory carries Paul into chapters 8 and 9 and helps prepare the ground for his appeal concerning the collection.

◀ *left*

SERAPIS

▶ The Asclepion of Corinth

Dedicated to Asclepius, the god of healing, the Asclepion of Corinth was the ancient equivalent of the modern hospital. Here the ailing person offered a sacrifice and waited for a vision from the deity prescribing a cure. The remains of the temple of Aclepius in Corinth reveal spacious courtyards, baths, fountains, kitchens, and dining rooms. The dining facilities were used for both religious and social functions. Within the main sanctuary stood the cult statues of Asclepius and Hygieia (goddess of health), along with a table for offerings. Located at the entrance of the temple was a stone collection box, in which archaeologists have discovered thirteen copper coins. Also unearthed from the Asclepion was a vast collection of terra-cotta ex-votos, representing bodily parts in need of healing: hands, ears, feet, breasts, and so on.[A-20]

Make room for us in your hearts . . . you have such a place in our hearts that we would live or die with you (7:2 – 3). Paul does not want his appeal for reciprocated affection to be interpreted as a veiled criticism, and so he reiterates the depth of his commitment to their well-being by means of one of his favorite images, life and death. As a pastor, Paul's unrestrained self-investment in the lives of the Corinthians serves as a cord that binds their fates together. When they suffer, so does Paul; when they rejoice, so does Paul (see 11:28 – 29). Popular Stoicism, a philosophy vying for the attention of the Corinthians, would have despised such vulnerability as moral weakness:

> This is what you ought to practice from morning till evening: Begin with the most trifling things . . . like a pot, or a cup, and then advance to a tunic, a paltry dog, a mere horse, a bit of land; thence to yourself, your body, and its members, your children, wife, brothers. Look about on every side and cast these things away from you. Purify your judgments, for fear lest [you] be attached to them or grown together with them, and may give you pain when it is torn loose.[94]

I have great confidence in you (7:4). Many commentaries and translations recognize a technical expression in the opening phrase of verse 4 and so render

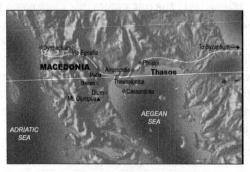

it, "I can speak quite candidly with you" (cf. 6:11). In the Greco-Roman world of Paul's day, *parrēsia*, candid speech (NIV "confidence"), was the right of every citizen and one of the defining virtues of true friendship. The glories of sincere *parrēsia* were commonly extolled by philosophers; according to Musonius Rufus, the chief disadvantage of being enslaved or in exile was the loss of *parrēsia* (Fragment 9). Perhaps the most detailed treatment of the subject comes from the pen of Philodemus (c. 110 – 35 B.C.) in his essay "On Frank Criticism" (*Peri parrēsia*), who remarks:

> In short, a wise man will employ frankness (*parrēsia*) toward his friends. . . . Although many fine things result from friendship, there is nothing so grand as having one to whom one will say what is in one's heart and who will listen when one speaks.[95]

As 11:11 – 12 will reveal, the Corinthians have begun to doubt Paul's affection for them. His choice of words in this verse would be heard by the Corinthians as a profound compliment and a reaffirmation of his committed friendship.

For when we came into Macedonia . . . we were harassed at every turn — conflicts on the outside, fears within (7:5). We have no information on the precise nature of these stressful events, though the "fears within" undoubtedly include his concern over Titus's reception (see comments on 2:12 – 13).

But God, who comforts the downcast, comforted us by the coming of Titus. . . . He told us about your longing for me, your deep sorrow (7:6 – 7). Comfort in affliction is a central theme in 2 Corinthians (1:3 – 11; 2:2 – 3, 14 – 17;

4:7 – 12, 16 – 17; 6:3 – 10) and arises from the relief Paul felt at the gracious treatment Titus received in Corinth. As Paul's emissary, Titus was charged with a difficult task: to confront the Corinthians with Paul's forceful letter, to heal the broken relationship without ignoring the grievous offense, and to rekindle enthusiasm for the stalled collection.

Paul's choice of Titus was shrewd. He was Greek (Gal. 2:3) and so shared many cultural affinities with the Corinthians. He was also experienced in politically sensitive missions, having accompanied Paul on his embassy to Jerusalem in resolution of the Gentile question (Gal. 2:1 – 10). His splendid success in Corinth is perhaps one reason why we later see him commissioned to go to Crete and "straighten out what was left unfinished" (Titus 1:5).

Even if I caused you sorrow by my letter, I do not regret it . . . because your sorrow led you to repentance (7:8 – 9). The rebuke that aims at edification was commended in Hebrew wisdom literature (Prov. 3:11 – 12; Sir. 30:1 – 13) and was considered crucial for moral formation by Greco-Roman philosophers. It was closely associated with *parrēsia*, "frank criticism," and was called "a caring admonition" by Philodemus.[96] According to Plutarch, the painful wound of frank criticism "is healed by the very words which inflicted the hurt. For this reason he who is taken to task must feel and suffer some smart, yet not be crushed or dispirited."[97] Paul's fatherly affection required fatherly discipline, and on this point the Hebrew sage and the pagan moralist were in hearty agreement.

Godly sorrow brings repentance that leads to salvation and leaves no regret, but worldly sorrow brings death **(7:10 – 11).** "Salvation" (Gk. *sōtērion*) commonly refers to deliverance from calamity. In this context it may denote fullness of life rather than final eternal life. The sincere repentance described here is delightfully illustrated by one of Paul's Jewish contemporaries, who pictures repentance as a beautiful angel who "renews all who repent and waits on them herself forever and ever."[98]

You were all obedient, receiving him with fear and trembling (7:15). Cultural protocol — Jewish and Roman — dictated that an envoy be afforded the same respect as the person he or she represented.[99] Thus, the Corinthians' warm reception of Titus is particularly comforting for Paul. Philo expresses the matter like this: "Whatever insults ambassadors are subjected to are at all times referred to those who sent them."[100] The principle was stated positively by Jesus: "Whoever receives me, receives the one who sent me" (John 13:20).

REFLECTIONS

CHRISTIANS TYPICALLY THINK OF REPENTANCE AS something necessary for beginning the Christian life, but it should also be an activity that characterizes the Christian life. Like the pilot who continually makes slight course adjustments to keep his aircraft on track, repentance and renewal should characterize our daily walk with Christ. In this passage Paul commends the Christians in Corinth for repenting when confronted with their sin, and in the process makes an important distinction between healthy and unhealthy remorse. In contrast to genuine contrition ("godly sorrow," 7:10), which restores life, stands disingenuous, worldly sorrow, which is closer to resentment than repentance. This kind of sorrow regrets the discovery of the sin more than the sin itself and leads to bitterness and ultimately death (7:11).

Remembering the Poor (8:1 – 9:15)

The collection for the poor in Jerusalem is a critical venture for Paul, one that the Corinthians have already committed themselves to (see "The Collection"). However, the unstable situation in Corinth, especially the church's strained relationship with Paul, has caused their enthusiasm for the project to wane. The earlier visit of Titus with the "tearful letter" helped get the Corinthians back on board, and in these two chapters Paul gives further advice on the subject prior to his arrival.

The grace that God has given the Macedonian churches (8:1). Paul's ministry in Macedonia began as a result of a vision the apostle received while in Troas, in which he saw a Macedonian pleading for help (Acts 16:6 – 10). Paul and his companions established churches in Philippi, Thessalonica, and Berea (Acts 16:6 – 17:15), and by the time of this writing the Macedonians were now offering help to others, in the form of a monetary donation to the Jerusalem fund.

Out of the most severe trial, their overflowing joy and their extreme poverty welled up in rich generosity (8:2).

▶ The Collection

Although Paul is remembered primarily as an evangelist and theologian, he also devoted a great deal of time and energy to organizing a collection to help relieve the economic hardship of the churches in Judea. Following the request of Peter and the leadership of the Jerusalem church that he "continue to remember the poor" (Gal. 2:10; cf. Acts 11:27 – 30), Paul began actively promoting this charitable contribution in his ministry throughout the Aegean basin.

The scope of this endeavor was truly significant. In the letters that have survived, Paul first explicitly mentions it in 1 Corinthians 16:1 – 4, though it is clear from this reference that the Corinthians have already been participating in the project, as were the churches in Galatia. In Romans 15:26 Paul confirms that the churches of Achaia are contributing, as well as those of Macedonia (cf. 2 Cor. 8:1 – 5). From 2 Corinthians 8:19 – 20 (cf. 1 Cor. 16:3 – 4) we learn that the apostle himself is going to accompany delegates from the churches to deliver the relief aid to Jerusalem.

As Paul sets out for Jerusalem, Acts records that he is accompanied by representatives from Derbe, Lystra, Berea, Thessalonica, and Ephesus (Acts 20:4). It is commonly assumed that these men are the local

delegates chosen to travel with Paul and the collection. According to Romans 15:28 – 29, Paul's plan is to escort the gift to Jerusalem and then journey to Rome "in the full measure of the blessing of Christ."

While the primary purpose of this charitable gift is to relieve the poverty of the Jerusalem church, in 2 Corinthians 9:12 – 14 Paul indicates that more is involved than mere financial assistance: "In their prayers [of thanksgiving] for you their hearts will go out to you because of the surpassing grace God has given you."[A-21] Paul reasons that such a generous gift will cause the Jewish believers in Jerusalem to grow in their affection for the expanding Gentile church, thus promoting the unity of Jew and Gentile in Christ and, by implication, strengthening his Gentile mission.

Although the goals of this philanthropic endeavor are noble, the outcome of the collection is not what Paul has anticipated (but see Rom. 15:30 – 31). After a warm reception by the leaders of the Jerusalem church (Acts 21:17 – 25), Paul's visit to the temple causes a riot that led to his arrest and subsequent transferal to Rome to stand trial. Paul does indeed make it to Rome, but he arrives there in shackles.

Although Paul does not mention the details of the severe trials in Macedonia or the cause of their poverty, his letters to the Christian communities in this province confirm these hardships. Intense persecution accompanied Paul's proclamation of the gospel in the Macedonian city of Thessalonica, and it seems likely that this contributed significantly to their economic deprivation.[101]

It is important to remember that the distribution of wealth in ancient Mediterranean society was enormously lopsided compared with modern Western societies, and Paul's report of the Macedonians' "extreme poverty" needs to be understood in this light. Considering that there was virtually no middle class in the first-century Roman world of Achaia and Macedonia and that the vast majority of the population lived at or below the subsistence level, the colloquialism "dirt poor" would not be an inappropriate description of the Macedonian communities responsible for this generous gift.

They gave as much as they were able, and even beyond their ability (8:3). Perhaps it was their own low estate that allowed the Macedonians to feel more keenly the deprivation of their brothers and sisters in Judea. Dio Chrysostom, who was once clothed, fed, and given shelter by a local peasant and his family after being shipwrecked on Euboea (an island south of Macedonia, off the coast of Greece) reflects on the openhanded generosity of the poor:

> They light a fire more promptly than the rich and guide one on the way without reluctance . . . and often they share what they have more readily. When will you find a rich man

who will give the victim of a shipwreck his wife's or his daughter's purple gown or any article of clothing far cheaper than that: a mantle, a tunic, though he has thousand of them, or even a cloak from one of his slaves?[102]

This service to the saints (8:4). The word rendered "saints" represents the Greek term *hagioi* (lit., "holy ones"), which is one of Paul's favorite designations for those who have placed their faith in Christ.[103] This language is common in the Old Testament, where it denotes persons or objects separated and consecrated to the Lord's service.[104] It later came to refer to God's elect people as a whole, particularly in distinction from the pagan nations.[105] Paul's frequent use of such rich and powerful language serves to reinforce the new personal identity of the believer ("a new creation," 2 Cor. 5:17), while also helping to reorient the social identity of the believing community as God's elect and holy people.

So we urged Titus, since he had earlier made a beginning, to bring also to completion this act of grace on your part (8:6). Apparently during his previous visit, after successfully representing Paul's grievance, Titus was also able to revive the stalled collection. Paul's

ERASTUS INSCRIPTION IN CORINTH

Erastus was a well-known patron in Corinth, a city administrator, and a Christian.

decision to send Titus ahead of him with the present letter may have been a result of his progress on this front.

But just as you excel in everything — in faith, in speech, in knowledge . . . see that you also excel in this grace of giving (8:7). Paul probably refers here to those remarkable manifestations of the Spirit discussed in his earlier correspondence: glossalalia (1 Cor. 12:10; 14:1 – 19), miracle-working faith (12:9 – 10; 13:2), and supernatural discernment (12:8; 13:2). Paul uses the same word here (*perisseuō*) to describe the Corinthians' excelling in charismata as he did earlier (2 Cor. 8:3) to describe Macedonians' excelling in generosity. He wants the Corinthians to abound not only in the spectacular gifts that inspire awe and are focused on the local assembly, but also in the less dramatic gifts that benefit the larger body of Christ.

For if the willingness is there, the gift is acceptable according to what one has (8:12). The sentiment expressed here was widely held in the Jewish and Greco-Roman world and is illustrated in the story of "the widow's mite" in Mark 12:41 – 44. On the Jewish side, Tobit 4:8 is relevant: "Measure your alms by what you have; if you have much, give more; if you have little, do not be afraid to give less in alms." The enlightened pagan moralist Dio Chrysostom thought along similar lines: "No gift is inadequate which is prompted by affection."[106]

Our desire is . . . that there might be equality (8:13). "Equality" was deeply

▶ Social Stratification in Ancient Mediterranean Society

Most people in the first-century were relatively poor by modern standards.[A-22] At the top of the social hierarchy were the Roman imperial aristocracy, senators, equestrians, the provincial aristocracy, and the (relatively few) men and women who had made their fortune through successful trade, or other skills. Those dependent on the elite upper strata for their livelihood included slaves, freedmen, and some freeborn who assumed important offices for their master or patron — administrative, cultic, or military. Beneath these were those artisans, teachers, small landowners, shopkeepers, and certain members of the military establishment, who worked hard and enjoyed seasons of modest success, but were still relatively poor by today's standards.

Roughly 70 percent of the populace survived at or below the subsistence level. They lived hand to mouth and spent their day hoping to earn enough to feed themselves and their dependents. In this group we would find less successful craftsmen, clients of patrons, day laborers, slaves, and tenant farmers. Lucian vividly depicts the unhappy lot of this large majority of the populace: "Toiling and moiling from morning till night, doubled over their tasks, they merely eke out a bare existence."[A-23] At the very bottom were the outcasts: orphans, widows, and those unable to work because of illness or physical impairment.

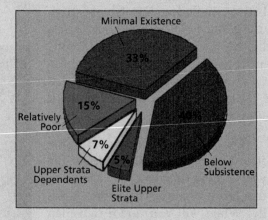

imbedded in the ideals of Greek democracy and was copiously extolled by the great thinkers of Greece: Plato, Aristotle, Demosthenes, Isocrates, and so on. The playwright Euripides advised: "It is better, my son, to honor Equality, who always joins friend to friend, city to city, allies to allies . . . but the lesser is always in opposition to the greater, and so begins the dawn of hatred."[107] Philo, Paul's older contemporary in Alexandria, devoted a lengthy essay to this theme, defining equality as "the parent of peace."[108] In a similar vein, Paul also understands that extreme economic disparity will engender discord and disunity, and this recognition seems to have played a role in his strenuous campaign for this relief fund.

Your plenty will supply what they need, so that in turn their plenty will supply what you need. Then there will be equality (8:14). Paul's concern for equality should not be construed in terms of strict economic parity. Paul does not command wealthy converts to liquidate their assets. Rather, he exhorts them not to put their trust in ephemeral wealth but instead to be eager to share (1 Tim. 6:17 – 19). Both Paul and the local assemblies benefited from the hospitality of wealthy church members (Rom. 16:23), and Paul himself experienced seasons of plenty (Phil. 4:12). As the citation of Ex. 16:18 in verse 15 indicates, Paul's concern is that everyone's basic needs are met.

More important are the implications of these verses for Paul's theology of work. According to Paul, the goal of work is not the *accumulation* of wealth,

REFLECTIONS

IN ROMANS 12:8 PAUL MENTIONS THE SPIRITUAL gift of philanthropy, though in 2 Corinthians 8 and 9 he speaks more generally of a Christian grace in which all believers are called to abound: generosity. Paul couches his discussion in language designed to communicate that generosity as an act of spirituality and a necessary consequence of faith in Christ. He calls it a *grace* (8:1, 6) and a *spiritual endowment* (8:7) *given from God* (8:1). It is a *ministry* (9:12) and *service to the saints* (8:4 – 7; 9:1), modeled on *the sacrificial offering of Christ* (8:8) which brings *glory to God* (8:19; 9:14). In Paul's view, willingness to contribute financially to the needs of others is a concrete measure of the sincerity of the believer's love (8:9). This judgment is a natural application of the principle enunciated by Jesus: "For where your treasure is, there your heart will be also" (Matt. 6:21).

▸ *Aequitas* ("Equality")

Roman imperial society, with its elitist oligarchy and rigid hierarchical structure, showed little enthusiasm for the democratic principles of Greek culture. The Roman emperors, however, made shrewd use of the virtue of Equality (Lat., *Aequitas*) on their coinage, which served as imperial propaganda. *Aequitas* is personified as a beautiful woman holding scales (symbolic of justice and equity) and a cornucopia (symbolic of prosperity). The inscription on many coins depicting *Aequitas* typically reads "Augustan Equality." It is entirely possible that at least some coins of this type were contributed to the Jerusalem relief fund, whose goal, Paul tells us, was "equality."

◀

THE GODDESS
AEQUITAS

but its *dissemination*: "He who has been stealing . . . must work, doing something useful with his hands, *that he might have something to share with those in need.*"[109] Paul ardently commends personal industry, not for personal gain, but in order to be a blessing to others: "You will be made rich . . . so that you can be generous on every occasion."[110]

The brother who is praised by all the churches . . . [and] our brother who has often proved to us in many ways that he is zealous (8:18, 22). It is curious that Paul does not mention the names of the brothers he is recommending. Some commentators suppose that their names were recorded in the original, but were subsequently expunged after some moral failure on their part. This is an unnecessary conjecture. Since these individuals will be present with Titus when this letter is delivered and read, there is no need for their names to be mentioned here. To us, their identity will remain a mystery, though Luke, Timothy, and Apollos are frequently suggested as possibilities. The brother of verse 22 may have been one of the representatives from Macedonia who accompanied Paul to Jerusalem with the collection: Sopater, Aristarchus, or Secundus (Acts 20:4).

He was chosen by the churches to accompany us as we carry the offering (8:19). The method of selection used by the Macedonian churches was probably some kind of an electoral procedure, as suggested by the verb *cheirotoneō*, which originally meant to elect by a show of hands. This would have been a natural course of action for the democratically oriented Macedonian assemblies; it was also practiced in the primitive church: *Didache* 15:1; Ignatius, *To the Philadelphians* 10:1;

To the Smyrneans 11:2. Other methods of selection attested in New Testament include direct appointment (Titus 1:9), casting lots (Acts 1:26), and direct revelation from the Spirit (13:2 – 3). The selection of this traveling companion ensures that all propriety is observed in handling the donations (8:20 – 22), as well as for safety along the journey.

For if any Macedonians come with me and find you unprepared . . . we would be ashamed of having been so confident (9:4). The possible embarrassment felt by Paul and the Corinthians will be all the greater, given the poverty of the Macedonians and the relative prosperity of at least some of the members of the Achaean-Corinthian assemblies. Erastus was able to donate an expensive pavement near the theater in return for his election to public office (see "Erastus Inscription" at 3:1). Titius Justus owned a home near the synagogue and hosted Paul (Acts 18:7). The home of Gaius was large enough to accommodate all the Corinthian house churches at once (Rom. 16:23).

The ability to travel is a good indicator of financial means, and we see many Corinthians on the move. Phoebe, a deaconess and patroness of the assembly in Cenchrea,[111] had the resources to travel to Rome (on business?) and deliver Paul's letter to the Romans (Rom. 16:1 – 2). Chloe was able to dispatch servants or family members to Ephesus (perhaps on other business) and keep Paul abreast of developments in Corinth (1 Cor. 1:11). Stephanas is also able to visit Paul in Ephesus, along with Fortunatus and Achaicus (his slaves?), and offer encouragement (16:15 – 18). Certainly the Corinthians had the wherewithal to contribute to those destitute believers in Jerusalem.

The generous gift you had promised (9:5). Not only were some of the Corinthians evidently persons of substance, but the region itself was almost legendary for its prosperity. Corinth's location, commerce, festivals, and fertile agricultural regions provide the background for the assessment of Favorinus (A.D. 85 – 155) that the city was "both prow and stern of Hellas, having been called prosperous and wealthy and the like by poets and gods from olden days."[112] This is not to say that the Corinthian church as a whole was affluent (see 1 Cor. 1:26 – 29; 11:22). Yet the evidence from Paul's letters suggests that they were better off than the Macedonian assemblies and more than capable of a generous donation.

REFLECTIONS

ALTHOUGH PAUL'S COMMENTS HERE and in 1 Corinthians 16:1 – 4 concern a special collection for the poor in Jerusalem, they also have important implications for the modern practice of *tithing*, giving from our income to support the ministry of the church. (1) Our giving should be *regular*: "On the first day of every week . . . set aside a sum of money" (1 Cor. 16:2). (2) It should be *proportionate*: "in keeping with one's income" (1 Cor. 16:2); "according to your means" (2 Cor. 8:11). (3) It should be *generous*: "Whoever sows generously will reap generously" (2 Cor. 9:6). (4) Finally, it should be done *joyfully*: "not reluctantly . . . for God loves a cheerful giver" (2 Cor. 9:7 – 8). As in all things, our model is Jesus: "Though he was rich, yet for your sake he became poor" (8:9).

Whoever sows sparingly will also reap sparingly, and whoever sows generously will also reap generously (9:6). Although the local economy of Roman Corinth was not agriculturally based, nor was Paul, as far as we know, ever deeply involved in rural life, ancient societies were more vitally connected to the field and farm than modern Western societies and so also with the agrarian wisdom that thrived in such a setting. The image of a farmer sowing seed in the field, harvesting, and bearing his produce to the market would have been a daily reality for both Paul and the Corinthians.

He who supplies seed to the sower and bread for food . . . will increase your store of seed (9:10). Paul takes for granted that the Creator has supplied his creation with everything necessary for life and abundance. Yet this Jewish conviction clashes dramatically with the religious ideas of Greece and Rome, and this collision provides an opportunity for Paul to reeducate his pagan converts. In Corinth and throughout the Greco-Roman world, Demeter was worshiped as the goddess of grain, agriculture, and bountiful

FARMING IMPLEMENTS

A sickle, scraper, hoe, and other tools found in Samaria.

harvests, along with her daughter Kore. An ancient temple dedicated to these two goddesses was located on the north slope of the Acrocorinth and was remodeled during the first century B.C. This cult was especially popular among the poor of Corinth, judging from the large number of inexpensive votives found in the excavation.[113] Demeter is commonly pictured with grain, fruit, cornucopia, and other symbols of agricultural fertility.

Paul Defends His Ministry (10:1 – 18)

In chapters 10 – 13 Paul focuses his attention on the claims of his opponents, certain Jewish-Christian missionaries who have recently arrived in Corinth and are challenging Paul's apostolic credentials. While formally addressing the Corinthians, Paul takes up the objections of his rivals, and the tone of the polemic often bristles with sarcasm. Such an approach was deemed appropriate for the moralist when the souls of his listeners hung in the balance: "partly by persuading and exhorting, partly by abusing and reproaching, in the hope that he may thereby rescue somebody from folly . . . with gentle words and at other times harsh."[114]

By the meekness and gentleness of Christ, I appeal to you (10:1). The character of the Messiah (Gk. *Christos*) as gentle, meek, and lowly was anticipated in many Old Testament prophecies and was exemplified in the life and teaching of the earthly Jesus.[115] In Peter's recollection of Jesus he was a "lamb" (1 Peter 1:19), and this image dominates the apocalypse of John.[116] Not surprisingly, this picture was carried on in the writings of the early church fathers:

For Christ is with those who are humble, not with those who exalt themselves over his flock. The majestic scepter of God, our Lord Jesus Christ did not come with the pomp of arrogance or pride, but in humility . . . like a sheep he was led to the slaughter.[117]

I, Paul, who am "timid" when face to face with you, but "bold" when away! (10:1). The words placed in quotation marks in the NIV indicate that Paul is probably alluding to accusations of his opponents that he is courageous only from a distance (see comments on 10:10 – 12). Paul's opponents have confused his Christ-like demeanor with weakness, and it is this inverted value system he seeks to correct.

Some people who think that we live by the standards of this world (10:2). We encounter here another charge, which can be translated literally as "walking according to the flesh." This language represents Paul's assessment of his opponents' accusation(s), which he leaves unspecified.[118] It may relate to his seemingly fickle change of travel plans (2 Cor. 1:15 – 2:4), to an alleged mishandling of the collection (12:16 – 18), or to something else altogether. It is certain, however, that Paul's character is under indictment.

We do not wage war as the world does. The weapons we fight with are not the weapons of the world (10:3b – 4a). The warfare imagery Paul adopts was particularly popular among philosophers of the Stoic-Cynic variety, who depicted their way of life and philosophy in terms of a battle for moral advancement. According to Dio Chrysostom, the wise man continually fights "a stubborn battle against lusts and opinions and all mankind."[119] The development of character could be likened to capturing "the citadel within" and expelling the inner tyrants: "How then is a citadel destroyed? Not by iron, nor by fire, but by sound judgments."[120] The ultimate goal of the contest against the inner and outer foe is eloquently described by Seneca: "Though earthworks rise to match the loftiest citadel, yet no war-engines can be devised that will shake the firm-fixed soul."[121]

They have divine power to demolish strongholds (10:4b). By the first century A.D., Roman siege warfare had developed sophisticated machinery and treacherous tactics. Siege equipment included a complex variety of artillery, catapults, battering rams, mobile towers, mechanical ladders, movable protective sheds, and vehicles and tools specifically designed for maintaining a siege. The remains of an impressive siege ramp are still visible at Masada, and if the Romans could not go over or through a wall, they also developed methods for tunneling under the wall. Sometimes tunnels were constructed simply to undermine the foundation of the defensive fortification. Corinth itself was besieged and ravaged by the Roman General Lucius Mummius in 146 B.C., though by Paul's day the city walls had been restored. However, the

walls of the Acrocorinth, the fortress situated above Corinth, still lay in rubble and served as a poignant illustration of a "demolished stronghold".

We demolish arguments and every pretension that sets itself up against the knowledge of God (10:5). In speaking of pretentious reasoning that exalts itself over the truth, Paul echoes a common caricature of the Sophists, who were known for their crafty argumentation and affected style. In an earlier letter Paul refers to them as "the debaters of this age" whose (pseudo-)wisdom God has shown as foolishness (1 Cor. 1:20).

Philo is especially scornful of these "lovers of disputations," who "raise themselves up to heaven in pride and arrogance" and who are constantly "stirring up a quarrelsome confusion, which tends to the adulteration of the truth."[122] These pseudo-philosophers "annoy the ears of those whom they meet by discussing with minute accuracy . . . all expressions of a double and ambiguous character."[123] Through convoluted argumentation they erect "impregnable fortifications" and labor "to devise what is persuasive for the establishment of a false opinion."[124] Indeed, Philo labels the entire Sophistic

bottom left

BALLISTA

Large stones for launching in a siege engine. These were found at Masada.

bottom right

SIEGE ENGINES

Replicas of these Roman mechanisms of war.

▼

endeavor as "studying the art of words in opposition to truth."[125] Like many Greco-Roman cities, Corinth was deeply influenced by the Sophistic movement,[126] which compelled Paul to adopt an anti-Sophistic posture in Corinth in order to distinguish himself clearly from these other traveling preachers.[127]

We take captive every thought to make it obedient to Christ (10:5). Continuing the combat imagery, Paul pictures himself as a commander who has vanquished his foe and presented the survivors to his Lord as captives. The military success of Rome from 200 B.C.-A.D. 100 produced vast numbers of captives who were then sold as slaves in the slave markets. Like Rome itself, Corinth was undoubtedly teeming with these kinds of slaves or descendants of such captured slaves. One of the more common images on imperial coinage and other imperially commissioned statuary was the captive, bound and stooped under the boot of imperial Rome.

The authority the Lord gave us for building you up rather than pulling you down (10:8). In Galatians 1:15 Paul describes his conversion in terms reminiscent of the prophet Jeremiah's call from the womb (Jer. 1:5); here he depicts his ministry in language that also echoes Jeremiah's commission (1:10). As the herald of Jeremiah's new covenant (2 Cor. 3:6; cf. Jer. 31:31), Paul takes this heroic prophet as a role model exemplifying perseverance in opposition. It is not surprising, then, to see Paul look to Jeremiah for an indictment of his boasting adversaries: "Let him who boasts boast in the Lord."[128]

For some say, "His letters are weighty and forceful" (10:10). This verse is significant if for no other reason than that it is the only time Paul actually cites his opponents. It is difficult to determine, however, which group is voicing this objection. We know that the Corinthians themselves were already grumbling about Paul's unimpressive oratory, which

he defends in 1 Corinthians 1 – 4. Yet we also know that subsequently other missionaries arrived in Corinth and challenged Paul's leadership (2 Cor. 11 – 13).

Paul's opposition concedes that his letters are impressive examples of persuasive discourse, and this perspective is borne out by modern research on the structure and strategy of Paul's letters.[129] While far from the rhetorical showpieces of Cicero and Seneca, Paul's letters creatively adapt conventional features of Hellenistic letter-writing to address the needs of his churches and provide a powerful witness to the genius and passion of Paul the apostle.

"But in person he is unimpressive" (10:10). A more literal translation reads, "but his bodily presence is weak," indicating that some in Corinth are criticizing Paul's personal appearance — be it the opposing missionaries or the disgruntled among the Corinthians. The only physical description of Paul from antiquity comes to us from the second-century document, *The Acts of Paul and Thecla:* "small of stature, with a bald head and crooked legs, in a good state of body, with eyebrows meeting and nose somewhat hooked." While certainly fictitious, this depiction corresponds to what we might expect of a hard-working artisan, a tentmaker who labored at his workbench "night and day" (1 Thess. 2:9) in the cities he evangelized, including Corinth.[130]

But it is precisely this kind of public image that would repel those from the privileged classes in Corinth. Some of these may have agreed with the elitist perspective of Cicero, who looked down on all manual laborers, small shopkeepers, and artisans engaged in "vulgar trades, for no workshop can have anything liberal about it."[131] Often it was the dress and physical appearance of such workers that was deemed so distasteful. Lucian, in choosing his profession, purposely opts for the "dignified appearance" of the orator over the "servile appearance" of a sculptor, with his tunic covered in marble dust, hunched over his work, toting sledges and chisels in his calloused hands.[132]

To be sure, the working class judged matters differently, as did some philosophers, who believed certain kinds of manual labor could be good for the body and soul.[133] Yet even an enlightened spirit like Epictetus argued that in order for the philosopher-moralist to be compelling, "such a man needs also a certain kind of body, since if a consumptive man comes forward, thin and pale, his testimony no longer carries the same weight" (*Discourses* 3.22.86). Epictetus goes on to explain that in order to gain a hearing for his message, the philosopher should be able to say, "Look, both I and my body are witnesses to the truth of my contention" (3.22.88). Such a maxim would have carried much weight in Corinth,

REFLECTIONS

IN 10:7 PAUL ACCUSES THE CORINTHIANS OF "LOOK-ing only on the surface"; this may be regarded as the fundamental problem in Corinth. Like many today, the Corinthians were more concerned with externals, such as social status, physical appearance, and flashy demonstrations of the Spirit, and neglected the deeper issues of character, humility, and the inner beauty of a Spirit-filled life. Even mature believers struggle with this from time to time. It is somewhat comforting to recall that even the prophet Samuel had to be reminded of this fundamental spiritual principle: "But the LORD said to Samuel, 'Do not consider his appearance or his height. . . . The LORD does not look at the things man looks at. Man looks at the outward appearance, but the LORD looks at the heart' " (1 Sam. 16:7).

where physical appearance was valued at a premium.[134]

In his discourse *On Personal Adornment*, Epictetus describes a young student of rhetoric from Corinth who was "elaborately dressed . . . and whose attire in general was highly embellished" (3.1.1). Bedecked in jewelry and sporting a lavish hairstyle (3.1.14), this Corinthian even plucked out all his bodily hair to enhance his physical appeal (3.1.27 – 35). Martial's description of another Corinthian, Charmenion, is similar: "You stroll about with sleek and curled hair. . . . You are smoothed with depilatory [hair removal lotion] daily."[135] It is no wonder that Paul began this section with the reproof, "[O Corinthians,] you are looking only on the surface of things" (10:7).

And his speaking amounts to nothing (10:10). The accusation of poor rhetorical ability permeates Paul's extant correspondence with this church and appears to be the main complaint leveled against Paul in Corinth.[136] The Corinthians, like typical citizens of any Greco-Roman city in this era, had been fed a rich diet of oratory from birth and were true connoisseurs of the art (see comments on 5:11 – 13). What Dio Chrysostom says of the Phrygians was even more true of the Corinthians: "You are devoted to oratory . . . and you tolerate as speakers only those who are very clever."[137]

The Corinthians prided themselves on their expertise in evaluating public speakers, who were expected to be exemplary in word and appearance. Lucian advises anyone aspiring to be a Sophist, "First of all, you must pay special attention to outward appearance," which reveals why Paul's physical appearance and his rhetorical ability are both under attack here: The Corinthians are comparing Paul to the orators who entertain them at their banquets and in their lecture halls, and are giving him poor marks on their scorecards.[138]

When they measure themselves by themselves and compare themselves with themselves, they are not wise (10:12). The art of comparison was taught as a rudimentary exercise of rhetorical technique and is defined by Paul's contemporary Quintilian as the determination of "which of two characters are the better or worse."[139] The practice was particularly common among the Sophists as a means of self-advertisement. Indeed, Plutarch virtually defines Sophists by the excessive use of comparison in attracting

---

▶ Reflections of a Jewish Scribe on Leisure and Manual Labor (c. 180 B.C.)

The wisdom of the scribe depends on the opportunity of leisure; only the one who has little business can become wise. How can one become wise who handles the plow, and who glories in the shaft of a goad, who drives oxen and is occupied with their work, and whose talk is about bulls? . . . So it is with every artisan and master artisan who labors by night as well as by day; those who cut the signets of seals . . . the smith . . . the potter. . . . All these rely on their hands, and all are skillful in their own work. Without them no city can be inhabited, and wherever they live, they will not go hungry. Yet they are not sought out for the council of the people, nor do they attain eminence in the public assembly. They do not sit in the judge's seat, nor do they understand the decisions of the courts; they cannot expound discipline or judgment, and they are not found among the rulers. (Sir. 38:24 – 33)

attention: "For it is not like friendship, but sophistry to seek for glory in other men's faults."[140] A good example of what Paul is opposing comes from Lucian, who sarcastically relates the words of a Sophist recruiting a student: "Do not expect to see something that you can compare with So-and-so, or So-and-so. . . . Indeed you will find that I drown them out as effectively as trumpets drown flutes."[141]

The field God has assigned to us, a field that reaches even to you (10:13). From the time of his calling on the Damascus road, God made clear to Paul that his commission was primarily to the Gentiles.[142] This was confirmed by Peter, James, and John, the leadership in Jerusalem (Gal. 2:7 – 9). In introducing the gospel to a Gentile city, Paul often began by preaching in the local synagogue, as he did in Corinth (Acts 18:4; cf. Acts 17:1 – 2). This approach allowed him to proclaim the Messiah first to his fellow Jews, while also gaining a hearing for his message among the God-fearing Gentiles who frequented the synagogue.

God-fearers were not full converts to Judaism, yet they were attracted to the faith, tradition, and ethic of the Jewish religion. In this verse and in one that follows, Paul is reminding the Corinthians that God himself has assigned him apostolic jurisdiction among the Gentiles. No matter what his opponents may claim, in bringing the gospel to Corinth he is not reaching beyond his divinely granted commission.

As your faith continues to grow . . . we can preach the gospel in the regions beyond you. For we do not want to boast about work already done in another man's territory (10:15 – 16). Two principles of Paul's missionary strategy are enunciated here: to use established churches as a base for further advancing the gospel, and to preach Christ in regions hitherto unevangelized, "where Christ is not known" (Rom. 15:20). Paul also implies that a healthy church will be a *sending church*, one whose growing faith inevitably involves a desire to see Christ's kingdom expand.

Paul's passion for evangelism was particularly focused on unreached peoples, so that he could claim in Romans 15:19 – 23: "From Jerusalem all the way around to Illyricum, I have fully proclaimed the gospel of Christ . . . there is no more place for me to work in these regions" — referring to a vast swath of the Roman world in which there was certainly more work to be done. As a pioneer evangelist, Paul's goal was to proclaim the gospel *extensively*, in as many regions as possible, rather than *intensively*, to everyone within a particular region. Of course, Paul made a great effort to ensure that churches were established and believers nourished. But as his letters indicate, with their frequent travel itineraries, visions of Spain, and so on, Paul's eye was ever on the road, always planning his next missionary enterprise.

Let him who boasts boast in the Lord (10:17). See comments on 10:8.

Paul's "Foolish" Boasting (11:1 – 12:13)

Continuing his defense of his ministry, Paul is forced into the awkward position of adopting a practice he has just censured in his opponents: boasting. Paul calls this maneuver "foolishness" (11:1) and being "out of [his] mind" (11:23), but the effectiveness of his opponents' libel campaign compels him to fight fire with fire. Paul refuses, however, to engage in petty Sophistic one-upmanship. Rather, he peppers his boasting with tongue-in-cheek irony in order to expose the absurdity of his opponents' position: They arrogantly proclaim a Messiah who, in fact, exemplified meekness and humility in his earthly life!

The climax of this parody is Paul's preposterous (to his rivals) insistence on boasting in his weakness (11:30) and his nonsensical contention that weakness is strength (12:10). But concealed in the apostle's hand is a trump card his opponents are not expecting: the example of Jesus, crucified in weakness (13:4). Paul concentrates his boasting in three areas: his proclamation of the gospel free of charge (11:7 – 15), his suffering as an apostle (11:16 – 33), and his mystical experiences (12:1 – 10).

I am jealous for you with a godly jealousy. I promised you to one husband, to Christ (11:2). In order to communicate his outrage at the infatuation that some in Corinth feel toward the intruding missionaries, Paul portrays himself as a father who has pledged his daughter (the Corinthians) in marriage, only to hear rumors that she has transferred her affections. The imagery is that of a betrothal (*harmozō*; NIV, "I promised"). While both Roman and Jewish marriage customs included a betrothal period, Paul is probably assuming a Jewish framework, which involved a ceremony with witnesses and an exchange of gifts and could precede the actual marriage by as much as twelve months.

Not all these details are relevant here, but the Jewish betrothal differs from our modern Western engagement period in that it was legally binding. As we see with Joseph and Mary, terminating the relationship constituted a divorce (Matt. 1:18 – 20). According to the Mishnah, the death of the betrothed male prior to the wedding rendered the virgin a widow and prohibited her from marrying a high priest.[143]

So that I might present you as a pure virgin to him (11:2). Following the betrothal, the bride was presented to the groom by her family and friends, which sometimes involved a joyous procession to the groom's house (1 Macc. 9:39; Matt. 25:6 – 10). It was the obligation of the father of the bride to safeguard his daughter's chastity, which was a serious matter. The sages of the Mishnah provided detailed legislation regarding the bride's obligation to furnish proof of her purity after cohabitation and the husband's right to sue her family if such evidence was not forthcoming.[144] Purity during the betrothal period was especially revered in Jewish circles, and the mishnaic rabbis stipulated that any man violating a betrothed virgin still under the protection of her father should be stoned or strangled.[145]

These Jewish sources help us understand the gravity of the situation in Corinth as Paul sees it and the appropriateness of his analogy to illustrate the matter. Paul feels the outrage of a father whose daughter has been seduced by another man on the eve of her wedding. The analogy also alludes to the consummation of redemptive history, when the presentation of the bride (the church) to the groom (Christ) is made (Eph. 5:27; Rev. 19:6 – 9; 21:2).

As Eve was deceived by the serpent's cunning (11:3). Jewish writers of the period describe the serpent of Genesis 3 as Satan, as his mouthpiece, or as one of the fallen angels.[146] The context (esp. 2 Cor. 11:13 – 15) suggests that Paul may be making a similar assumption. The abundant evidence — archaeological and literary — of a pervasive Jewish presence throughout the Mediterranean leaves little doubt that the average Roman was familiar with the major stories and characters of the Jewish Scriptures, including the serpent in Eden.

A Jesus other than the Jesus we preached . . . a different spirit . . . a different gospel . . . "super-apostles" (11:4 – 5). See "Paul's Opponents in Corinth" at 11:6 and comments on 12:11.

I may not be a trained speaker, but I do have knowledge (11:6). Once again Paul singles out his oratory as one of the central points of contention between him and his detractors. The NIV captures well the sense of the Greek expression *idiōtēs tō logō* ("not a trained speaker"), which indicates only that Paul has not received formal training as a rhetorician; he is an amateur. Yet we need not suppose that he is a complete bungler, rhetorically. Acts presents the apostle as a competent speaker, if not always compelling (Acts 17:18; 20:9), and we can assume that after many years of preaching in synagogues and in other public venues he developed some proficiency in his delivery. As 2 Corinthians 10:10 – 12 indicates, the problem is that the Corinthians, perhaps encouraged by Paul's opponents, are comparing Paul with polished professional orators and judging him inadequate.

But Paul is not merely battling snooty Corinthians with overly sensitive rhetorical tastes. Rather, he is confronting a cultural value that judges a person's knowledge and character on the basis of his or her oratorical prowess. From the time of Isocrates (436 – 338 B.C.), who reasoned that "the power to speak well is the surest index of sound understanding," to the time of Aristides (A.D. 117 – 181), who contended that "the title of 'wise' and the ability to speak well are attributes of the same man," wisdom and eloquence were intimately connected; this helps explain Paul's insistence that he does in fact possess knowledge, even though his oratory may be less than brilliant.[147] Stoic philosophy in particular connected oratory and knowledge, and in such way as to make eloquence a gauge of character:

- What is he [the listener] to think of their souls, when their speech is sent into the charge in utter disorder, and cannot be kept in hand?[148]
- They [the Stoics] say that only the wise man is a good prophet, poet, and orator.[149]

Aristides, quoting a widely circulated proverb, makes the connection explicit and illustrates well the difficulty Paul finds himself in: "As character is, such is the speech. The reverse is also true."[150]

Was it a sin for me to lower myself in order to elevate you by preaching the gospel of God to you free of charge? (11:7 – 10). Paul is responding to a complaint issuing from his refusal to accept financial remuneration from the Corinthians. As the context indicates, what the Corinthians are objecting to is Paul "lowering himself" through manual labor in order not to be "a burden" on any of them (11:8).[151] Paul's insistence on plying his trade as a leather worker in order to support himself is a source of embarrassment to some in Corinth (see comments on 2 Cor. 10:10). While manual labor was more esteemed in Jewish circles, even here it had its cultured despisers (see "Reflections of a Jewish Scribe" at 10:10).

Among Greeks and Romans in Paul's day there was a fair amount of debate concerning the appropriate means of livelihood for philosophers and ethical moralists.[152] Cynics begged, Sophists charged fees, philosophers attached themselves to wealthy patrons, and Stoics might do any of the above but were also known to support themselves through manual labor.[153]

▶ Paul's Opponents in Corinth

The identity of Paul's opponents in Corinth has been a major point of dispute among New Testament scholars for much of the twentieth century. The various profiles that have been offered include Jewish-Christians from Palestine who want Gentile Christians to keep the law, Gnostics, and Christian evangelists with roots in Hellenistic Judaism. Deciding among the alternatives requires reckoning with a whole host of methodological and historical issues, as well as a circumspect analysis of the text. Any reconstruction must recognize that, while 2 Corinthians 10 – 13 provide firm evidence of intruders, we know from 1 Corinthians that complaints about Paul had already been voiced among the Corinthians themselves, so we cannot assume that every objection Paul answers in 2 Corinthians is directed toward a single front.

What we do know about Paul's opponents can be summarized briefly. (1) They are Jewish (11:22), but there is no evidence that they are advocating obedience to the Mosaic law. (2) They profess Christ (11:23) and claim the title "apostle" (11:5, 13; 12:11). (3) They relish oratorical display (11:5 – 6) and rhetorical technique (11:12). (4) They boast excessively (10:12 – 17; 11:16 – 12:11) and are abusive in their leadership style (11:20). (5) They take money from the Corinthians (11:7 – 15, 20; 12:14 – 15).

Paul never attacks their teaching but focuses rather on their arrogant, bombastic style. This suggests that the primary heresy of these intruders, in Paul's eyes, is not one of doctrine, but one of demeanor. Based on what we know with certainty about these interlopers, it appears that they are Jewish-Christian evangelists who have adopted the methods and style of the popular Hellenistic Sophist-philosophers for their own financial gain and have severely compromised the gospel in the process.

Paul, by contrast, understands that the medium and the message are inextricably connected, so that proclaiming a humble, self-sacrificing Messiah in an inflated, self-promoting way represents a distortion of the message itself. It is, in fact, preaching another Jesus and proclaiming another gospel (11:4). Paul resolved to preach Christ "not with eloquent words of wisdom" lest the gospel be robbed of its power and attention be focused on the preacher rather than on the one preached (1 Cor. 2:1 – 5). As James Denny put it, "No man can give the impression that he himself is clever, and that Christ is mighty to save."[A-24] Anyone who pretends otherwise, in Paul's view, is a mere charlatan with a counterfeit faith and truncated gospel (11:13 – 15).[A-25]

The exorbitant fees charged by Sophists frequently led to accusations of greed and avarice.[154] Sophists were widely known as lovers of luxury who were "strangers to labor," and Paul was certainly not willing to be confused with this lot.[155]

Yet cultivating a relationship with a wealthy patron as a means of financial support would involve Paul in a whole host of reciprocal obligations that would severely limit his freedom (see below). This kind of relationship was regarded by Paul's contemporaries as virtual slavery, turning the philosopher into his patron's yes-man.[156] On this issue Paul is in agreement with his Stoic contemporary Musonius Rufus: "One should endure hardships and suffer the pains of labor with his own body, rather than depend upon another for sustenance" (Fragment 11).

Paul is willing to accept limited support from the Macedonians to make up for his lack (11:9), but the support the Corinthians offer either had patron-client strings attached or was offered merely as a way of avoiding the shameful spectacle of their founding apostle setting up shop in the market. Paul, however, is less concerned about offending patrician sensibilities than he is about modeling the servanthood of Christ (Phil. 2:6 – 11), who made himself poor so that others might become rich (2 Cor. 8:9).[157]

Why? Because I do not love you? God knows I do! (11:11 – 12). In justifying his refusal to accept the Corinthians' offer of financial support, Paul inadvertently divulges their interpretation of his action: It is tantamount to rejecting their friendship.

Greco-Roman society was governed by a complex system of patronage and benefaction, in which the offer of a gift constituted an offer of friendship and obligated the recipient to respond in some tangible and proportionate fashion.[158] Often gifts were proffered to a weaker party in order to create a power relationship, thus enhancing the status and honor of the benefactor. There was something of a moral obligation to accept such gifts when offered, and refusal could result in animosity on the part of the one declined. A person might refuse benefaction if the giver were deemed unworthy, if the recipient was unwilling to return the favor, or if accepting might put the recipient in a difficult situation with respect to some other party. In refusing their support, Paul has violated certain cultural conventions relating to giving and receiving gifts, and some Corinthians have taken grave offense.

False apostles, deceitful workmen, masquerading as apostles of Christ . . . [Satan's] servants (11:13 – 15). Although many questions would be answered had Paul specifically identified the targets of his attack, his use of polemical epithets to describe his opponents is widely attested

MASK

Flask in the form of the head of an actor wearing a female mask.

in the literature of Second Temple Judaism. In *Jubilees*, the oppressing Gentiles are labeled as "sons of Beliar," "children of perdition," "idol worshipers," and "the hated ones," among other things. In the Dead Sea Scrolls the chief opponent of the sect at Qumran (presumably the high priest in Jerusalem) is never actually named, but instead is referred to contemptuously as "the Scoffer," "the Liar," "the Spouter of Lies," and "the Wicked Priest." While Paul's invective may sound harsh to our ears, the situation in Corinth demands a sharp response from him, which he renders in accordance with the polemical conventions of his day.

Satan himself masquerades as an angel of light (11:14). In some Jewish traditions, Satan transformed himself into an angel of light and deceived Eve a second time:

> Then Satan was angry and transformed himself into the brightness of angels and went away to the Tigris River to Eve and found her weeping. And the devil himself, as if to grieve with her began to weep and said to her, "Step out of the river and cry no more . . . come out to the water and I will lead you to the place where your food has been prepared."[159]

Since many are boasting in the way the world does, I too will boast (11:18). Although Paul does not explicitly reveal who the "many" are who are boasting "according to the flesh" (NIV, "as the world does"), we can safely assume he has one eye on the Sophists and other fashionable rhetoricians, who made boasting a regular feature of their oratorical repertoire, and another eye on

his opponents, who have adopted this trendy style of declamation (see "Paul's Opponents in Corinth" at 11:6).

Like Paul, Plutarch regarded Sophistic self-praise as "odious and offensive," yet accepted that boasting could be legitimately employed when done in the service of a noble cause or in defense of one's character.[160] Self-praise could be rendered inoffensive if one's own shortcomings are also mentioned, if the speaker recounts his or her hardships, or if credit is given to others or to God.[161] The correspondences between Plutarch's advice and Paul's self-acknowledged foolish boasting ("I am out of my mind to talk like this," 11:23) are remarkable, though the basis of their abhorrence of boasting is very different. For Plutarch, boasting was tasteless self-display. For Paul, informed by the Jewish Scriptures (Ps. 94:4 – 7; 103:3 – 4; Jer. 9:23), it represents the quintessential expression of humanity in opposition to God (Rom. 3:27; 1 Cor. 1:28 – 31).

You even put up with anyone who enslaves you or exploits you or takes advantage of you or pushes himself forward or slaps you in the face (11:20). Paul provides important information on the deportment of the intruding missionaries, which essentially amounts to an abusive manner, with overtones of financial exploitation. Although it may sound incredible that some in Corinth would tolerate such a demeanor, this kind of hard-hitting public persona was very much in vogue in Paul's day. Cynic philosophers had a reputation for verbally accosting passersby, and Sophists likewise were known to be ruthless in advancing their point of view.

Dio Chrysostom describes a scene in Isthmia, some six miles from Corinth, in which "crowds of wretched sophists [stand] around Poseidon's temple shouting and reviling one another, and their disciples too . . . fighting with one another."[162] Philo paints a similar picture of Sophists as "lovers of self" who, like gladiators, descend into the arena to battle men of virtue and "never cease struggling against them with every kind of weapon, till they compel them to succumb, or else utterly destroy them."[163] What Paul describes is a heavy-handed leadership style, which is the antithesis of what he has modeled for the Corinthians in his own ministry (10:1; 11:22).

Are they Hebrews . . . Israelites . . . Abraham's descendants? So am I (11:22). "They" refers to the intruders, and it seems that one of their boasts concerned their pristine Jewish lineage (see "Paul's Opponents in Corinth" at 11:6). The terms Paul uses here are roughly synonymous in this context and are piled up for rhetorical effect. If Paul's opponents are *Palestinian* Jewish-Christians, which seems likely, it is conceivable that they drew attention to Paul's Diaspora roots (Tarsus, Acts 21:39; 22:3) in contrast to their own origins in the Jewish heartland, so as to discredit him. This kind of comparison was a routine practice of Sophists and rhetoricians (see comments on 10:12) and is explained by Theon (late first century A.D.) in the following way:

In the comparison of people, one firstly juxtaposes their status, education, offspring, positions held, prestige and physique; if there is any other physical matter, or external merit, it should be stated beforehand in the material for the encomia.[164]

In the face of such carnal self-promotion, Paul counters that he is every bit as "Jewish" as they are.

I have worked much harder (11:23). Hardship catalogs, like the one that follows, were commonly employed by Stoics in order to demonstrate their superior character and fortitude. For a discussion of Paul's hardship catalogs in relation to his Stoic contemporaries, see comments on 6:3 – 13.

In prison more frequently (11:23). Acts mentions only one imprisonment prior to the time of this letter (in Philippi, Acts 16:16 – 40), which illustrates the selective nature of Luke's account. Imprisonment could occur for reasons other than being judged guilty (with or without a trial) of some criminal offence.[165] Confinement sometimes took place to protect an individual or to hold an accused offender on remand while authorities determined if charges were appropriate. At other times imprisonment was used by magistrates to coerce a stubborn provincial to divulge information or to comply with a command.

The conditions in which prisoners were typically held would be considered inhumane by modern standards.[166] Locked away in over-crowded, lice-infested, unsanitary, and lightless hovels, prisoners routinely contracted disease through incarceration and sometimes died as a result of a prolonged stay in a Roman jail. Heavy iron manacles were

◀ *left*

CAPTIVES

Coin depicting Germanic captives with the inscription "Victor."

bound around wrists, feet, and often the neck, which grated through the flesh and caused all manner of pain and infection. Paul's frequent mention of his "chains," should conjure up images too distressful to contemplate.[167]

Five times I received from the Jews the forty lashes minus one. Three times I was beaten with rods, once I was stoned, three times I was shipwrecked (11:24 – 25). Paul's words read like a parody of the famous inscription of Augustus in which he catalogs the glories of his reign, the achievements he wanted all to remember:

> Twice have I had the lesser triumph . . . three times the [full] curule triumph; twenty-one times have I been saluted as "Imperator." . . . Fifty-five times has the Senate decreed a thanksgiving unto the Immortal Gods . . . Nine kings, or children of kings, have been led before my chariot in my triumphs . . . thirteen times had I been consul.[168]

The original inscription was erected on bronze pillars at the emperor's mausoleum in Rome, and copies were distributed throughout the provinces. Portions have been found in Ancyra (capital of Galatia), Apollonia (in Illyricum), and Antioch (in Pisidia). Such chronicles of glory would have been familiar to Paul and the Corinthians, rendering Paul's "boast" all the more ironic.

Forty lashes minus one (11:24). Deuteronomy 25:2 – 3 prescribes flogging as a means of punishment, up to a maximum of forty strokes. Receiving one less than forty may have been to ensure that the Mosaic stipulations were not exceeded through miscount. The later mishnaic

rabbis offered detailed instruction on what crimes were punishable by flogging, which included moral, cultic, and civil infractions.[169] As the passage from the Mishnah indicates, this was a painful and humiliating ordeal:

> How do they flog him? One ties his two hands on either side of a pillar, and the minister of the community grabs his clothing — if it is torn, it is torn, and if it is ripped to pieces, it is ripped to pieces — until he bares his chest. A stone is set down behind him, on which the minister of the community stands. And a strap of cowhide is in his hand, doubled and redoubled, with two straps that rise and fall [fastened] to it. . . . And he who hits him hits with one hand, with all his might.[170]

That Paul received this "from the Jews" indicates his continued missionary activities in the synagogues (Acts 17:1 – 3).

Beaten with rods (11:25). This punishment was a distinctively Roman way of dealing with a malefactor. The rods were made of wood, and the sentence would be executed by the *lictor*, who assisted the magistrate with the enforcement of corporal punishment. Acts records that Paul and Silas were severely beaten with rods in Philippi (Acts 16:22 – 23), even though it was illegal to flog a Roman citizen. Numerous examples can be found where the law was ignored by a magistrate.[171] As Romans, the Corinthians would have been keenly aware of the social stigma attached to this punishment, which underscores again Paul's determination to undermine the inverted value system of the Corinthians by boasting in the very things they would have regarded as shameful (11:30; 12:9 – 10).

Once I was stoned (11:25). Stoning was a common brand of punishment among Jews and was occasionally practiced by Romans.[172] While it could be an officially administered form of capital punishment, it was more often the result of mob violence.[173] The specific incident Paul refers to occurred in Lystra at the instigation of Jews from Antioch and Iconium (14:19).

Three times I was shipwrecked, I spent a night and a day in the open sea (11:25). Although Acts records only one shipwreck involving Paul (during his later journey to Rome), it mentions a number of other voyages on which such calamities may have occurred. Even these, however, do not comprise all of Paul seafaring journeys. Traveling by ship was especially dangerous in the first century, and countless instances of nautical misfortune are chronicled in the surviving literature and inscriptions.[174]

Since passenger ships were not in existence, Paul would have booked passage on a merchant ship heading to his desired destination and slept on the deck with other passengers and crew. Only the captain had a separate sleeping quarters. The causes of maritime disasters were numerous. Ancient merchant ships were considerably less sturdy than later sailing vessels and were propelled by only one mainsail, with possibly a smaller sail on the bowsprit. The ability to sail into the wind (tacking) was a later achievement, which meant that ancient mariners were largely at the mercy of prevailing winds.

In addition, these vessels were controlled by a steering oar, not a rudder, which further inhibited maneuverability. If one combines all this with the absence of (modern) detailed navigational charts, which display currents, depths, and hazards, the abundance of dedicatory epigrams like the following is not surprising:

> To Glaucus, Nereus, and Melicertes, Ino's son [mythological figures associated with the sea], to the Lord of the Depths, the son of Cronos, and to the Samothracian gods, do I, Lucillius, saved from the deep, offer these locks clipped from my head, for I have nothing else.[175]

> Dionysius, the only one saved out of forty sailors, dedicates here the image of a cele [possibly part of the ship's rigging], tying which close to his thighs he swam to shore. So even a cele brings luck on some occasions.[176]

bottom left

MERCHANT SHIPS

A column in Rome in honor of the emperor Marcus Aurelius (A.D. 161 – 180) depicting Roman merchant ships.

bottom right

ST. PAUL'S BAY, MALTA

The place where Paul survived a dramatic shipwreck.
▼

I have been constantly on the move. I have been in danger from rivers . . . from bandits . . . from my own countrymen . . . from Gentiles . . . in danger in the city, in danger in the country (11:26). Paul recounts in short staccato salvos the occupational hazards of an itinerant evangelist. These center around travel, which has always (until recent history) been a risky undertaking. Like most, Paul would have traveled on foot and been subject to cold, heat, dust, mud, and all the vicissitudes of capricious weather.[177]

For accommodation, Paul and his traveling companions (he would not have traveled alone, if at all possible) would have relied on the hospitality of local residents, inns, or sleeping in the open, if need be. Horace (65 – 8 B.C.) describes a journey that involved all three at various points.[178] Though decent lodging could occasionally be found, inns were notorious for bed bugs, rough characters, and promiscuity.[179] Bandits, too, were a perennial threat (Luke 10:30 – 35), and every precaution was taken to ensure safe passage:

> This is the way also with the more cautious among travelers. A man has heard that the road which he is taking is infested with robbers; he does

not venture to set forth alone, but he waits for company, either that of a quaestor or proconsul, and when he has attached himself to them he travels along the road in safety.[180]

The first-century traveler, well aware of the all the dangers involved, would have made vows to his/her patron deity for protection while traveling and looked for roadside shrines en route, as this inscription attests:

> Artemis, goddess of the road, Antiphilus dedicates to thee this hat from his head, a token of his wayfaring; for thou hast hearkened to his vows, thou has blessed his paths. The gift is not great, but given in piety, and let no covetous traveler lay his hand on my offering; it is not safe to despoil a shrine or even little gifts.[181]

I have labored and toiled and have often gone without sleep; I have known hunger and thirst and have often gone without food; I have been cold and naked (11:27). Choosing to support himself through his trade, Paul was forced to work longer hours than other artisans and to face even worse deprivation. The observation of Jesus ben Sirach that all craftsmen could be found "toiling day and night" (Sir. 38:27) would have been even more true of a bivocational evangelist. Paul labored "night and day" (1 Thess. 2:9; 2 Thess. 3:7 – 10) in the cities he evangelized in order to be a model for the Christian communities he established. His policy was to "gladly spend . . . and expend [himself]" on behalf of his spiritual children (12:15). On Paul's life as a tentmaker, see comments on 10:10 and 11:7 – 10.

I face daily the pressure of my concern for all the churches. Who is weak, and I

CENCHRAE

This was the site of the eastern port of Corinth.

▼

do not feel weak? Who is led into sin, and I do not inwardly burn? (11:28 – 29). As a pastor, Paul identifies with his flock to the point of suffering with them through their weaknesses and temptations. As we emphasized in our comments on 6:3 – 13, although both Paul and his Stoic contemporaries make use of hardship catalogs to commend themselves to their followers, the underlying presuppositions of each are very different.

For the Stoics, the whole point of adversity was to render the philosopher impervious to sorrow, fear, anxiety, or distress. According to Epictetus, philosophy beckons her pupils with the words, "Men, if you heed me, wherever you may be, whatever you may be doing, you will feel no pain, no anger, no compulsion, no hindrance, but you will pass your lives in tranquility and in freedom from every disturbance."[182]

Paul's open admission of anxiety is diametrically opposed to the doctrine and ideals of popular Stoic teaching and reflects a level of transparency that many of his day would despise as weakness. According to Dio Chrysostom, Diogenes represented the model to which all should aspire:

> . . . disclosing no weakness even though he must endure the lash or give his body to be burned . . . he holds [hardships] as mere trifles, and while in their very grip the perfect man is often as sportive as boys with their dice and their colored balls.[183]

With irony as his chief weapon, Paul is redefining for the Corinthians what true strength is. As the following verses illustrate, weakness and vulnerability play a major role in his definition.

In Damascus the governor under King Aretas had the city of the Damascenes guarded in order to arrest me. But I was lowered in a basket from a window in the wall and slipped through his hands (11:32 – 33). This incident is also related in Acts 9:23 – 25, which implicates the Jews of Damascus in the plot as well. Aretas was the ruler of the Arabic kingdom of the Nabateans to the south of the ancient city of Damascus, and it is unclear what kind of authority he exercised in Damascus at this time. The Greek word *ethnarch*, however, has a much broader range of meanings than the NIV's "governor" and may indicate simply that Aretas's consul in Roman controlled Damascus.[184] If Paul's time in Arabia (Gal. 1:17) included an unwelcomed mission among the Nabateans, this could explain the hostility on the part of Aretas.

The biting irony of Paul's boast becomes clear when we understand that the highest military honor in the Roman army was the *corona muralis*, the "wall crown," given to the first soldier to scale the wall and enter a besieged city. The pitiful picture of Paul being lowered in a basket contrasts dramatically with the glorious image of soldier battling his way over the wall and is offered as a scolding parody of the Corinthians' inverted value system.

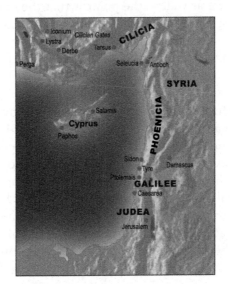

◀

SYRIA

I know a man in Christ (12:2). Paul adopts the third person to relate an experience we later discover is his own (12:6 – 10). This is indicative of his reticence to "boast" of such remarkable occurrences in his own life and his commitment to proclaim Christ, not himself (2 Cor. 4:5). Interestingly, the experience of Paul's heavenly ascent has many parallels in Jewish literature, and there too the revelation is always ascribed to another, usually a hero of Israel's past.[185]

Fourteen years ago (12:2). That Paul must go back a full fourteen years to this occurrence indicates it is not a regular feature of his religious experience. If 2 Corinthians was written in the mid – 50s, then the event Paul narrates occurred around 40 A.D., some seven years after his conversion and at least several years before he founded the church in Corinth.

Caught up to the third heaven . . . to paradise (12:2 – 4). Jewish literature of the period refers to one, three, five, seven, and even 955 heavens.[186] In each instance — and this seems to be the case here as well — the point is that the one ascending has reached the *highest* heavens, the very abode of God. In this passage, "third heaven" and "paradise" refer to the same locale.

He heard inexpressible things, things that man is not permitted to tell (12:4). Quite contrary to other heavenly ascent texts of Second Temple Judaism, whose whole point was to reveal the cosmological secrets of the universe or describe the ineffable mysteries of God, Paul comes back with nothing to say. Once again, the irony of Paul's "boast" is barely concealed by the exceptional nature of the event he recounts.

A thorn in my flesh, a messenger of Satan, to torment me (12:7). In order to keep Paul humble, God allows him to be plagued by a "thorn in [his] flesh." Many have suggested that this was some type of physical or mental ailment (poor eyesight, a speech impediment, epilepsy, depression), while others have seen in the mention of Satan an allusion to Paul's opponents and his persecution for the gospel (cf. 11:13 – 15). The reference to the "flesh" makes one think of a physical impairment of some kind, though anything beyond this is conjecture. Paul must have been of reasonably sound physical constitution in order to endure the hardships he has just described (11:23 – 28) and to maintain his arduous travel itinerary. Whatever this ailment was, it is probably more of a chronic burden than a completely debilitating affliction.

right ▶

A WALL AT THE MODERN CITY OF DAMASCUS

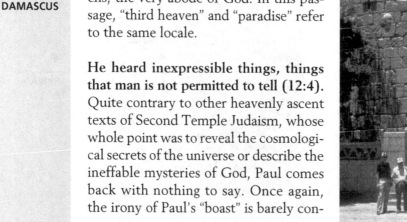

For Christ's sake, I delight in weaknesses . . . for when I am weak, then I am strong (12:10). This single, most important verse in 2 Corinthians crystallizes the argument of chapters 10 – 13 in a paradox of profound magnitude. In the crucible of affliction Paul has learned that the presence of the crucified Christ is mediated more perfectly through suffering and weakness than through glory and strength. This principle he has made emblematic of his ministry. Living his life in the shadow of the cross, Paul's ministry assumes a cruciform character, which rejects the path of status, position, power, and prestige and embraces the folly and humiliation of the cross as God's deepest wisdom (cf. 1 Cor. 1:18 – 2:5).

I am not in the least inferior to the "super-apostles" (12:11). "Super-apostles" represents Paul's own cynical designation of the intruders — with their imposing manner, pretentious oratory, and eccentric claims to apostolic status. See "Paul's Opponents in Corinth" at 11:6.

Signs, wonders and miracles (12:12). Part of Paul's proof of his apostleship is the miraculous deeds he performs in the service of the gospel. Acts attributes to Paul various healings (14:8 – 10; 28:7 – 9), exorcisms (16:16 – 18), and even raising the dead (20:7 – 12), though none of those described in Acts occurred in Corinth.

Paul's Impending Visit and a Final Warning (12:14 – 13:13)

In concluding his letter, Paul warns the Corinthians of his upcoming visit and exhorts them to perform a thorough spiritual inventory, lest he have to deal with them more harshly than he would like.

Now I am ready to visit you for the third time (12:14). Paul's first visit was his founding visit (Acts 18), and his second visit was the painful visit described in 2:1 – 5 and 7:12.

Not your possessions, but you (12:14). In reiterating his determination to support himself, Paul again alludes to the

REFLECTIONS

PERHAPS NOTHING IS MORE PAINFUL THAN TO HEAR God say "No." We can be sure that Paul's earnest prayers that this unnamed physical burden be removed were offered for all the right reasons. How could he endure the rigors of his ministry — the preaching, the travel, the public debates — if his own body often recoiled at the mundane tasks of daily life? We can also be certain that the outcome of this affliction — experiencing the power of the risen Christ — was the deepest desire of Paul's heart (Phil. 3:10), even though the means God chose to accomplish this end sent him staggering to his knees for relief. As Jesus was made perfect through suffering (Heb. 2:10), so too must his followers. The lesson Paul learned came at a heavy price, and it is one we all must face in our journey toward Christ-likeness. God cannot use a person greatly until he wounds him deeply.

mercenary tactics of his opponents, who proclaim the gospel with a view to monetary gain (see 2:17; 11:7 – 15).

Children should not have to save up for their parents, but parents for their children (12:14). As today, Greek, Roman, and Jewish societies emphasized the parents' responsibility in providing for their children. A variety of formal and informal laws of inheritance guarded this custom. The proverbial nature of Paul's statement reflects the universality of the principle, which the apostle applies to himself (the parent) and the Corinthians (the children). Whereas the Corinthians would have liked to have been Paul's patron/benefactor, providing for his needs and thus placing him under certain obligations, Paul explains their relationship with the metaphor of a family. Within this model, the emphasis lies on self-sacrifice and love, not on debits, credits, and reciprocal obligations.

Did I exploit you through any of the men I sent you? (12:17). Likely concealed beneath this rhetorical question is the suspicion on the part of some in Corinth that Paul has been siphoning funds from the collection (see "The Collection" at 8:1). While giving the appearance of financial propriety (they allege), the third parties involved are really working in concert with Paul to defraud them. Paul's confident, even incredulous tone in 12:16 – 18 indicates his certainty that few in Corinth will take this charge seriously.

Quarreling, jealousy, outbursts of anger, factions, slander, gossip, arrogance and disorder (12:20). Vice catalogs, like the one here, were a traditional component of first-century ethical discourse and have many parallels in the New Testament and in pagan philosophical literature.[187] This should caution us against assuming that the scenario Paul is contemplating in Corinth upon his arrival is truly as bleak as it may appear from this verse. Yet there is evidence in 1 Corinthians that many of these vices were wreaking havoc in the community, and we can understand why Paul is bracing himself for the worst.

"The testimony of two or three witnesses" (13:1). Paul intends to arbitrate disputes and put to rest any allegations against him when he arrives. He invokes the juridical principle of Deuteronomy 19:5, which

he also applies in relation to church discipline in 1 Timothy 5:19 (cf. Matt 18:16).

Since you are demanding proof that Christ is speaking through me (13:3). One more time before he signs off Paul brings up the Corinthian complaint regarding his oratory and their skepticism concerning his claim to be a divine spokesman. Yet Paul's continued insistence that Christ (2:17; 12:19; 13:3) or God (5:21) is speaking through him can only have provided his skeptics with fuel for their fire.

Sophists and professors of rhetoric regularly ascribed their eloquence to divine giftedness, portraying the orator as "a god among men."[188] In an address to the Corinthians, the Sophist Favorinus (A.D. 80 – 150) explains that his wisdom and eloquence are evidence that he has been "equipped by the gods for this express purpose."[189] Given the popular understanding of oratory as "a divine thing,"[190] anyone claiming to be a divine spokesman would have fairly large sandals to fill. When seen in this light, the Corinthian expectation that Paul should excel in the rhetorical arts is not as eccentric as it may at first appear.

He was crucified in weakness (13:4). The Roman practice of crucifixion was a gruesome and agonizing form of capital punishment, typically reserved for slaves and noncitizens. The ordeal began with the flogging of the condemned, who was then forced to carry the cross-beam to the place of execution. The victim's wrists would be nailed or bound with cords to the horizontal cross-beam, and the feet were similarly bound to the vertical beam.

Often there was a small ledge affixed to the vertical beam to partially support the body and prolong the torture. The

victim would not die from the wounds inflicted during the crucifixion, but from exhaustion or suffocation. Recent archaeological excavations near Jerusalem uncovered the tomb of a certain Jehohanan, crucified sometime between A.D. 7 and 66.[191] During his crucifixion Jehohanan's legs were shattered with a heavy object, probably to prevent him from being able to raise himself up for breath, thus hastening death. The large nail used to secure Jehohanan's legs to the cross was still lodged in the heel bone. As a portrait of "weakness," no more potent image could be offered than the humiliating spectacle of a victim of crucifixion.

Examine yourselves . . . test yourselves . . . do what is right (13:5 – 7). The exhortation to self-scrutiny was popular among Hellenistic philosophers from at least the time of Socrates, as witnessed by Epictetus (A.D. 55 – 135): "Socrates used to tell us not to live a life unsubjected to examination."[192] The goal of this moral introspection was knowledge of "the good" (*to kalon*; NIV, "what is right"), which should lead to right conduct:

> For the gods did not withhold from non-Greeks the ability to know the good. It is possible, through reasoned examination, to test whether

◀ *left*

HEELBONE OF A CRUCIFIED MAN

The iron nail that pierced the bone is still fixed in the heel. The bone was found in an ossuary in a Jerusalem tomb.

▶ Weakness and Strength: A Corinthian Perspective

In a city whose heritage, culture, and worldview were shaped by athletic competition and the triumph of strength over weakness, Paul's proclamation of a Savior crucified in weakness and his insistence that weakness is strength must have left many Corinthians staring in confused bewilderment. As the proud host of the Isthmian games, the victorious athlete stood at the center of Corinth's civic pride. A visitor to first-century Corinth would stroll past exquisite marble statues of wrestlers grappling, sprinters poised for flight, plaques enumerating victors, and a colossal sculpture of the goddess herself, Nike/Victoria, with triumphant wings outstretched.

The coins exchanged in the market bore similar images of contestants and victors' wreaths, and upon leaving the forum along the Lechaeum road, an imposing bronze of Herakles/Hercules would bid the traveler farewell. In fact, Hercules, the "savior of the earth and humanity," performed six of his famous twelve labors in the region and served as the patron saint of the Peloponnese.[A-26] Embodying the ideal of bravery and brute strength, his brawny physique graced Corinthian coins and statuary, and his temple was located near the center of the city. Half mortal, half divine, this mythic hero conquered death itself by descending into the underworld and bringing back the infernal watchdog, Cerberus. In death he was equally glorious, for he mounted his own funeral pyre, set it alight, and offered himself sacrificially to Zeus, his father.

When compared to mighty Hercules or the victors at the games, Jesus the crucified criminal cut a rather poor figure, and Paul's strenuous campaign in 2 Corinthians 10 – 13 to redefine strength and weakness is actually a daring exercise in resocialization.

we think good thoughts, and to investigate whether our words correspond to our actions, and whether we are like those who live morally.[193]

Paul has phrased this bold challenge in the parlance of popular Greco-Roman philosophy in order to render his appeal all the more intelligible and convicting to his Greco-Roman audience.

Do you not realize that Christ Jesus is in you — unless, of course, you fail the test? (13:5). While the form of Paul's exhortation conforms to the general pattern of Hellenistic philosophers (see above), the criterion for evaluation is not inner fortitude or moral progress, but the presence of the indwelling Christ: "If anyone does not have the Spirit of Christ, he does not belong to Christ" (Rom. 8:9).

This is why I write these things when I am absent, that when I come I may not have to be harsh in my use of authority (13:10). It is probably right to read this verse in reference to the entire letter (see 2:3 – 4). Paul's fatherly affection leads him to take every measure possible to avoid an unnecessary display of his parental authority, including penning this lengthy letter. From this verse we can conclude that 2 Corinthians has been written primarily to preempt another "painful visit" and to effect reconciliation with the minority, who have come under the influence of the intruding missionaries.

For building you up, not tearing you down (13:10). See comments on 10:8.

Finally, brothers, good-by. Aim for perfection, listen to my appeal, be of one mind, live in peace. And the God of love and peace will be with you (13:11). Using brief maxim-like exhortations, Paul summarizes his prayer for the Corinthians: *maturity* ("aim at perfection"), *obedience* ("listen to my appeal"), *unity* ("be of one mind"), and *harmony* ("live in peace"). Sadly, many of the same problems Paul addressed in 1 and 2 Corinthians were still present a generation later. According to *1 Clement*, written around A.D. 95 by the leadership of the church in Rome to the congregation in Corinth, once again the Corinthian church was torn by "jealousy and envy, strife and sedition, persecution and anarchy."[194]

Greet one another with a holy kiss (13:12). In Paul's day, kisses were given to express affection (between relatives, close friends, or lovers), homage (to the emperor or a patron), congratulation (to the victor in athletic competition), and sometimes upon entrance to a guild or religious sect. There is some evidence that rural communities differed from urban populations with respect to kissing, as evidenced by the embarrassing situation recounted by Dio Chrysostom, in which a farmer greets an old acquaintance he meets in the city with a kiss, only to be laughed at by bystanders: "Then I understood that in the cities, they do not kiss."[195]

REFLECTIONS

PAUL'S PROMISE THAT THE GOD OF love and peace would make his presence felt in the lives of the Corinthians (13:11) is contingent on their active pursuit of holiness. The blessings of God's love and peace can be hindered by obstinacy and spiritual laziness, which is why Paul enjoins his readers, "Examine yourselves!" (13:5).

Paul elsewhere recommends a kiss of greeting between believers, which later became a regular part of community worship.[196] This expression of intimacy cut across social barriers and served to both promote and symbolize the genuine sense of community experienced among believers, regardless of rank or status.

All the saints send their greetings (13:13). Although the precise identity of "the saints" is uncertain, more than likely Paul refers to the Macedonian believers in his company as the letter was penned. Paul typically includes greetings from others in his farewell.[197] This serves to reinforce the unity of the dispersed body of Christ, while also placing the local community in the context of something much larger, the church universal.

The grace of our Lord Jesus Christ, and the love of God, and the fellowship of the Holy Spirit (13:13). This final blessing is expressed in a Trinitarian formula that suggestively unites Father, Son, and Spirit as coworkers in the process of sanctification. Such triadic expressions are not uncommon in Paul's letters and imply a Trinitarian conception of the Godhead, at least in embryonic form.[198]

ANNOTATED BIBLIOGRAPHY

Commentaries

Barrett, C. K. *A Commentary to the Second Epistle to the Corinthians.* BNTC. London: Black, 1973.

A concise and circumspect exegesis of 2 Corinthians from one of the leading New Testament scholars of this century.

Furnish, Victor Paul. *II Corinthians.* AB 32A. New York: Doubleday, 1984.

A detailed, technical commentary rich in primary source research. Includes a fresh translation of the text.

Garland, David E. *2 Corinthians.* NAC 29. Nashville: Broadman & Holman, 1999.

A full-scale exegetical commentary mindful of the contemporary application of the text. Pastoral and theological in tone.

Witherington, Ben III. *Conflict and Community in Corinth: A Socio-Rhetorical Commentary on 1 and 2 Corinthians.* Grand Rapids: Eerdmans, 1995.

Focuses on the rhetorical dimensions of 1 and 2 Corinthians and the social context of Paul's ministry. Contains numerous helpful excurses on important issues.

Important Studies

Hafemann, Scott J. *Suffering and Ministry in the Spirit: Paul's Defense of His Ministry in II Corinthians 2:14 – 3:3.* Grand Rapids: Eerdmans, 1990.

A detailed exegesis of 2 Corinthians 2 – 3 with profound insights into Paul's perception of his apostolic ministry.

Hubbard, Moyer. *New Creation.* SNTSMS. Cambridge: Cambridge University Press, forthcoming.

An examination of the motif of new creation in 2 Corinthians and Galatians, with special reference to the Jewish background of this theme.

Savage, Timothy B. *Power Through Weakness: Paul's Understanding of the Christian Ministry in 2 Corinthians.* SNTSMS 86, 1996.

An exploration of the motif of strength in weakness in 2 Corinthians, with an illuminating depiction of Corinth and the Corinthians.

Sumney, Jerry L. *Identifying Paul's Opponents: The Question of Method in 2 Corinthians.* JSNTSup 40. Sheffield: JSOT Press.

A level-headed, textually based study of one on the most difficult issues in 2 Corinthians: the identity of Paul's opponents.

Winter, Bruce W. *Paul and Philo Among the Sophists.* SNTSMS 96. Cambridge: Cambridge University Press, 1997.

An examination of Paul and the Corinthian correspondence in light of the rise of the second Sophistic movement.

Main Text Notes

1. For example, Francis Young and David Ford, *Meaning and Truth in 2 Corinthians* (London: SCM, 1987); Ben Witherington, *Conflict and Community in Corinth* (Grand Rapids: Eerdmans, 1995); Paul Barnett, *The Second Epistle to the Corinthians* (NICNT. Grand Rapids: Eerdmans, 1997); Jerry McCant, *2 Corinthians* (Sheffield: Sheffield Academic, 1999); J. D. H. Amador, "Revisiting 2 Corinthians: Rhetoric and the Case for Unity," *NTS* 46 (2000): 92 – 111.
2. On this see Amador, "Revisiting 2 Corinthians."
3. See 1:17 – 23; 6:1 – 3, 11 – 13; 6:14 – 7:2.
4. Amador, "Revisiting 2 Corinthians," 94.
5. Jerome Murphy-O'Connor, *St. Paul's Corinth* (Collegeville, Minn.: Liturgical), 161 – 69.
6. Martial, *Epigrams* 3.60.
7. See Dennis Pardee, "Hebrew Letters," *ABD*, 4:282 – 85; Paul E. Dion, "Aramaic Letters" *ABD*, 4:285 – 90.
8. Isa. 63:16; cf. 64:8; Jer. 31:9; Mal. 2:10.
9. Rom. 8:15; Gal. 4:6; cf. Mark 14:36.
10. 1QH 17:35 – 36; see also Sir. 23:1; *T. Job* 33:3, 9; *Jos. Asen.* 12:7 – 11.
11. Tacitus, *Hist.* 5.3.
12. For the Christian objection, see *Didache* 2:2; 5:2. More forceful is the moving essay by the first-century Stoic philosopher Musonius Rufus entitled, "Should Every Child That Is Born Be Raised?"
13. Dio Chrysostom, *Oration* 32.10.
14. Arius Didymus, *Epitome of Stoic Ethics* 11m.
15. 1 Sam. 16:13; 1 Kings 19:16; Ps. 105:15; Zech. 4:14.
16. *Planting* 18; cf. *Creation* 134; *Alleg. Interp.* 1.133 – 33; *Flight* 11 – 13.
17. Cf. Rom. 1:9; Phil. 1:8. On this construction see BAGD, 288.
18. Cited in Walter A. Elwell and Robert W. Yarborough, *Readings from the First-Century World* (Grand Rapids: Baker, 1998), 136.
19. *Description of Greece* 2.2.1.
20. See the account by Dio Cassius, *Roman History* 65.13, who notes that Musonius Rufus was exempted.
21. Lucian, *Icarmenippus* 29 – 30. See also his *A Professor of Public Speaking* and *The Runaways*.
22. See BAGD, 689, which cites 2 Cor. 9:2 and Phil. 1:14 as further instances of this usage. Note also Paul's use of "all" as a synonym for "the many" in Rom. 5:15 – 21.
23. See James C. VanderKam, *The Dead Sea Scrolls Today* (Grand Rapids: Eerdmans, 1994), 164 – 65; 1QS 6:13 – 14.
24. *Jub.* 17:16; 18:12; 2 Cor. 48:1 – 4; cf. Ex 4.24 – 25; 49:2 – 4; 48:9.
25. Scott J. Hafemann, *Suffering and Ministry in the Spirit: Paul's Defense of his Ministry in II Corinthians 2:14 – 3:3* (Grand Rapids: Eerdmans, 1990), 16 – 34.
26. *Aemelius Paulus* 32.
27. *Did.* 11:6.
28. Plato, *Protagoras* 313D.
29. *The Life of Moses* 2.212.
30. *Oration* 32.10.
31. Ibid., 32.9.
32. John Harvey Kent, *Corinth, Volume 8, Part 3: The Inscriptions, 1926 – 1950* (Princeton: American School of Classical Studies at Athens, 1966).
33. Numerous examples of such letters survive. See the examples in Chan-Hie Kim, *The Familiar Greek Letter of Recommendation* (SBLDS 4; Missoula, Mont.: Society of Biblical Literature, 1972). For relevant New Testament references, see Acts 9:2; 15:23 – 29; 18:27; 22:5; Rom. 16:1 – 2; 1 Cor. 16:10 – 11; 2 Cor. 8:22 – 24; Col. 4:10.
34. CD 6:19; 8:21; 20:12; 1QpHab 2:3 – 4.
35. 1QS 8:20 – 22.
36. See also 2 Macc. 7:23; Wisd. Sol. 15:11; *T. Abr.* 18:11; Philo, *Creation* 32.
37. *1 En.* 99:2; *Let. Aris.* 144 – 45.
38. *Eighteen Benedictions*; cf. Wisd. Sol. 17:11; 45:5; *4 Ezra* 14:30; *2 Bar.* 38:2.
39. *2 Bar.* 78:16; Ps. Philo 9:8.
40. *4 Ezra* 9:37.
41. Dio Chrysostom, *Oration* 32.11. See also Plutarch's amusing "How to Tell a Friend from a Flatterer" and the lengthy treatise by Philodemus, *On Frank Criticism*.
42. Philo, *Good Person* 81 – 82.
43. Cited in Elwell and Yarbrough, *Readings*, 87.
44. *1 En.* 90:37 – 39; *2 Bar.* 51:1 – 3; 1QS 4:6 – 8; Wisd. Sol. 3:7; *Jos Asen.* 8 – 21; 1QH; 4Q434 – 37.
45. Lucian, *Hermotimus* 59.
46. Gal. 1:4; cf. Rom. 12:2; 1 Cor. 1:20; Eph. 1:21; also Isa. 19 – 20; Hos. 2:18; Amos 9:11.
47. *1 En.* 16; CD 6:10 – 14; *4 Ezra* 4:9; *2 Bar.* 15:8; *Jub.* 1:16.
48. *Jub.* 12:20.
49. 1QH 4:24.
50. 11Q5 19.
51. 1QS 4:22 – 23; CD 3:18 – 20; 1QH 4:15.
52. Dio Chrysostom, *Discourse* 13:11.
53. *Discourses* 2:28.

54. Seneca, *Ep.* 40.4, 8, 14.

55. Cicero, *Tusc. Disp.* 4.14; Propertius 3.5.6; Petronius, *Satyr.* 50; Josephus, *J.W.* 5.5.3 §201; Suetonius, *Aug.* 70.

56. Cited in Margaret Thrall, *The Second Epistle to the Corinthians* (Edinburgh: T. & T. Clark, 1994), 1:326.

57. Seneca, *Epistle* 24.19 – 20 (italics added).

58. Marcus Aurelius, *Meditations* 10.

59. See Albert A. Bell Jr., *A Guide to the New Testament World* (Scottsdale, Pa.: Herald, 1994), 214 – 17.

60. Plotinus, *The Animate and the Man* 10.

61. From a letter dated A.D. 99. See MM, 192.

62. Oscar Broneer (ed.), *Ancient Corinth: A Guide to the Excavations* (Athens: Hestia, 1947), 55.

63. On the background and influence of *peithō* in Greek literature see R. G. A. Buxton, *Persuasion in Greek Tragedy: A Study of* Peitho (Cambridge: Cambridge Univ. Press, 1982); George Kennedy, *The Art of Persuasion in Greece* (London: Routledge and Keegan Paul, 1963).

64. *Descriptions of Greece* 2.7.7 – 9.

65. Cicero, *Orator* 97.

66. Dio Chrysostom, *Discourses* 33.1.

67. For an excellent discussion of this subject, see Duane Litfin's *St. Paul's Theology of Proclamation* (SNTSMS 79; Cambridge: Cambridge Univ. Press, 1994).

68. See the account by Philostratus, *Lives of the Sophists* 491.

69. Philo, *Lives of the Sophists* 532.

70. Ibid., 616.

71. This speech has been passed down under the name of Dio Chrysostom (see his *Discourses* 37.26).

72. See Moyer Hubbard, "Was Paul Out of His Mind? Re-reading 2 Cor 5:13," *JSNT* 70 (1998) 39 – 64.

73. See Aristotle's influential *The Art of Rhetoric* 1408b; 1418a.

74. *Jubilees* 1:15 – 29; cf. *1 En.* 72:1.

75. *Gen. Rab.* 39:4.

76. *Jos. Asen.* 8:9.

77. See Cilliers Breytenbach, *Versöhnung: Eine Studie zur paulinischen Soteriologie* (WMANT 60; Neukirchener: Neukirchen-Vluyn, 1989).

78. *Rom. Ant.* 5.49.6.

79. *Lives of the Sophists* 489, 520 – 33.

80. Dio Chrysostom, *Oration* 37.7 – 9.

81. See Seneca's "On Despising Death" (*Epistle* 24), or Musonius Rufus's "That One Should Disdain Hardships" (*Fragment* 7); Dio Chrysostom, *Oration* 3.3.

82. Epictetus, *Discourses* 30.2 – 3.

83. Musonius Rufus, *Fragment* 9; Epictetus, *Discourses* 1.29.4.

84. Rom. 13:12; Eph. 6:10 – 18; 1 Thess. 5:8; 1 Tim. 3:3 – 4.

85. Dio Chrysostom, *Oration* 8:16.

86. Arius Didymus, *Stoic Ethics* 5a.

87. Seneca, *On Firmness* 6.3.

88. Epictetus, *Discourses* 2.19.24.

89. Seneca, *On Firmness* 6.5 – 6.

90. See *New Documents Illustrating Early Christianity*, ed. Richard Horsley (New Ryde: Macquarie University), 1.5.

91. For details and primary sources see Ramsay MacMullen, *Paganism in the Roman Empire* (New Haven: Yale Univ. Press, 1981), 18 – 48.

92. From *New Documents Illustrating Early Christianity*, 1.5. The Thoereion was probably a banquet room connected to the temple of Isis or Serapis.

93. Tacitus, *Ann.* 15.44; Tertullian, *Apology* 35 – 37.

94. Epictetus, *Discourses* 4.1.111 – 12.

95. Philodemus, *On Frank Criticism* 15, 28.

96. Ibid., 26.

97. Plutarch, *On Listening to Lectures* 47A.

98. *Jos. Asen.* 15:7.

99. See Margaret M. Mitchell, "New Testament Envoys in the Context of Greco-Roman Diplomatic and Epistolary Conventions: The Example of Timothy and Titus," *JBL* 111 (1992): 641 – 62.

100. Philo, *Embassy* 369.

101. 1 Thess. 1:6; 2:14; 3:2 – 4; 2 Thess. 1:4 – 10; cf. Phil. 1:29 – 30.

102. *Oration* 7.82.

103. Rom. 12:15; 1 Cor. 1:2; Eph. 1:18.

104. Ex. 19:6; Lev. 21:7; Ex. 28:2; Lev. 16:32 – 33.

105. Ps. 34:9; Dan. 7:18 – 27; cf. Tobit 8:15.

106. Dio Chrysostom, *Oration* 7.93.

107. Although a fifth-century B.C. playwright, Euripides's perennial popularity is illustrated by Dio Chrysostom (A.D. 40 – 120), who cites this passage from memory in *Oration* 17; Euripides, *Phoenician Women* 535.

108. Philo, *Heir* 162.

109. Eph. 4:28, italics added; cf. Rom. 12:13; 1 Tim. 6:18.

110. 1 Thess. 4:11 – 12; 2 Thess. 3:6 – 13; 1 Tim. 6:6 – 10; 2 Cor. 8:11; cf. Phil. 4:10 – 19.

111. On the patroness status of Phoebe, see Wayne Meeks, *The First Urban Christians* (New Haven: Yale Univ. Press, 1983), 60.

112. This oration has been passed down under Dio Chrysostom's name (see his *Discourses* 37.36).

113. Donald Engels, *Roman Corinth: An Alternative Model for the Classical City* (Chicago: Univ. of Chicago Press, 1994), 101.

114. Dio Chrysostom, *Oration* 77.38.
115. E.g., Ps. 45:4; Isa. 40:11; 42:3; 53:7; Zech. 9:9 (cited in Matt. 21:5); Matt. 5:5; 11:29; John 1:29.
116. Rev. 5:6 – 13; 6:1 – 7; 21:9 – 22.
117. *1 Clem.* 16:1, 7; cf. *Barn.* 5:2.
118. Cf. Rom. 8:4 – 5, 12 – 13; 2 Cor. 1:17; 5:16; 11:18.
119. Dio Chrysostom, *Oration* 77/78.40.
120. Epictetus, *Discourses* 4.1.86.
121. Seneca, *On the Firmness of the Wise Man* 6.4.
122. Philo, QG 3.27; *Migration* 172; *Planting* 159.
123. Philo, *Planting* 136.
124. Philo, *Rewards* 25; *Cherubim* 9.
125. Philo, *Posterity* 101.
126. See Litfin, *Proclamation*.
127. See Bruce Winter, *Paul and Philo Among the Sophists* (SNTSMS 96; Cambridge: Cambridge Univ. Press, 1997).
128. 2 Cor. 10:17; cf. Jer. 9:24; 1 Cor. 1:31.
129. An insightful treatment of this topic can be found in Calvin Roetzel, *Paul: The Man and the Myth* (Philadelphia: Fortress, 1999), ch. 3, "The Letter Writer."
130. Acts 18:1 – 3; 1 Cor. 4:12; 9:3 – 18; 2 Cor. 11:7 – 9.
131. Cicero, *Off.* 150.
132. Lucian, *Dream* 6 – 13.
133. The life of the farmer was particularly admired; see Musonius Rufus, *Fragment* 11; Dio Chrysostom, *Oration* 7.103 – 52.
134. On the importance of beauty in Corinth see Timothy B. Savage, *Power Through Weakness: Paul's Understanding of the Christian Ministry in 2 Corinthians* (SNTSMS 86; Cambridge: Cambridge Univ. Press, 1996), 46 – 47.
135. Martial, *Ep.* 10.65.
136. 1 Cor. 1 – 4; 2 Cor. 2:17; 5:11 – 13; 10:10; 11:6; 12:19; 13:3.
137. Dio Chrysostom, *Oration* 35.1.
138. Lucian, *Professor of Public Speaking* 16.
139. Cited in Peter Marshall, *Enmity in Corinth: Social Conventions in Paul's Relations with the Corinthians* (WUNT 2.23; Tübingen: J.C.B. Mohr [Paul Siebeck] 1987), 54; Quintilian, *Inst. Or.* 2.4.21.
140. Plutarch, *How to Tell a Friend from a Flatterer* 71.
141. Lucian, *Professor of Public Speaking* 13.
142. Acts 22:21; 26:17 – 18; Gal. 1:16.
143. *m. Yebam.* 6:4.
144. *m. Ketub.*
145. Deut. 22:22 – 27; Philo, *Spec. Laws* 1.107; 3.72; *m. Sanh.* 7:9.
146. Wisd. Sol. 2:24; *Apoc. Mos.* 16; *1 En.* 69:6, which names the angel Gader'el.
147. Isocrates, *Nicoles* 7; Aristides, *To Plato* 391.
148. Seneca, *Ep.* 40.6.
149. Arius Dydimus, *Epitome* 5b12.
150. Aristides, *To Plato* 392. This proverb surfaces in one form or another in Plato, Cicero, Seneca, Quintilian, and Juvenal. Seneca, in fact, devoted an entire essay to its exposition: "On Style as a Mirror of Character" (*Epistle* 114).
151. Cf. Acts 18:1 – 3; 1 Cor. 4:12; 9:3 – 18; 2 Cor. 12:15.
152. See, e.g., Musonius Rufus, Fragment 11, "What Means of Livelihood Is Appropriate for a Philosopher?"; Dio Chrysostom, *Oration* 7; Arius Didymus 11m; Diogenes Laertius 7.188.
153. For a more nuanced appraisal, see Ronald F. Hock, *The Social Context of Paul's Ministry: Tentmaking and Apostleship* (Philadelphia: Fortress, 1980), 50 – 65.
154. Dio Chrysostom, *Oration* 4.132; Philo, *Posterity* 150; Lucian, *Professor of Public Speaking* 6 – 8.
155. Philo, *Worse* 34.
156. See, e.g., Lucian, *On Salaried Posts*; Dio Chrysostom, *Oration* 77/78.37.
157. For the view that Paul refused support primarily to model a life of self-imposed poverty before the materialistic Corinthians, see Savage, *Power Through Weakness*, 80 – 99.
158. On Greco-Roman gift-giving conventions, see Peter Marshall's *Enmity in Corinth*. My comments rely on his detailed analysis.
159. *Life of Adam and Eve* 9:1 – 5.
160. Plutarch, *On Inoffensive Self-Praise* 547 D; 539 E-F; 540 C.
161. Ibid., 543 F – 544 C; cf. 12:9 – 10; 544 C; cf. 11:23 – 29; 542 E – 543 A; cf. 11:32 – 33; 12:9 – 10.
162. Dio Chrysostom, *Oration* 8:9.
163. Philo, *Worse* 33.
164. Cited in C. Forbes, "Comparison, Self-Praise, and Irony: Paul's Boasting and the Conventions of Hellenistic Rhetoric," *NTS* 32 (1986): 7.
165. For a full discussion, see Brian Rapske's study, *The Book of Acts and Paul in Roman Custody* (BAFCS 3; Grand Rapids: Eerdmans, 1994), 10 – 20.
166. Ibid., 195 – 225.
167. Eph. 6:20; Phil. 1:7, 13 – 17; Col. 4:3, 18; 2 Tim. 2:9; Philem. 10, 13.
168. *Acts of Augustus* 1.4.
169. *m. Makkot* 3:1 – 16; *m. Šebuʿot* 3:7 – 11.
170. *m. Makkot* 3:12 – 13.
171. See Rapske, *Paul in Roman Custody*, 48 – 56.
172. Josh. 7:25; *Jub.* 30:7 – 9; *Lives of the Prophets* 2:1; Philo, *Flaccus* 66, 174; Petronius, *Satyr.* 90.
173. Deut. 13:7 – 12; *m. Sanh.* 6:1 – 4; John 10:31 – 33; Acts 7:58; 14:19.

174. E.g., Dio Chrysostom, *Oration* 7; Petronius, *Satyr.* 113 – 16; Seneca, *Ep.* 53; For inscriptional evidence see Horsley, *New Documents Illustrating Early Christianity*, 4. #26.

175. Lucillius, *Greek Anthology* 6.164.

176. Dionysius, *Greek Anthology* 6.166.

177. Cf. Seneca, *On the Trials of Travel*.

178. Horace, *Satires* 1.5.

179. Ibid.; Petronius, *Satyr.* 16 – 26.

180. Epictetus, *Discourses* 4.1.91.

181. Antiphilus, *Greek Anthology* 6.199.

182. Epictetus, *Discourses* 3.13.11.

183. Dio Chrysostom, *Oration* 8.15 – 16.

184. A comprehensive survey of this issue can be found in Rainer Riesner's, *Paul's Early Period: Chronology, Mission Strategy, Theology* (Grand Rapids: Eerdmans, 1998), 75 – 89.

185. E.g., *1 En.* 1 – 36; *2 En.*; *3 Bar.*; *The Apocalypse of Zephaniah*.

186. One heaven: *1 En.*; three heavens: *T. Levi* 3:1; *Apoc. Mos.* 37; five heavens: *3 Bar.* 11:1 – 2; seven heavens: *2 En.* 20:1; *Apoc. Ab.* 19:5 – 6; *Ascen. Isa.* 9:6; *3 En.* 17:1; 955 heavens: *3 En.* 48:1.

187. E.g., Rom. 1:29 – 30; 1 Tim. 6:4 – 5; Arius Didymus, *Epitome* 11k; Ps.-Anacharsis, *Ep.* 1.

188. Cicero, *De Oratore* 3.53.

189. This speech is found in the orations of Dio Chrysostom, 37.27.

190. Aelius Aristides, *In Defense of Oratory* 113.

191. James H. Charlesworth, "Jesus and Jehohanan: An Archaeological Note on Crucifixion," *ExpTim* 84/6 (February, 1973), 147 – 50.

192. Epictetus, *Discourses* 3.12.15.

193. Ps-Anacharsis, *Epistle* 2.

194. *1 Clem.* 3:2.

195. Dio Chrysostom, *Oration* 7.59.

196. Rom. 16:16; 1 Cor 16:20; 1 Thess. 5:26; cf. 1 Pet. 5:14.

197. Rom. 16:21 – 23; 1 Cor. 16:19 – 20; Phil. 4:22; Philem. 23 – 24.

198. Rom. 15:30; 1 Cor. 12:4 – 6; Gal. 4:4 – 6.

Sidebar and Chart Notes

A-1. See the extensive treatment by Hafemann in *Suffering and Ministry in the Spirit*.

A-2. Josephus, *J.W.* 7.5.5 §132.

A-3. *Acts of Augustus* 1.4.

A-4. Josephus, *J.W.* 7.5.6 §§153 – 54.

A-5. See the description of Pausanius, *Descriptions of Greece* 2.3.1 – 2.

A-6. Oscar Broneer (ed.), *Ancient Corinth: A Guide to the Excavations*, 39 – 40.

A-7. Philo, *Embassy* 281.

A-8. See *New Documents Illustrating Early Christianity*, 4:213 – 20.

A-9. Polycarp, *Martyrdom of Polycarp* 8:2.

A-10. Suetonius, *Dom.* 13.

A-11. Paul Zanker, "The Power of Images," in *Paul and Empire: Religion and Power in Roman Imperial Society*, ed. Richard A. Horsley (Harrisburg, Pa.: Trinity, 1997), 72 – 86.

A-12. Donald Engels, *Roman Corinth*, 101 – 2.

A-13. Kent, *Corinth: The Inscriptions*, #102.

A-14. Engels, *Roman Corinth*, 102.

A-15. Pliny, *Letters* 10.96 – 97.

A-16. Polycarp, *Mart. Pol.* 9 – 15.

A-17. Trimalchio, a fictitious character from Petronius' *Satyricon* (71).

A-18. Philo, *Creation* 135; Wisd. Sol. 3; *4 Macc.* 18:23.

A-19. Matt. 17:22 – 23; 1 Cor. 15; cf. 2 Macc. 7:14; *2 Bar.* 49 – 51.

A-20. On the Asclepion in Corinth, see Broneer, *Ancient Corinth*, 100 – 105; James Wisemann, "Corinth and Rome I: 228 BC – AD 267" in *ANRW* 2.7.1 (Berlin: Walter de Gruyter, 1979): 438 – 548.

A-21. Acts 24:17; Rom. 15:26; Gal. 2:10; 2 Cor. 8:13 – 15.

A-22. This data has been adapted from Ekkehard W. Stegemann and Wolfgang Stegemann, *The Jesus Movement: A Social History of its First Century* (Minneapolis: Fortress, 1999), 5 – 95. See also James S. Jeffers, *The Greco-Roman World of the New Testament Era: Exploring the Background of the New Testament* (Downers Grove: InterVarsity, 1999), 181 – 96.

A-23. Lucian, *Runaways* 17.

A-24. Cited in John Piper, *The Supremacy of God in Preaching* (Grand Rapids: Baker, 1990), 55.

A-25. The classic treatments of Paul's opponents in Corinth are those of C. K. Barrett ("Paul's Opponents in II Corinthians," *NTS* 17 [1971]: 233 – 54) and Ernst Käsemann ("Die Legitimität des Apostels: Eine Untersuchung zu II Korinther 10 – 13," *ZNW* 41 [1942]: 33 – 71). My own appraisal is closest to Jerry Sumney's in *Identifying Paul's Opponents: The Question of Method in 2 Corinthians* (JSNTSup 40; Sheffield: JSOT Press, 1990).

A-26. Dio Chrysostom, *Oration* 1.84.

CREDITS FOR PHOTOS AND MAPS

ALSO AVAILABLE

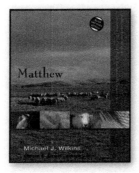

Matthew

Michael J. Wilkins

Mark

David E. Garland

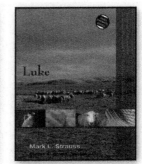

Luke

Mark L. Strauss

John

Andreas J. Köstenberger

Acts

Clinton E. Arnold

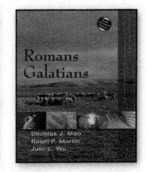

Romans
Galatians

Douglas J. Moo
Ralph P. Martin
Julie L. Wu

1 & 2
Corinthians

David W. J. Gill
Moyer V. Hubbard

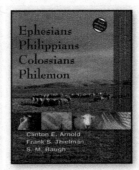

Ephesians
Philippians
Colossians
Philemon

Clinton E. Arnold
Frank S. Thielman
S. M. Baugh

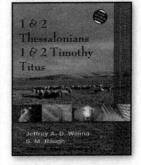

1 & 2
Thessalonians
1 & 2 Timothy
Titus

Jeffrey A. D. Weima
S. M. Baugh

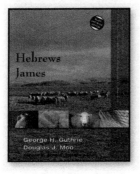

Hebrews
James

George H. Guthrie
Douglas J. Moo

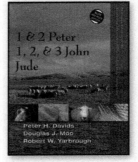

1 & 2 Peter
1, 2, & 3 John
Jude

Peter H. Davids
Douglas J. Moo
Robert W. Yarbrough

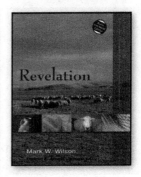

Revelation

Mark W. Wilson

CPSIA information can be obtained
at www.ICGtesting.com
Printed in the USA
LVOW03s0021151016
508852LV00007B/17/P